Handbook of Stock Brokerage Accounting

RICHARD ROSS

Compliance International, Inc.
165 Passaic Avenue, Fairfield New Jersey, 07004

10 9 8 7 6 5 4 3 2 1

Library of Congress Catalogue-in-Publication Data

Ross, Richard D.
The Handbook of Stock Brokerage Accounting, 2000 Edition / Richard Ross
p. cm.
Includes Index.
ISBN 0-9701067-0-X
1. Stock Brokerage Accounting-Accounting: I. Title II. Title: Stock Brokerage Accounting

ISBN 0-9701067-0-X

Compliance International Inc.
165 Passaic Avenue, Fairfield New Jersey, 07004

Printed in the United States of America

Contents

Contents

Handbook of

STOCK BROKERAGE ACCOUNTING

RICHARD ROSS

Introduction

At last there's a comprehensive Handbook that focuses almost *exclusively* on the specialized accounting practices and regulations of the securities industry.

This reference provides clear, understandable explanations of the most-often used financial instruments, as well as details of specific compliance issues generated by SEC regulations, including recordkeeping procedures, margin requirements, and Rules 15c3-3 and 15c3-1.

Designed for accountants and auditors at all levels - and also as a help for individuals studying for the Series 27 exam - this valuable guide is organized into four sections featuring:

PART I: OVERVIEW OF THE FINANCIAL MARKETS:

A detailed examination of the basic products bought and sold by broker-dealers, as well as the types of markets on which these products trade.

PART II: OPERATIONS OVERVIEW:

An Exclusive "insider's view" of the inner workings of a Wall Street broker-dealer "back office", with the real story of how transactions are processed.

PART III: ACCOUNTING AND RECORDKEEPING:

An in-depth analysis of the broker-dealer accounting process and a review of the accounts that comprise the Statement of Financial Condition, Income Statement, and Primary & Subsidiary Records.

PART IV: SYNDICATE ACCOUNTING:

Details on the Syndicate Accounting Process and the techniques and strategies broker-dealers use with Syndicate, Corporate Finance, and Investment Banking Activities.

PART V: BROKER-DEALER REGULATIONS

Overviews of the rules and regulations that govern the financial accounting world, including recordkeeping, Margin, the Net Capital Rule (recently amended by the SEC), and the Customer Protection Rule.

THE HANDBOOK OF STOCK BROKERAGE ACCOUNTING is one of the few references available that provides in-depth coverage of brokerage accounting and its related rules and regulations. For auditors, accountants, brokers - indeed, anyone connected with the security industry - it's a reference you can't afford to be without.

Author

About the Author

Richard D. Ross is President & CEO of Ross Asset Management, a financial advisory firm that provides financial institutions with investment, risk management, and strategic planning guidance.

Mr. Ross has over 15 years of experience advising global financial institutions, including Prudential Insurance, Lehman Brothers, and Bank of America. He also served as Chairman of the Securities Industry Association's Internal Audit Education Committee.

Mr. Ross is a Certified Internal Auditor and a Certified Fraud Examiner.

PART I: OVERVIEW OF THE FINANCIAL MARKETS

CHAPTER 1: OVERVIEW OF THE PRODUCTS

EQUITIES

Corporate common stocks or equities are the most typical form of financial asset. Common stock represents a share of ownership in a company. It provides the owner with a pro rata share of the earnings (via dividends) from the operation of the company and the benefit of capital gains from any rise in the price stock. Common stockholders control the firm through their right to elect the board of directors of the corporation. The board of directors, in turn, appoints the members of management who supervise the daily operations of the company.

Preferred stock is an intermediate form of financing between common stock and debt, since it has some of the properties of each. Preferred stockholders have a prior claim relative to common stockholders to the firm's income after interest and taxes and to the firm's assets in the event of bankruptcy. Preferred stock also pays dividends, however, the payments are fixed and quoted as a percentage of par, e.g., a dividend of 10% of par on preferred shares with a par of $100 would be $10 per year. The firm need not pay dividends on preferred stock if it chooses, so long as it also fails to pay dividends on its common stock. Usually, a cumulative dividend provision is included in the preferred stock agreement that requires all past unpaid dividends on the preferred stock must be met before any dividends can be declared on the common stock. Preferred stockholders are usually accorded only limited voting privileges.

FIXED INCOME SECURITIES

There are two methods that an entity can use to borrow money: bank debt and fixed income securities, more commonly known as bonds. Bond issuers include the federal government and its agencies, municipal governments, and private corporations.

A bond entitles the owner to a specific, contractually agreed upon series of payments, usually in the form of periodic interest payments, until some specified date in the future. At that time, the issuer will cease to make the periodic payments and will return to the bond holder the face or par value of the debt.

The key features of a bond include the maturity, the coupon, the price, and the yield.

Maturity

A bond's maturity is the number of years of life it has left until the interest payments cease and the principal is repaid by the issuer. A bond's maturity is important to investors for several reasons. First, it is the date which the investors will receive their principal back and will have to reinvest it in another financial instrument. Secondly, the yield or the investor's return on investment, depends substantially on the maturity. Third, the volatility of a bond's price depends greatly upon its maturity. Changes in interest rates will have larger effect on the price of a bond with long maturity than one with a short maturity.

When considering a bond's maturity, the investor should be aware of any provisions that modify, or permit the issuer to modify, the maturity. Many bonds give the issuer a call privilege, which permits the issuer to redeem the bond before the scheduled maturity date. Others have put features that allow investors to give their bonds to the issuer in exchange for the original principal. Many bonds have sinking fund provisions which mandate that the issuer must retire a large portion of the debt in a prearranged schedule before the stated maturity.

Coupon

A bond's coupon is the periodic interest payment made to owners during the life of the bond. The coupon rate is quoted as what investors will receive on a yearly basis, for instance: IBM 8 due in 2000 means that this bond will pay a coupon of 8% per year until the year 2000. Typically, bonds issued in the U.S., half of the coupon is paid in semiannual installments. Bonds may be bearer bonds or registered bonds. With bearer bonds, investors clip coupons and send them to the issuer for payment. For registered issues, bond owners receive the payment automatically at the appropriate time.

Zero coupon bonds have been issued by corporations and municipalities since the early 1980s. The investor in a zero coupon security receives interest by buying the security at a price below its principal value and holding it to the maturity date.

There are bonds that have coupons which do not remain fixed for the entire term-to-maturity, called *floating rate bonds*. The coupon on floating rate bonds is periodically reset based on some predetermined benchmark, such as the 30 year treasury bond rate or LIBOR.

Yields

The yield of a bond is a measure of an investor's return on their investment. There are three common methods used to measure a bond's yield: "current yield", "yield-to-maturity", and "yield-to-call". Current yield is the ratio of the bond's coupon to its current price. The current yield not an effective measure because it neglects the principal to be paid at maturity. The yield-to-maturity is the rate of interest an investor would earn if an investment equal to the price of the bond were capable of generating the semiannual coupon payments and the principal of the bond in the exact same pattern promised by the issuer. The yield-to-call is the same analytical technique as yield-to-maturity, except the yield-to-call uses the bond's potential call date as the maturity date.

Price

The prices of bonds are usually quoted as percentages of par or face value. To convert the price quote into a dollar figure, just multiply the price by the par value. Treasury notes and bonds are quoted in thirty-seconds of a percentage point. Corporate and municipal bonds are quoted in eighths of a percentage point.

Detailed below is a brief description of commonly fixed income instruments.

Money Market Instruments

Commercial Paper

Commercial paper is an unsecured promissory note with a fixed maturity. The issuer promises to pay the buyer some fixed amount on some future date but pledges no assets, only his liquidity and established earning power, to guarantee that promise. Commercial paper is exempt from SEC registration if the issuer meets one of several alternative sets of requirements. The maturity of the paper is 1 to 270 days.

Commercial paper can be issued in either bearer form or in registered form. Rates on commercial paper, like those on bills, are quoted on a discount basis. A small amount of commercial paper is issued in interest-bearing form; the rate paid on such paper is the quoted discount rate converted to the equivalent simple interest rate.

Commercial paper yields more than Treasury bills of comparable maturity. Normally, the spread is widest when money is tight - first because commercial paper exposes the investor to credit risk. Second, because it is less liquid than bills. The spread can also be affected by other factors, such as market corrections, political upheaval in other countries, and central bank interventions (both domestic and foreign).

The commercial paper market is a wholesale market; typically, the minimum sale is $100,000 to $200,000. A corporate liquidity portfolio might trade for $250,000, while a money fund for $50MM. Commercial paper is an unsecured promissory note with a fixed maturity. The issuer promises to pay the buyer some fixed amount on some future date but pledges no assets, only his liquidity and established earning power, to guarantee that promise. Commercial paper is exempt from SEC registration if the issuer meets one of several alternative sets of requirements. The maturity of the paper is 1 to 270 days.

Commercial paper can be issued in either bearer form or in registered form. Rates on commercial paper, like those on bills, are quoted on a discount basis. A small amount of commercial paper is issued in interest-bearing form; the rate paid on such paper is the quoted discount rate converted to the equivalent simple interest rate.

Commercial paper yields more than Treasury bills of comparable maturity. Normally, the spread is widest when money is tight - first because commercial paper exposes the investor to credit risk. Second, because it is less liquid than bills. The spread can also be affected by other factors, such as market corrections, political upheaval in other countries, and central bank interventions (both domestic and foreign).

The commercial paper market is a wholesale market; typically, the minimum sale is $100,000 to $200,000. A corporate liquidity portfolio might trade for $250,000, while a money fund for $50MM.

Banker Acceptances

A banker's acceptance (BA) is a time draft. In other words, it is an order to pay a specified amount of money to the acceptance holder on a specified date. BAs are drawn on and accepted by a bank that, by accepting the draft, assumes responsibility to make payment on the draft at maturity. BAs date back when early forms of this instrument were used to finance international trade.

Under current Fed regulations, BAs may be created by accepting banks to finance foreign trade, the domestic shipment of goods, domestic or foreign storage of readily marketable staples, and the provision of dollar exchange credits to banks in certain countries.

BAs, like T-bills, are discount instruments, and yields on them are quoted on a discount basis. Most BAs are backed by documents such as invoices, bills of lading, or independent terminal or warehouse receipts. This documentation is held by the accepting bank, so the instrument sold to investors is a simply drawn note. This note describes the nature of the transaction being financed and has been stamped "accepted" by the accepted bank. BAs are generally issued in bearer form. They may be drawn for varying maturities, but the largest volume of BAs traded in the market is in the 3-month area. Maturities of BAs at issue range from one to six months. A BA with an original maturity of more than six months becomes "ineligible", and therefore, trades at a concession to the market.

The initial Federal Reserve Act specified that BAs eligible for discount at or purchased by the Fed had to meet certain requirements. The spirit of the requirements are that for a BA to be eligible, it should finance a short-term (no longer than 6 months), self-liquidating commercial transaction of one of several specified types. Only BAs that are deemed eligible according to these requirements may be sold by member banks without incurring a reserve requirement.

Certificates of Deposit

A certificate of deposit is a negotiable instrument evidencing a time deposit made with a bank at a fixed rate of interest for a fixed period. CDs bear interest and are quoted on an interest-bearing rather than a discount basis. Normally, interest on a CD, which is calculated for actual days on a 360-day basis, is paid at maturity. However, on CDs issued with a maturity beyond one year, interest is paid semiannually. The maturities range from a few weeks to several years.

Banks have long needed dependable sources of long term funds to maintain their liquidity and to manage their interest rate exposure. Most money center banks have always received some large time deposits from individuals, partnerships, and smaller corporations. The total of such deposits was, however, small relative to the banks' needs for longer-term deposits. To fill the resulting gap, the banks use CDs, which allow them to buy longer-term funds in large volume.

U.S. Government Securities

U.S. Government securities are fixed income securities which are backed by the full faith and credit of the U.S. Government. These securities are viewed by investors as having no credit risk. The U.S. Department of the Treasury is the largest single issuer of debt in the world, with treasury securities accounting for over $2 trillion in debt in the financial marketplace. In addition, the large total volume of debt and the large size of any single issue have

contributed to making the Treasury market the most active and therefore the most liquid market in the world.

There are three major categories of treasury securities: bills, notes, and bonds. Treasury bills are securities which are issued with maturities of one year or less. Treasury securities with original maturities from 2 to ten years are called Treasury notes. Treasuries securities with original maturities greater than ten years are called Treasury bonds.

Treasury securities can be issued as either discount or coupon securities. Discount securities are issued at a discount to par and pay the face value of security at maturity. The difference between the discount price paid for the security and its par value is the interest earned by the holder. Treasury bills are issued in discount form. Coupon securities pay interest every six months. Treasury notes and bonds are issued in coupon form.

Interest income from treasury securities is subject to federal income taxation but is exempt from state and local taxes.

Municipal Bonds

Municipal bonds are securities issued by state and local governments and their creations such as authorities and special districts. The main incentive for investors to purchase municipal bonds is because the interest income from them are exempt from federal taxes.

There are two types of municipal bond structures: (i) *general obligation bonds*, and (ii) *revenue bonds*.

General obligation bonds are debt instruments issued by states, counties, special districts, cities, towns, and school districts. They are usually secured by the issuer's taxing power.

Revenue bonds are issued for either project or enterprise financings in which the bond issuers pledge to the bondholders the revenues generated by the operating projects financed. The types of revenue bonds issued by municipalities include Airport Revenue Bonds, College and University Revenue Bonds, Hospital and Nursing Home Revenue Bonds, Single-Family Mortgage Revenue

Bonds, and Multifamily Revenue Bonds.

Municipal Notes

Tax exempt debt issued for periods of three years and less are short term in nature and are called notes. These instruments, known as Tax, Revenue, Grant, and Bond Anticipation Notes (TANs, RANs, GANs, and BANs) are temporary borrowings by municipalities. Usually, notes are issued for a period of 12 months. TANs and RANs are issued in anticipation of the collection of taxes or other expected revenue. BANs are issued in anticipation of the sale of long term bonds.

Mortgage-Backed Securities

Mortgage Pass-Through Securities

Mortgage pass-through securities are created when mortgages are pooled together, and undivided interests or participations in the pool(s) are sold. The originator (or another that purchases the right) continues to service the mortgages, collecting principal and interest payments, and "passing through" the payments, less servicing, guarantee, and other fees, to the security holders. The security holders receive pro rata shares of the resulting cash flows.

A portion of the outstanding principal balance of the underlying loans is paid each month according to the amortization schedules established for each individual mortgage. The principal on individual mortgages can be prepaid without penalty in whole or in part at any time before the stated maturity of the security. Prepayments of mortgages shorten the stated maturity or mortgage-backed securities, and investors may not be able to find an similar investment with comparable yield when their investment dollars are returned. This is known as "prepayment risk".

The mortgages that collateralize mortgage-backed securities are more commonly known as "whole loans". Whole loans represent the mortgages that are sold by lending organizations to conduits (such as banks and broker-dealers) for eventual resale or securitization. By definition, a mortgage is a pledge of property to secure payment of a debt. Typically, the property refers to real estate, which can be either in the form of a house or a commercial property. If the property owner (mortgagor) fails to pay the lender (mortgagee), the lender has the right to foreclose the loan and seize the property in order to ensure that the loan is repaid.

Most mortgages have a fixed rate of interest on the loan for its entire term (although many mortgages today are "ARMs" or adjustable rate mortgages), and the loan is repaid in monthly installments of principal and interest. The loan is structured in such a way that the total each month (the sum of principal and interest) is equal or level. The principal portion of each payment is used to reduce the amount of the loan outstanding.

Mortgage pass-through securities are issued by the Government National Mortgage Association (GNMA or "Ginnie Mae"), the Federal National Mortgage Association (FNMA or "Fannie Mae"), and the Federal Home Loan Mortgage Corporation (FHLMC or Freddie Mac). In addition, mortgage pass-throughs may also be issued by private conduits. These securities are known as private-label issues.

Collateralized Mortgage Obligations ("CMOs")

CMOs are bonds that are collateralized by mortgage pass-throughs and packaged into various short, medium, or long term maturity tranches (bond classes) to meet the maturity and cash flow needs of a variety of different investors. The cash flows generated by the assets in the collateral pool are used to first pay interest and then pay principal to the CMO bondholders.

The CMO security structure was created to reduce the effects of the prepayment risk associated with traditional pass-through securities. The CMO structure divides the prepayment risk among classes of bonds. Instead of distributing the monthly cash flow on a pro rata basis, the distribution is performed on a prioritized basis to redistribute prepayment risk among the various bond classes.

Corporate Bonds

A corporate bond is a debt instrument setting forth the obligation of the issuer to satisfy the terms of the agreement, known as a "bond covenant". Failure to meet this obligation in accordance with the terms of the covenant constitute legal default, and court proceedings may be undertaken to enforce the contract.

In the event of a bankruptcy, bondholders, as creditors, have a prior legal claim to the income and assets of the corporation for the principal and interest due them.

The five broad categories of corporate bonds sold in the United States based on the type of issuer are public utilities, transportations, industrials, banks and finance companies, and international issues.

The covenants between investors and issuers are detailed in contracts known as indentures. The corporate trustee is responsible for ensuring that promises made by the issuer to the investors are kept, and that all facets of the indentures are adhered to. In essence, the trustee acts as a representative of the interests of bondholders. A bank or trust company is usually given the responsibility of acting as the corporate trustee. Many of the responsibilities and requirements of trustees are set forth in the Trust Indenture Act.

OPTIONS

An option is the right to buy or sell a particular security (known as the underlying security) at a certain price for a specified period of time. There are two types of options: calls and puts. A call option gives the owner the right to buy the underlying security at a given price, known as the strike price. A put option gives the owner the right to sell the underlying security at the strike price. An option owner who uses their right to buy or sell the underlying security is said to be exercising the option. Call holders may exercise to buy the underlying security, and put holders may exercise to sell the security.

The are four characteristics that describe an options contract: (1) the type, which is a put or a call; (2) the underlying security. Option contracts are issued for many types of securities, including stocks, and futures contracts; (3) the expiration date; and (4) the strike price. For instance, an ACME January 30 put is an option to sell

100 shares of the underlying ACME stock at $30 per share. The

price of a option is quoted on a per share or per contract basis regardless of the amount of the security that may purchase with an option.

Option Pricing

There are two terms which describe the relationship between the strike price on the call or put options contract and the price of the underlying security - "*in-the-money*" and "*out-of-the-money*". An in-the-money call option is an option where the market value of the underlying security is greater than the strike price. In this situation, the option holder may exercise the option to obtain the security at a cheaper-than-market price, then sell it on Street at the market price and make a profit. An out-of-the-money call option will have a strike price that is greater than the market price.

Conversely, an in-the-money put option will have a strike price that is greater than the market price, thus allowing the holder to purchase the underlying security at the market price, then exercise the option and sell the security at the higher strike price. An out-of-the-money put option will have a strike price that is lower than the market price.

The price of an option contract is comprised to two elements: (1) intrinsic value and (2) time value. The intrinsic value of an option is the amount that the option is "in the money". The time value of an option is the value the market places on the option based on the amount of time left before the option expires and the belief that the option may become profitable before that point. Other factors affecting options pricing include the volatility of the underlying security, the current risk-free interest rate, and the dividend rate of any underlying stocks.

FUTURES

A futures contract is an agreement for a seller to deliver a specified quantity of a particular grade of a certain commodity to a predetermined location on a certain date. The particular characteristics of a futures contract are standardized so that the only negotiable aspect of a contract is the price.

The standardization of a futures contract makes the contract "liquid" because any given buyer or seller can expect a minimum level of quality and amount with each contract. The contracts are standardized according to factors like quantity, grade, delivery month, and delivery point.

Standardization and liquidity of the contracts allows them to be traded on the floor of a commodities futures exchange.

A typical futures contract - one that is traded presently at the Chicago Mercantile Exchange ("CME") - is the contract for frozen pork bellies. This contract calls for 40,000 of green, square cut, clear bellies with 75 or fewer minor defects, cut from barrows, gilts, and smoother sows (no stags or boars permitted) to be delivered from a federally inspected packing plant in Chicago during the months February, March, May, July or August. Anyone who trades in pork bellies at the CME will trade that particular contract. Only the price per pound will be negotiated on the trading floor.

CHAPTER 2: THE MARKETPLACES

The markets for securities provide the arenas, valuations, liquidity, and familiarity that encourages institutional and public interest in investing. The existence of these ready markets assures investors that their investments are worthwhile and will be saleable should the need or desire arise. These trades occur in either listed securities exchanges, NASDAQ, or the various over-the-counter marketplaces.

LISTED EQUITIES

The securities exchanges in the United States include the New York Stock Exchange, the American Stock Exchange, the Boston Stock Exchange, the Philadelphia Stock Exchange, the Chicago Stock Exchange, and the Pacific Stock Exchange. Trades on these exchanges are primarily executed on an "agency" basis. The trade begins when a customer calls his stock broker and requests that a listed security be bought or sold. The stockbroker then transmits the order (via wire or telephone) to a trading desk which would usually be responsible for all trades executed in listed securities. Most firms call this desk the "Block Trading Desk". The trading desk will then forward the order to a "runner" on the floor who will hand it to a floor broker. The New York Stock Exchange also utilizes an automated system to send orders to the exchange floor (and the specialists) called the Designated Order Turnaround System (DOT). The other exchanges also utilized automated trade reporting systems. The floor brokers' responsibility is to negotiate a price with the specialist for the security and execute the trade with the specialist. There is only one specialist for each security listed on an exchange and the specialists' responsibility is to fill purchase and sale orders for a designated security and maintain an orderly market in that security. Once the order is executed, the price, share quantity, and other trade facts are sent back to the desk trader which then forwards the information to the stockbroker, and eventually the customer. When the DOT system is utilized, the entire execution process is automated.

OVER-THE-COUNTER (OTC) EQUITIES

Trades in OTC equity securities are usually executed on a firm's OTC Trading Desk. OTC equities are traded on the NASDAQ system and through the pink sheets or the non-NASDAQ Reporting System, otherwise known as the "bulletin board". With NASDAQ listed securities, the stockbroker will again contact the trader with the customer order, however, the trader will not call the stock exchange floor. The trader, using a computer monitor linked to the NASDAQ system, will determine the other firms willing to buy and sell the appropriate security at the most advantageous price for the customer.

In purchase situations, if the trader has the security in his trading inventory, he can sell to the customer, but at the best price listed on the NASDAQ screen. If the trader believes selling his inventory at this price would not be advantageous, then he can consult the NASDAQ screen to determine which broker has the price, then buy the security from that broker. Broker-dealers executing transactions in a NASDAQ listed securities can act either as principal or agent.

When a customer wants to sell a NASDAQ-listed security, the trader will decide whether he will purchase the security into his own inventory or sell to the broker giving the best quote on the system.

With pink sheet securities, the trader is still obligated to give customers the best price possible. However, instead of consulting their NASDAQ screen, the trader is required to call at least three market makers in the security to determine the best price for the security at that moment. The trader can determine which brokers are making a market in a security by consulting the pink sheets.

The bulletin board is used to provide quotations, trade and report the price and volume of securities that are not listed on the NASDAQ System or on a listed exchange. Basically, the bulletin board is automated means for trading in former pink sheet stocks. The trading activity and sales practices of broker-dealers using the bulletin board are monitored the same way as firms using the NASDAQ System.

FIXED INCOME SECURITIES

Fixed income securities are usually traded in the OTC market, which means that traders either buy and sell securities out of their inventory accounts or execute these trades with other brokers. However, some of these securities are traded on the exchanges. These securities include *corporate bonds, municipal bonds, government bonds,* and *mortgage-backed securities*. Frequently, there are independent pricing sources for these securities to help the traders determine what the best price for these securities are at the time of the transaction, such as the J.J. Kenney Pricing Service, IDSI, Telerate, Bloomberg, Cantor Fitzgerald, and Standard and Poors.

Fixed income securities entitle the owner to specific, contractually agreed upon series of payments, usually in the form of periodic interest payments, and the return of the principal investment. Fixed income securities usually have fixed maturity dates and coupon rates. The coupon rate is stated as a percentage of the par value, and most corporate bonds are issued in $1,000 or $5,000 par values. Thus, a 15% percent annual coupon rate implies that total annual interest payments of $150 are promised on bonds with a par value of $1,000. The claims of fixed income or debt security holders are superior to those of common stock holders and preferred stock holders in the case of bankruptcy.

OPTIONS

The options exchanges in the U.S. include The Chicago Board Options Exchange, the American Stock Exchange, the Philadelphia Stock Exchange, the Pacific Stock Exchange, and the New York Stock Exchange.

The trading of options on exchanges is similar to the trading of equities. Each option is assigned to a particular location on the trading floor and negotiations between buyer and seller take place at that spot. Some of the exchanges use the specialist system, where the specialist acts as both agent (for client orders), and principal (for his own account). Other exchanges separate these functions to prevent potential conflicts of interest.

FUTURES

The modern futures exchange exists for the purpose of bringing buyers and sellers together and providing a place where trading can happen. In most exchanges, this trading occurs in a place called the "pit".

Although some of the U.S. major futures exchanges have established some electronically traded contracts, most futures trading still occurs by open outcry in the "pit" of the exchange.

The major U.S. futures exchanges include The Chicago Board of Trade, The Chicago Mercantile Exchange, The Coffee, Sugar, and Cocoa Exchange, The Commodity Exchange, The New York Cotton Exchange, and the New York Futures Exchange.

PART II: OPERATIONS OVERVIEW

CHAPTER 3: HOW ORDERS ARE PROCESSED

TRANSACTIONS

There are two types of transactions that can be posted to the books and records of a broker-dealer: principal and agency.

Principal Transactions

A principal transaction involves the purchase or sale of a security to or from the proprietary account of the broker-dealer. For instance, a customer wants to purchase 100 shares of XYZ. In a principal trade, the broker-dealer will sell the customer the 100 shares of XYZ from its own inventory account. The broker-dealers' profit will come from the marking-up of the security a fraction of a point above the current market price (ask price). In the case of a customer's sell transaction, the broker-dealer will mark-down the security a fraction of a point below the current market price (bid price). The mark-up/mark-down is compensation for the market risk and financing costs the broker-dealer incurs by holding the position in its inventory.

Agency Transactions

An agency transaction involves the purchase or sale of a security between a customer and another financial institution, with the broker-dealer acting as the middle man or agent. The broker-dealer's profit will come from the charging of a commission to the customer for finding a counter party for the transaction.

THE ORDER ROOM

All customer orders are sent to the order room by the various branch offices where the stockbrokers work. The order room is responsible for receiving the order, recording the details of the order, executing the order in a timely manner, the reporting the execution price and time back to the branch office.

Types of Orders

There are various types of orders that a customer may place with a stockbroker for execution, including:

❑ Market Orders

A "market order" is an order to buy or sell a security at the prevailing market price at the time the order was placed. Usually, a customer will ask their stockbroker what price a security is trading at before placing the order. A complete price quote includes the bid and the ask prices. The bid is the price which a customer can sell their security for, and the ask is the price at which a customer may purchase a security. The bid is usually lower than the ask.

❑ Limit Orders

A "limit order" places a limit on the price at which a customer is willing buy or sell a security. If it is a buy limit order, then the customer will buy a security at the limit price or lower. If it is a sell limit, then the customer will sell the security at the limit price or higher.

❑ Stop Order

A "stop order" is an order to buy or sell a security at the market price once the security reaches a certain price. If a buy stop order is placed, then the customer will have an order to purchase at the market once the security price reaches the price specified by the customer or higher. A sell stop order will be executed once the security falls below the price specified by the customer or lower.

❑ Fill-or-Kill

A "fill-or-kill" order must be executed for the entire quantity specified by the customer at once or the order will be canceled.

❑ Immediate-or-Cancel

An "immediate-or-cancel" order may be partially filled immediately but the balance of the order must be canceled.

❑ All-or-None

An "all-or-none" order must be filled within time constraints (set by the customer) or the entire order will be canceled.

❑ Stop Limit Order

A "stop limit" order becomes a limit order once the buy stop or sell stop price is reached.

Whether a trade is listed or over-the-counter, all orders are sent to an order room where the orders are filled the processed manually or via trading systems. While small firms may have a single order room to trade all products, larger firms will use specialized trading desks where each product (corporate bonds, OTC stocks, etc.) will be traded at a separate location. If the order is processed manually, then order tickets are used to record all of the necessary and required details of the trades. The information on the tickets are then recorded on a trading blotters which will detail of all the activity for that day.

The Order Room's two main responsibilities are to:

1) Reconcile executed trades with execution reports from the exchange floors and NASDAQ execution reports from the OTC market; and

2) Confirming and tracking customer's open orders.

The information obtained from the Order Room's activities is given, usually systematically, to the Purchase and Sales Department for processing on the broker-dealer's books and records.

PURCHASE AND SALES (P&S) DEPARTMENT

The P&S department is responsible for four functions: 1) Recording 2) Figuration 3) Comparison 4) Booking

RECORDING

Every transaction in a broker/dealer is assigned a CUSIP number or in-house security number and a unique transaction number. All of the trade details my be recorded manually or via systems. Many firms will perform an additional comparison between the trade tickets from the order room and the P&S records to ensure the accurate recording of the trade on the books and records.

FIGURATION

When a trade is processed by a broker/dealer there are several computations that must be performed to determine the final settlement balance. These calculations include the amount due to the broker/dealer, the amount of money/securities due the customer, and the amount of money/securities due the counterparty. Also, in regards to bond transactions, the accrued interest, if any, must be determined. The customer or broker/dealer who has been holding an interest-paying bond is due the interest earned on the bond from the time the last interest payment was made.

COMPARISON

The comparison process consists of the reconciliation of customer trades against the trade of the opposing or contra-broker. Manual comparison consists of trades being separated by the exchanges on which they were executed, i.e., NYSE, AMEX, OTC, etc. The trades are coded, dated, then sent to the computer center for processing. The P&S Department will produce trading runs that will be sent out to the appropriate clearing house of each of the exchanges for additional processing. For most securities, this is done on trade date "plus one" (plus one additional day). On trade date plus two, P&S will pair-off customer trades with its corresponding streetside trade. All problems and non-reconciling items should be corrected and adjustments made by trade date plus two.

Balancing of trades used to be performed manually, but in today's automated environment this is no longer necessary. The development and computerization of clearing organizations has been instrumental in automating the clearing of trades.

National Securities Clearing Corporation (NSCC) is the major trade clearing organization in the U.S. Its history began with the formation of the Stock Clearing Corporation or SCC in 1892. The SCC was the clearing house for the New York Stock Exchange. The American Stock Exchange formed the American Stock Exchange Clearing Corporation in 1931. And in 1971, the NASD formed the National Clearing Corporation to facilitate clearing of over-the-counter stocks.

Finally, in 1978, the three exchanges decided to merge the three clearing organizations into what is known today as NSCC.

One major impetus to this merger was the "paper-work crises" from 1968-1970 when many broker-dealers went bankrupt because of their inability reconcile their books and records in the face of the raging bull market of the 1960s.

The main purpose of clearing organizations is to operate cost-effective systems for trade processing, clearance, delivery, and settlement of trades. Clearing organizations issues computer runs, known as contract sheets, which detail trade information from both sides of a transaction (buyer and seller). Trades in which both parties agree appear on the compared section of the sheet. Trades which do not agree appear on the uncompared section of the sheet.

The NSCC, which is the premier clearing organization for equity and equity-related products, operates cost-effective systems for trade processing, clearance, delivery and settlement. NSCC also interfaces with the other registered clearing agencies to ensure efficient national clearance and settlement.

The trade clearing process for transactions executed via NSCC is as follows:

<u>Trade Input and Deletion</u>

Trade activity is submitted to the clearing corporation by (i) the corresponding exchanges or NASDAQ, and (ii) the broker-dealer.

All transactions are submitted to NSCC via computer.

Clearance & Settlement

Trade Date - T

The three-day cycle of clearance and settlement begins on the trade date, which is known as "T". On T, all details of trading activity is transmitted to NSCC via computer. Most of these trades are transmitted by automated marketplace systems as "locked in" trades, meaning the details of the trades from buyer and seller have already been matched by computer. An exception process exists for the remaining trades, in which NSCC compares and matches the trade details submitted directly by broker participants.

NSCC's guarantee of settlement begins after midnight on the day that the trade is reported to the participant as compared. Now NSCC assumes the responsibility of settling the trade, even in the event of bankruptcy of either counterparty.

At this point, NSCC is now the point of contact for each counterparty. Net sellers deliver securities to NSCC, and net buyers deliver funds to settle transactions.

T+1

NSCC transmits to the participants computerized reports known as T contracts. T contracts, which are legally binding trade records, detail every buy and sell reported by the broker and the marketplace on trade date and confirm that the trades have compared and are ready for settlement in CNS. Trades that fail to match are reported back to the participants for corrections. Firms may then make corrections and transmit the information back to NSCC.

T+2

On T+2, CNS summarizes settlement information on trades that have already been matched on T and T+1. The net settlement information is then sent to participants. Also, NSCC continues to help firms reconcile still-open unmatched trades.

T+3

T+3 is settlement date. NSCC completes the settlement cycle by delivering securities top net buyers and payments to net sellers.

The final phase of the cycle is money settlement. NSCC nets the financial obligations of each participant so that settlement can be achieved in a single payment to a participant, or receipt from a participant.

The netting of financial obligations into one net payment brings greater efficiency and reduced risk to capital markets.

BOOKING

Once a transaction has been processed and balanced, it must be entered onto the broker-dealer's records, or booked. Most firms have automated accounting systems that are fed information from their P&S systems and are updated automatically. Most of the manual work in booking trades involves trade corrections.

THE CASHIER'S DEPARTMENT

Cashier Department Overview

The Cashier's Department, more commonly known as the "cage", has physical custody of securities in the possession of the broker-dealer and physically handles all receipts, deliveries, and transfers of securities and money in connection with the business of the firm. Cashier's maintains records of securities due to or from, or held by, other brokers, banks, and transfers agents. Also, it arranges loans from banks and others and initiates the accounting for receipts and disbursements of funds. In addition, the Cashier's area may be responsible for tracking the reorganization of stocks owned by the firm or their customers. The Cashier's Department has a broad range of responsibilities, but its main duties are the settlement of security transactions.

In small broker-dealers, the Cashier's Department may be divided into a Security Cage and a Money Cage. The Security Cage is responsible for the custody, receipt, and delivery of securities, and for the segregation of securities between those available for use of the firm and those held in safekeeping and other segregated status for the customer. The responsibilities for the Money Cage include the receipt, deposit and payment of funds; processing bank loans; transfer of funds between banks; daily balancing of money transactions; and custody of funds on the premises. In smaller firms, the Stock Record and Dividend Departments may be part of the Cashier's Department.

In larger firms, the Cashier's area will be further divided into functions and sub-functions of the duties described above. The securities cage will be divided into a Box and Vault section, a Receive and Deliver section, a Transfer section and a Reorganization section.

Securities balanced by Cashiering may be in the vault, at depositories, or at a custodial bank. For securities in the vault, the Cashiering Department's procedures begin with the receipt, prior to settlement day, of blotters or computer runs detailing purchases and sales to be settled or cleared. Accompanying the reports are clearing corporation balance orders for the settlement of regular-way transactions on the exchanges and NASDAQ, individual security orders for other transactions to be settled through the clearing corporations, and receive and deliver reports for trades to be settled with other firms. Each receive or deliver ticket details the name or identifying symbol of the security to be received or delivered, the name or identifying symbol of the contra-party, and the amount to be received or paid.

The Receive and Deliver area receives the runs or blotters summarizing receive and deliver activity from the P&S Department. Although P&S is responsible for the accuracy and completeness of the reports, Receive and Delivery will check them again before preparing for receipts and deliveries. In some firms, R&D prepares the receive and delivery reports from information provided by P&S.

After verification of the summary reports, the reports are given to the Box and Vault area to request the securities needed for delivery. The clerks remove the requested securities from the box the day before settlement date. If the securities are not on hand, the box is rechecked to verify that the securities are not on location or that they have not been received in the meantime. The securities removed from the box are attached to the orders or tickets and sent to the delivery clerk, who check them, enter the certificate number on the form, and prepare them for delivery. Orders or tickets that cannot be matched to securities in the box are returned to the deliver clerk. If the securities are not delivered in time, the transaction becomes a "fail to deliver". A fail to delivery is a receivable on the balance sheet, because when the securities are delivered, the firm will receive cash.

Receive orders and tickets are retained by the receive clerks for use on settlement date. As securities are received through the clearing corporations or from other brokers, the receive clerks match them to the orders and tickets and enter the certificate numbers. Any orders or tickets not matched to securities received represent "fails to receive". Fails to receive are payables on the balance sheet because when the securities are delivered, the firm must pay out cash.

The National Securities Clearing Corporation (NSCC) provides its participants with a report known as the projection report. It informs the Cashiers area of remaining settlement positions due that day and the net settlement positions for the next day. All day, receives and delivers are posted to the projection report. At the end of the day, receives or delivers that have not been completed are placed on tomorrow's projection report. Since the positions on the report are part of "continuous net settlement" (CNS), one day's uncompleted delivery or receive position is simply netted into the next day's positions. In CNS, open fail items are updated daily. In a given security, a firm can only have one fail to receive or one fail to deliver at a time or be flat. This system eliminates the multiple fails that non-CNS securities experience.

Continuous Net Settlement

The Continuous Net Settlement System operated by NSCC was developed in recognition of the need for complete automation in the area of processing securities transactions.

Incorporated in CNS are functions which allow for the consolidation of transactions and automated book-entry movement of securities in a centralized and controlled environment. Compared transactions enter CNS through various front-end systems, such as NSCC's comparison and trade recording services, Depository Trust Company's Institutional Delivery System (ID), and interfaces of compared trades from other clearing corporations. As these compared transactions are processed through CNS, reports are generated, providing a complete audit trail.

The key features of CNS include the following:

❑ All trades in CNS eligible securities may be included in the system, regardless of size.

❑ Continuous recycling permits securities received by participants on settlement day to be turned around for delivery on a same-day basis.

❑ Deliveries between CNS and participants' depository positions are automatic.

❑ All deliveries are made through the Depository Trust Company by book-entry procedures, allowing CNS to operate in a certificateless environment.

❑ Closing positions are marked-to-market daily, giving protection to all participants in the event of a failure of any individual firm.

The CNS Process

The CNS process is designed to be completely automatic and minimize manual intervention by the participating broker-dealer. On settlement date, all transactions in each security are combined to produce a net position representing the number of shares or bonds to be settled by the participants. Once transactions are recorded in CNS, NSCC becomes the opposite side to all long and short positions, eliminating any need for participants to maintain streetside records on a trade-for-trade basis.

CNS short positions, representing securities owed by the participants to NSCC, are passed against the participant's DTC account and delivered to NSCC. This automatic delivery process occurs once during the night and is repeated continuously on settlement day (T+3). In order for participants to avoid segregation violations and effectively meet other delivery needs, an override procedure is provided to modify this automatic system.

CNS long positions, representing position owed by NSCC to the participant, are processed in an order determined by an algorithm involving the age of the position and a computer generated random number. As securities are received by NSCC in CNS, they are automatically allocated to the participant's long position. The automatic allocation process can be modified through specific instructions submitted by the participant for a particular trade or through standing instructions maintained in the CNS accounting system.

Since all CNS movements are made by book entry and the system operates without certificates, therefore, there are no denominational considerations in the short cover or long allocation functions.

Key CNS Reports

The CNS Compared Trade Summary

This report, which is issued on the morning of trade date + 2, summarizes all transactions due to settle on the following business day. In addition to hard copy, the CNS Compared Trade Summary is available in machine readable form.

The Projection Report

This report, produced every morning, details the participant's current net position in each security issue, transactions due to settle on the following business day, plus any stock dividends due for payment. The combination of these three items results in a single net position due for settlement.

The Accounting Summary

The Accounting Summary provides a comprehensive review of the participant's CNS account on a daily basis. Included in the report is information regarding activity, open positions, and money balances. Broker-dealers seeking to automate their securities and money movement procedures can request this report in machine-readable form.

Dividend and Interest Accounting

CNS also provides a dividend and interest accounting system which requires little or no intervention by the participant. It provides payments, eliminates fail claims, automatically protects as-of transactions and avoids the use of due bills.

On the dividend or interest record date, the CNS system scans each participants long and short positions. These positions, along with the anticipated dividends or interest to be paid or charged are shown on a Record Date Report. On the day before payable date, the Dividend Activity Report is issued, showing all dividend activity which will be applied to the participant's account on the following day.

Money Settlement

In CNS processing, money settlement is effected on the basis of comparing the participant's closing money balance for the previous day to the net market value of the CNS account today. Each participant either collects or pays NSCC one figure representing the amount necessary to bring the CNS account into balance with the net market value of the open positions.

DELIVERY OF SECURITIES

The method of delivery of securities varies based on the customers' needs and the delivery instructions given to the broker-dealer. These methods include:

Deliver Versus Payment

With Delivery Versus Payment (DVP) accounts, or Cash on Delivery (COD) accounts, the customer pays for the purchase of securities upon delivery and get paid for their sales upon the receipt of securities by the broker-dealer. Institutional customers, such as banks, pension funds, and insurance companies, use these accounts.

The Institutional Delivery System

The Institutional Delivery (ID) System is a service designed by DTC for confirming, authorizing, and settling trades initiated by an institution in a automated manner that reduces errors, time delay, and costs and simplifies settlements. Simply stated, the ID System works as follows:

* A broker-dealer executing an institutional trade furnished DTC with trade data (price, quantity, issue, etc.). DTC routes this information to the institution in a form that is recognized as a legal confirmation.

* If the ID confirmation accurately reflects the institutions order, the

institution sends an affirmation to DTC. If the confirmation does not agree with the institutions records, the institution can act early enough in the settlement process so that the broker-dealer can enter the correct trade information into the ID System.

* Upon receiving the affirmation, DTC forwards an Eligible Trade Report to both the agent bank and the broker-dealer to schedule settlement.

* If the delivering participant has sufficient securities in its DTC account, DTC will automatically complete the delivery by book-entry on the morning of settlement date and process the related money settlement.

If the delivering institution does not have sufficient securities in its DTC account, it will be notified early in the morning on settlement date. The participant still has the opportunity to provide the securities for delivery later on settlement date.

If the security is not DTC eligible, the deliverer and receiver may use special deliver/receive instructions to settle the transaction outside the depository system.

Other depositories offer services that are similar to DTC's ID System that may have some differences but are also designed to facilitate the settlement process.

Custody of Securities

Over time, custody procedures have changed to match changes in technology and increased efficiency in trade processing. For instance, most corporate securities and many municipal are issued in DTC eligible form and transactions can be processed via book entry, requiring no on site vaulting by broker-dealers. Government securities are also issued in book entry form. In addition, listed options are certificateless, so vaulting is not necessary. However, many securities still trade in physical form and requiring vaulting in order to process transactions.

The Vault area maintains custody of all securities in the possession of the firm. Those securities that may be used for deliveries, loans, or collateral are kept in a active box. Each morning, the active box securities are moved from the vault to the processing areas, and at night the securities are returned to the vault. Vault personnel are responsible for recording security movements to or from the active box each day. The record is forwarded to the Stock Record Department as a basis for the entry to box positions on the stock record.

Segregated or safekeeping positions will remain in the vault until their removal is requested. Vault personnel remove securities from segregation or safekeeping on instructions from the Margin Department.

Securities received during the day by the Receive and Deliver area are checked for negotiability, matched to the appropriate tickets, and sent to the vault personnel. However, if the securities are required for delivery the same day, they will be given directly to the delivery clerks. The vault clerks will enter securities received on the vault record, and file the securities in the active box. The clerks remove securities from the active box on the basis of deliver orders or tickets, enter the quantity on the vault records, and send the securities to the delivery clerks. The clerks also remove securities on the basis of transfer tickets or segregation or safekeeping instructions, and send them to the Transfer area or the vault.

According to Regulation T, there are two situations where securities must be segregated and cannot be commingled with the securities of the broker-dealer:

* customer fully paid securities; and

* customer excess margin securities (the market value of securities in excess of 140% of the customer's debit balance).

Segregated securities cannot be used for loans, short sales, or hypothecation. Securities at DTC that should be segregated will be highlighted with "seg" memo field on their reports and on the broker-dealer's stock record.

Securities in "safekeeping" are customer securities as to which the broker-dealer is only acting as custodian.

THE TRANSFER DEPARTMENT

The Transfer area is responsible for sending securities to the transfer agents for reissue in the name of the new security holder of record or for reissue in different denominations. The transfer agent is usually bank and is selected by the security issuer. Transfer personnel also ensure that the securities are returned promptly from the transfer agent. In addition, Transfer maintains records detailing which securities are currently in transfer.

Customers may request that their fully paid securities be transferred into their name, or they can remain in the name of the broker-dealer. Securities purchased on margin are usually transferred into "street name".

For securities to be transferred into the name of a customer, transfer instruction forms are prepared according to the instructions given by the customer. Instructions are given by the customer either at the time of purchase, transfer, or the customer may issue standing instructions for all of their inventory holdings.

When securities are to be transferred in the name of the firm, the Cashier's Department will prepare the form.

There are two forms of transfer that securities may be placed in: 1) regular transfer; and 2) legal transfer.

Regular Transfer

A regular transfer is a transfer of the securities of an individual investor who submits the issue with all of the required paperwork (power of attorney, etc.). Negotiable securities will be sent directly from the Cashier's area to Transfer for processing. Securities which are not fully negotiable will be held in the vault while notice is sent to the appropriate branch office to obtain the necessary documents.

Legal Transfer

Legal transfers are transfers which require additional documentation because the customer is a corporation or an estate. The documentation for corporations includes a corporate resolution and the corporate by-laws or charter. The documentation required for estates includes a copy of the death certificate, tax waivers, and an affidavit of domicile.

When securities are fully prepared for transfer, they are delivered to the transfer agent with a copy of the transfer form. The transfer agent destroys the current certificate, issues a new certificate with a new certificate number, registers the securities in accordance with the instructions, and returns them to the broker-dealer.

Depository Trust Company (DTC) offers transfer services to its members which greater reduces time and the chances of error on the transfer. Given instruction from a broker-dealer, DTC gives the securities to the transfer agent who follows the usual procedures.

When the newly issued securities are ready, DTC returns them to the member firm.

THE RECEIPT AND DELIVERY DEPARTMENT

The Receipt and Delivery area is responsible for the processing of receipts and deliveries of securities to and from customers.

When securities are received from customers, various parties are notified to update the firm's records for the delivery, including Stock Record, and the Margin Department. Then securities are used by Cashier's for deliveries, to be sent to transfer, or to be put in safekeeping.

Deliveries of securities to customer's accounts can be made only with the approval of the Margin Department. Only fully paid securities can be delivered to customers. Prior to delivery, the securities must be transferred into the name of the customer.

This area is also responsible for preparing a Securities Received and Delivered Blotter to ensure that receipts and deliveries are properly monitored.

CASH RECEIPTS AND DISBURSEMENTS

The Cash Receipts and Disbursements area is responsible for receiving payments and making disbursements and for preparing a record of transactions. Checks and cash are received from customers, banks, and brokers either through the window or over the wire. The funds are received either for payment of a securities purchase, additional equity for their margin accounts (in the event of a margin call), or for deposit in their cash accounts. Cash receipts are recorded on the Cash Receipts Blotter and are usually reconciled to the bank statement at least once a month.

Cash disbursements are usually made by check or over the wire. Cash disbursements may be monitored via the checking account statement.

THE STOCK RECORD DEPARTMENT

The Stock Record Department is the focal point at which all of the reporting, security movements, and accountibilities for securities by the firm converges. The Stock Record Department determine movements and accountibilities of individual securities in and out of the firm. In summary, through the use of various records and reports, the Stock Record Department keeps an inventory of securities that are within the firms possession or control.

The major control record used to track inventory is called the stock record. The stock record reflects positions in all securities within the firm's possession or control. It is maintained by the double-entry principal, similar to accounting records, with entries booked as either "long" or "short".

Long positions are payables of the firm for securities held for or owed to others. Long positions include ownership of or claims to securities by customers, the firm, individual partners of the firm, and other broker-dealers (including securities borrower from other broker-dealers and securities that the firm failed to deliver to other broker-dealers).

Short positions consist of securities physically held by the firm and receivables from others for securities held for or due to the firm.

Short positions include physical possession by the firm in the active box, in custody as segregated or safekeeping items, items in transfer, securities loaned to other broker-dealers, and securities failed to receive from other broker dealers.

Every securities transaction or movement results in both a long and short entry to the stock record. In other words, every long entry is offset by a short entry, just like in accounting, every credit is offset by a debit. The total longs for each security in the stock record must equal the total shorts, otherwise, there is a stock record break which must be researched and "cleaned-up".

The stock record is usually maintained in security order (either alphabetically, by CUSIP number, or by a firm-assigned security number), and accounts appear within each security. There are two types of stock records: 1) the daily take-off, and 2) the main stock record. The daily take-off details accounts that experienced movements or transactions on a particular day. Each daily take-off record updates the main stock record. The main stock record (produced weekly or monthly) shows all accounts for which a position existed on a given day.

Frequently, the stock record will detail memo fields, such as segregation, safekeeping, etc. These memo fields are used by different areas of the Cashier's Department to locate securities for deliveries, loans, and other uses.

PART III: ACCOUNTING AND RECORDKEEPING

CHAPTER 4: ACCOUNTING OVERVIEW

THE NATURE OF ACCOUNTING

The purpose of any business is to make a profit. The profit motive is the major consideration that guides a business in choosing certain market segments, allocating resources, hiring employees and managers, and selecting a marketing strategy. In essence, the stability and viability of a company is dependent upon the profitability of its various units.

Profitability is not just important to those who work for and manage companies, but also to the investors (stockholders, other owners, and creditors) who commit money to the company. Stability and profitability are necessary to entice investors to give money to a company.

The concern for profitability by managers, employees, and investors creates the need for financial information. People need to know information like net income, total liabilities, shareholders equity, the amount of goods and services sold, and how much liquid assets are available. Financial information helps interested parties evaluate the profitability, and therefore, the ultimate success of a business venture. The primary purpose of accounting is to provide decision makers and interested parties with financial information that will help them make good decisions concerning a business.

Accounting may be defined as the process of (i) collecting financial information; (ii) analyzing it to determine what information is relevant to particular decisions; (iii) presenting the relevant information in a meaningful form to the user; and (iv) assisting the user in interpreting the information and applying it in the decision making process. Because a significant portion of the accounting process involves the communication of information concerning business activity, accounting is known as the "language of business". Information presented through the accounting process is often the primary line of communication between a business and its managers, employees, and investors.

THE TYPES OF ACCOUNTING

Because of the varying types of information needed by

organizations, there are differing fields of accounting. The fields of accounting associated with these different uses are:

- ❑ Financial Accounting
- ❑ Managerial Accounting
- ❑ Tax Accounting

Although individual accountants may perform different functions than those noted above, they are the most common functional sub-divisions.

FINANCIAL ACCOUNTING

A large number of individuals and organizations require financial information on companies, especially publicly traded companies. These individuals are usually not involved in the day-to-day management, but still require periodic financial updates on the performance of the company. Such information is the focus of financial accounting and is communicated on a quarterly and/or annual basis by means of reports called financial statements. They are used for external reporting, that is, to report information to those outside company.

Financial statements consist of (i) a balance sheet; (ii) an income statement; (iii) a statement of changes in financial position. Additional financial information is also provided in the notes to the financial statements.

Interpretive and analytical information and further discussions of items listed in the financial statement are also contained in the notes. The individuals and entities interested in the financial statements include absentee owners, stockholders, creditors, financial analysts, unions, taxing authorities, regulatory agencies, and the state and federal government.

One other aspect of financial accounting is that the preparation of financial statements and the information presented therein must adhere to certain procedures and rules called generally accepted accounting principals ("GAAP"). The primary users of financial statements do not have access to all the information that is developed within the company. GAAP helps to standardize the reporting of information within financial statements. Also, GAAP gives the user some assurance about the methods used to prepare the financial statements.

MANAGERIAL ACCOUNTING

Managerial accounting relates to the accounting for the day-to-day management of a business.

Managerial accounting is intra-company in nature because it deals with information that is collected, organized, analyzed and presented by the organization's accountants to management. Managerial accounting consists of the following functions:

Cost Accounting

Cost Accounting determines the costs involved in a business. For instance, the cost in manufacturing a product, developing a process, or operating a department. Cost accounting data are necessary to establish profitable sales prices and profitable production or sales functions.

Budgeting

Budgeting is important for three reasons. First, it requires management to establish goals and plans for the future operations of the business. Second, budgets hold management accountable for the company's results. Third, it provides a yardstick by which the actual results can be measured.

Capital Budgeting

Capital budgeting refers to the process whereby decisions are made concerning the company's acquisition of major resources such as buildings, computers, and land.

Evaluation of Operations

One of management's key responsibilities is to evaluate the operations of a specific department, plant, or division within a company. Using a brokerage firm as an example, the risk arbitrage area within the Block Trading Desk may be evaluated for its profitability. Unprofitable operations can be identified and attended to, and if need be terminated. Outstanding managers of profitable departments can be rewarded. Managerial accounting plays an important role in obtaining and assisting in the evaluation of the data necessary for such decisions.

Internal Control

All organizations have resources, especially cash, that must be protected against fraud or misappropriation. In addition, checks and balances should be built into the accounting system so that data collected by the system can be relied upon to produce accurate internal and external reports. The safeguarding of resources and the controls included in the accounting system are called internal controls.

Internal controls also monitor the company's compliance with company policies and outside laws and regulations, the completeness and accuracy of financial data, and the efficiency and effectiveness of operations. Internal controls are implemented by management with the assistance of the firm's accountants, internal auditors, and external auditors.

All effective systems of internal control have certain features in common. These features or principles summarize the key concepts used to appraise any function or system. The following list reviews the techniques and concepts necessary for an effective review of internal controls.

❑ Reliable Personnel with Clear Responsibilities

A key element in the success of a internal control system is people, for they are the ones who have the capability to undermine the system. Procedures to hire, train, motivate, and supervise employees are essential. Most importantly, is the character and integrity of the people who run the organization. Management of corporations set the tone for the organizations they run. If management tolerates unstructured, undisciplined, and poorly controlled departments, then they are responsible for any losses and frauds that are certain to occur in that environment.

❑ Separation of Duties

The separation of duties not only helps ensure the accurate compilation of information but also limits the opportunities for fraud that require the collusion of two or more individuals. The separation of duties can be divided into four parts:

❑ Separation of Operational Responsibility from Recordkeeping Responsibility.

The entire accounting function should be separated from operating departments so that objective, independent records may be kept by other operating people or clerks.

❑ Separation of the Custody of Assets from Recordkeeping.

This is prime area for lower level employees to perpetrate frauds repeatedly without detection.

For example, the bookkeeper should not handle cash, and the cashier should not have access to ledger accounts such as the individual records of customers, or the ledger of their own daily receipts.

❑ Separation of the Authorization of Transactions from the Custody of Related Assets.

To the extent possible, persons who authorize transactions should not have control over the related asset. For example, a bookkeeper opens the mail, removes a $1,000 check from a customer, and somehow cashes it. To hide the theft, the bookkeeper debits the firm's Allowance for Bad Debt Account and credits Accounts Receivable to write-off the amount owed to the firm. This way, the firm will not chase the customer for the money, and the customer will not know that the firm never deposited his check.

❑ Separation of Duties from the Accounting Function

An employee should not be able to record a transaction from its origin to its ultimate posting in a ledger. Independent performance of various phases of transaction processing will help ensure control over errors.

❑ Proper Authorization

Authorization simply means that the activities of a company must be reviewed and approved by the appropriate level of employee.

Authorization can be general or specific. General authorization is usually found in writing. It often sets definite limits on spending, capital investments, or credit extension to customers. There may also be complete prohibitions of certain types of illegal or unethical activities. Specific authorization means that a superior manager must permit (usually in writing) any deviations from the limits set by general authorization.

❑ Adequate Documents

Documentation of the activities of the company is important to maintain adequate internal control. Immediate, complete, and tamper-proof recording is the goal. The documentation includes maintaining original sales invoices, cash register tapes, and posting journals and ledgers.

❑ Proper Procedures

Many organizations develop procedures manuals which specify the specific flow of documents and processes and provide information and instructions to facilitate adequate recordkeeping. Procedures manuals reduce the number of errors made by employees and serve as valuable training tools.

❑ Physical Safeguards

Losses of assets (cash, inventory, securities, furniture, computers, and records) can be prevented by physical safeguards such as safes, locks, security guards, security cameras, and limited access. Small businesses are especially vulnerable to thefts, and use safeguards such as guard dogs, alarm systems, and special lighting.

❑ Bonding, Vacations, and Rotation of Duties

Key people may be subject to excessive temptation. Top executives, branch managers, and individuals who handle cash or inventories should have understudies, be forced to take vacations, and be bonded.

❑ Independent Checks

All phases of the system should be subjected to periodic review by outsiders (e.g., external auditors) and internal auditors who do not ordinarily have contact with the operation under review. Auditors have a degree of objectivity that allows them to spot weaknesses in controls overlooked by managers immersed in day-to-day operations.

❑ Cost-Benefit Analysis

New and existing businesses should be reviewed periodically to determine their contribution to the organization. Cost-benefit analyses help the company decide whether it should continue with a particular business or use its resources in other, more potentiality profitable activities.

Internal Auditing

Once a company has established procedures for recordkeeping and internal control, it is important that those procedures be followed by each employee of the company. In addition, it is important that the internal controls in place are continuing to function properly, and are the most efficient and effective controls affordable by the company. The function of maintaining and improving proper internal control and monitoring the economical and efficient use of resources within a company is called internal auditing.

❑ Internal auditing is the control over all other controls in the company.

Most of the larger broker-dealers have at least one internal auditor to ensure that management's objectives, policies, and procedures are followed, and to ensure compliance with the myriad of securities rules and regulations. The role of the internal auditor is different from the role of the external auditor, whose job it is to verify the external financial statements of a company.

TAX ACCOUNTING

Tax accounting includes the preparation of tax reports and tax planning. Tax reporting includes calculating the estimated income tax liability on a quarterly basis, and supervising payment to the local, state, and federal government. The purpose of tax planning is to arrange business operations in order to minimize the amount of taxes paid. Tax accounting requires an intimate knowledge of state and federal tax laws and of the company's operations and tax status.

"GAAP" and Tax Reporting

There is a difference between GAAP for financial statement preparation and the Internal Revenue Code that governs the manner in which income tax returns are prepared.

The purpose of GAAP is to ensure that the financial status and profitability of a company are fairly presented in the company's financial statements. Generally accepted accounting principles are based on the foundations of accounting theory and are logically developed from them.

The Internal Revenue Code has two basic objectives:

(i) to raise funds for the operation of the federal government and its programs, and

(ii) to influence different segments of the economy.

Neither of these objectives relates to fairness of financial reporting. The first objective is met by taxing the profits of a business and income of an individual within limits defined by the Code. The second goal is accomplished by giving advantages to, or taking away advantages from, different segments of the economy. Tax advantages and disadvantages are not based on any fundamental theories of accounting (such as GAAP), but on the desired effects they will have on the economy.

Because of these differences in objectives, GAAP and the Internal Revenue Code have many procedural differences. These differences must be known by preparers of financial statements and tax reports because adjustments have to be made from one system to another.

There are GAAP pronouncements directed specifically at broker-dealers to tailor official accounting requirements to their special situations. We won't detail every broker-dealer related pronouncement, but there are two that should be mentioned.

First, GAAP requires that all broker-dealer transactions be booked on trade date. Many broker-dealers keep their books on a settlement date basis and accrue payables, receivables, and income expense items on unsettled trades when financial statements are prepared. We will further discuss trade date and settlement date accounting during the Recordkeeping chapter.

Second, GAAP requires all positions held by a broker-dealer to be marked-to-market daily. The traditional GAAP method of valuation involves pricing investments at the lower of cost or market. In order to compute unrealized profits/losses, an inventory costing methodology must be chosen. Gains and losses on firm trading accounts will be computed using either the "first in, first out" method (FIFO), or the "last in, first out" method, (LIFO).

Other broker-dealer related GAAP pronouncements can be found in the AICPA Audit and Accounting Guide titled "Audits of Brokers and Dealers In Securities", which is prepared by the Stockbrokerage Auditing Subcommittee.

This section has provided a brief overview of the nature of accounting and some of the basic concepts within accounting. Next, we will review some of the key components of financial statements, the balance sheet and the income statement.

CHAPTER 5: THE BALANCE SHEET

The balance sheet is a photograph of financial status at an instant in time. The balance sheet of a company consists of its assets, liabilities, and owner's or stockholder's equity. The easiest way to remember the components is to utilize the accountant's balance sheet equation:

Assets = Liabilities + Owner's Equity

ASSETS

Assets are economic resources that are expected to benefit future cash inflows or help reduce future cash outflows. Some common examples of assets on the balance sheet of a securities broker-dealer are:

- Cash
- Clearing organization deposits
- Clearing Firm Deposits
- Special Reserve Bank Account deposits
- Deposits from securities borrowed
- Securities purchased under agreements to resell
- Securities positions
- Broker-dealer receivables
- Customer receivables
- Dividend, principal, and interest receivable
- Membership in exchanges
- Computer equipment
- Furniture and fixtures
- Account receivables

We will explore some of the more liquid assets and discuss how the assets can be reviewed by accountants, analysts, and auditors.

Cash

Cash represents money on deposit in the firm's checking accounts and money in the vault determined to be owned by the firm. For auditors, any bank statements purported to represent cash owned by the firm should have the firm's name (and the firm's name only) as owner of the account. In addition, a bank reconciliation should have been performed as of the most recent month-end.

Clearing Organization Deposits

Clearing organizations net individual transactions in the same security to arrive at one position per security to be delivered or received between a clearing organization and a firm, and one net money balance to be received or paid. Money is received or paid on a daily basis, and the monetary balance in each firm's account typically equals the contract value, which approximates the market value, of all open positions. Examples of clearing organizations are National Securities Clearing Corporation, which clears equity transactions of member firms, and the Government Securities Clearing Corporation, which clears government securities trades.

Deposits at clearing corporations are receivables for advances made to secure open positions at the clearing organization. Deposits may be made in securities or cash. The types of securities suitable for this purpose are defined by each clearing organization and generally are comprised of U.S. Treasury Bills. For auditors, deposits at clearing organizations should be confirmed, and the prices of securities compared to the price provided by an independent pricing source.

Clearing Firm Deposits

Clearing firm deposits are monies placed on deposit by "introducing" broker-dealers with the firms that will clear their trades for them. These deposits are demanded by large, clearing broker-dealers as a form of security and a pledge that the smaller introducing firms will meet all of their obligations under the clearing agreement.

Special Reserve Bank Account Deposits

As required by SEC Rule 15c3-3 (The Customer Protection Rule), money or the equivalent amount of U.S. Treasury Bills must be set aside in a Special Reserve Bank Account. The amount required to be set aside will equal the net credit balance, as calculated by the Customer Reserve Formula, which is attributable to the firm's customers. Auditors should confirm the existence of the bank account, and verify that the account is subject to an agreement that in the event of liquidation the balance is to be used solely to satisfy customers' claims.

Deposits for Securities Borrowed

Deposits for securities borrowed represents amounts paid by a firm to lending brokers for securities that the firm has borrowed. The deposits are collateralized by the securities borrowed, and the deposit and securities should be approximately of the same value. The securities borrowed should be marked-to-market every day.

If the market value of the securities borrowed declines substantiality below the deposit, a portion of the deposit should be returned to the borrowing broker-dealer. If the value of the securities increases, the firm may be required to post additional monies to the deposit.

Auditors should confirm the existence of the deposit with the lending firm. In the addition, any significant differences between the deposit and the securities borrowed should questioned.

Securities Purchased Under Agreements to Resell

Repurchase agreements are formal contracts in which one broker-dealer sells securities, usually U.S. Treasury securities, to another firm, with the agreement to buy them back at a set price by a designated period of time. Any funds paid to another firm for the purchase of securities under the agreement are considered to be a receivable.

Securities Positions

Securities positions on the balance sheet are positions in firm inventory accounts and are owned by the firm. Firm inventory accounts can categorized as either trading accounts or investment accounts. Trading accounts hold securities earmarked for resale to customers or other broker-dealers. Investment securities are intended to be held for longer periods of time and are purchased with the expectation that dividends, interest, and capital gains will be earned on the investment.

Securities positions may be classified as marketable and not readily marketable securities on the balance sheet. Securities in firm inventory account are priced at the current market value for balance sheet purposes. Unrealized appreciation and depreciation in values are included in determining net income.

Auditors should compare the values for securities positions to independent pricing sources. Usually, broker-dealers have staff also comparing traders end-of-day marks to external pricing sources as an internal control.

Broker-Dealer Receivables and Receivables from Clearing Organizations

Broker-dealer receivables consist mainly of receivables due to fails to delivers, floor brokerage fees receivable, receivables due from clearing brokers (and to introducing broker-dealers), and receivables from clearing corporations.

Fails to Deliver

Fails to deliver are sell transactions to another broker-dealer in which the firm fails to deliver the securities sold by settlement date. The receivable is the money due to the firm when the securities are sent to the contra-party. The receivable amount is the contract dollar value of the securities sold.

The contra-transactions are usually fails to receive from another broker-dealer or short sales in customer or firm accounts.

Receivables due from Clearing Broker-Dealers (and to Introducing Broker-Dealers)

Broker-dealers that are small, not well capitalized, or do not choose to be bothered with the complications of running a back office operation, may opt to become "introducing broker-dealers".

An introducing broker-dealer elects not to hold customers' securities or funds but to send them to a larger, better capitalized firm for maintenance. The introducing firm may receive customers' funds and securities, but they must "promptly" forward them to the clearing broker-dealer within 24 hours. All deliveries of funds and securities must be made from the clearing firm.

There are three types of clearing firms, distinguished by the clearing methods they use: (i) self clearing; (ii) fully disclosed; and (iii) omnibus account arrangements.

Self-Clearing

A self-clearing firm receives and delivers securities and monies directive with the customer or contra broker-dealer. A firm may utilize the services of a clearing bank. A clearing bank's services include the physical receipt and delivery of securities, access to the book entry system of the Federal Reserve Banks (Fed Wire), and the extension of credit to finance the firm's positions. The specific arrangements between a firm and the clearing bank will usually be evidenced by a written agreement.

Fully Disclosed

A fully disclosed firm is one which places its order to purchase or sell securities through a clearing broker-dealer and completely identifies the customer to the clearing broker-dealer. The clearing broker-dealer usually maintains most of the required books and records for the introducing broker-dealer. The introducing broker-dealer's customers' accounts are carried on the books of the clearing firm, and the clearing firm treats those accounts as if they were its own. The clearing firm is responsible for ensuring that the accounts are collateralized and maintained in compliance with the appropriate regulatory requirements. The introducing firm and the clearing firm will have a written agreement detailing the specifics of their arrangements.

Omnibus Account Arrangements

In an omnibus account, an introducing firm maintains a single account with a clearing firm in its own name and does not disclose the identity of its customers whose purchases and sales of securities are cleared through the carrying firm. The introducing firm places the orders of its customers through the carrying firm that performs all back office and cashiering functions. The introducing firm may execute its own trades or use the carrying firm for execution. A carrying firm treats the omnibus account as a single account having an aggregate debit or credit balance. It is the introducing firm's responsibility to ensure that prompt payment is made on each customer's cash account and that each customer's margin account is properly margined.

Omnibus accounts must be reconciled no less than monthly. Auditors should independently verify a firm's reconciliation of the omnibus account. Unreconciled security positions and money balances in omnibus accounts could jeopardize a firm's calculation of net capital. Inaccurate positions can result in direct charges to the firm's capital.

Broker-dealers carry an account on the books which reflect the activity in the omnibus account. Frequently, the clearing firm supplies the member with daily runs of activity in the omnibus account.

Reconciliation of Omnibus Clearing Accounts

Reconciliation of the activity on a daily basis will prevent the development of more complex problems which have to be resolved at month end. The prompt reconciliation of discrepancies is especially significant because of the complex structure of the active omnibus account which can involve cash balances, securities positions, options positions, and option strategies. Also consider that all of this activity is taking place in the context of a margin account which requires the introducing firm to monitor the status of customer fully paid and excess margin securities.

Reconciling omnibus accounts involves the same mechanics as reconciling a bank account. This consists of adding back to the firm balance items booked in the firm account that have not cleared the bank or other type of account and subtracting charges made in the bank or other account which have not been booked in the firm account. Potential reconciliation items affecting the omnibus cash balance are:

1) initial clearing deposits

2) trades (options and securities)

3) margin deposits

4) cash received and disbursed

5) interest charges in debit balances

6) dividends paid on any security on deposit

7) proceeds from exercises and assignments of options

Some examples of reconciliation items are:

a) Differences in the calculation of proceeds and commissions on the part of the two brokers;

b) Checks or securities in transit between the two brokers;

c) Interest charges and dividend credits that have not been picked up on the introducing firms books;

d) As of trades; and

e) Unreconciled trades.

Security positions must also be reconciled. First, the total quantity for each security shown on the omnibus account statement must be compared to the introducing firm's position records and statement of account with the clearing broker-dealer, regardless of whether the security is "free" or "segregated". This is to ensure that positions agree in total. Next, check the location of each security to determine if it is free or segregated. The introducing firm notes on its own records the fully-paid securities that must be segregated. Segregation instructions are then sent to the clearing broker. SEC Rule 15c3-3 requires that broker-dealers reduce all customers' fully-paid and excess margin securities to its possession or control. An omnibus account is considered a good control location under the rule only to the extent that the broker "has instructed such carrying broker-dealer to maintain physical possession or control of them free of any charge, lien, or claim of any kind in favor of such carrying broker-dealer or any persons claiming through such carrying broker-dealer".

Whether such securities are free or segregated is the exclusive responsibility of the introducing firm. The carrying firm has no means of knowing what is fully-paid and what is not unless the introducing firm advises specifically on each item. Auditors can determine from the firm's books and records if customer fully-paid securities carried in an omnibus account are promptly segregated.

Receivables from Clearing Organizations

Clearing members are required by the clearing corporations to confirm, in writing, all open positions and money balances on a monthly basis. Therefore, it is necessary to perform periodic and timely reconciliations of activity in these accounts.

All trades cleared through the clearing corporation and all securities lodged with the depositories require multiple entries be made to the books and records of the member. This involves funneling through this account net money settlements on transactions, physical receipts and deliveries to and from the account, entries transferring securities to and from the depository, and dividend, interest, and credit entries.

All this activity occurring in the same account necessitates a daily reconciliation by the member. Failure to maintain daily reconciliations on the clearing account results in extremely complex differences which may become impossible to trace. To the extent that such differences exist, and are short differences (i.e., the clearing corporation shows the firm owes them the position, but the member firm does not reflect the position on its records, or conversely, the firm shows the clearing corporation owes shares to the member, but the clearing corporation does not reflect such a position) the market value of such position becomes a charge to net capital after it has been aged in accordance with the provisions of the Net Capital Rule. The Net Capital Rule is discussed in more detail in Chapter XX.

Clearing account money balances are a net combination of clearing deposits, settled transactions (both buys and sells), checks paid or received for daily net settlements, dividend, interest, or reorganization credits or charges, and clearing charges imposed on the member by the clearing entity.

Depository account money balances are a combination of funds received as the result of bank loans made against the member firm's collateral held by the depository, and/or funds received as a result of the depository's having loaned securities to other broker-dealers on behalf of the member firm, the dollar amount being the market value of such securities loaned. These balances would be adjusted by any payment of bank loans obtained, or the return of any securities borrowed by other broker-dealers.

Security position balances in the clearing account are netted by individual security for all transactions (both buys and sells), receipt and delivery of securities, stock dividend charges or credits, and transfer of securities positions to or from the depository.

The depository will make provisions for the segregation of customer's fully paid and excess margin securities; its daily record will indicate the location of such segregated securities, as well as securities for which the firm has provided transfer instructions. Member firms are responsible for generating these entries. Securities available to loan to other broker-dealers, or for bank hypothecation are identified based on information provided by the broker-dealer. Securities positions with national clearing and depository entities are marked-to-market on a daily basis. Adjusted prices on uncleared and settled security positions with the entity will affect daily net money balances due to or from the clearing corporation. The firm's books and records should be mirror image of the records supplied by the clearing corporation and depository, including net money balances, net security positions, and segregation and transfer locations for all securities.

A reconciliation of all such accounts is essential in order for the firm and the auditors to determine that the money balances and security positions are in agreement. Reconciliations of clearing and depository accounts include comparisons of money balances, and accounting for any differences between the records of the member and the clearing or depository statements. Also, each net security position must be compared and any differences must be resolved.

Items to be reconciled include securities in transit between the clearing or depository and the member; checks in transit; segregation instructions in transit; clearing charges made by the clearing entity but not booked by the member; dividend and interest charges and credits for cash, as well as charges or credits for stock dividends, made by the clearing entity but not booked by the member; reverse stock splits effected on the books of the clearing entity but not on the books of the member; and trade differences, i.e., trades reflected on the books and records of the member, but not on the records of the clearing entity; or trades reflected on the records of the clearing entity but not on the books of the member. When reconciliations of clearing accounts are made on a daily basis, errors and discrepancies are quickly located and resolved.

Auditors should confirm a sample of open fails to deliver, floor brokerage fees receivable, clearing firm receivables, and clearing corporation receivables with contra parties.

Customer Receivables

Customer receivables are composed of debit balances in customer accounts. Customer accounts exclude the accounts of other broker-dealers, and partners, officers, directors, and stockholders of the firm. Customers' debit balances exist because of purchases of securities by customers on margin, which is a form of credit.

Purchases on margin result in the firm lending the customer a portion of the purchase, which results in the customer owing the firm the amount borrowed. These receivables are collateralized by the securities purchased by the customer, which may be used by the firm for financing purposes.

Auditors should ensure that debit balances are adequately secured by the market value of the underlying securities.

Dividend, Principal, and Interest Receivables

These payments are owed to the firm due to securities maintained in firm inventory accounts. These payments should be accrued by the firm on a monthly basis.

LIABILITIES

Liabilities are economic obligations of the organization to outsiders. Some common examples of liabilities on the balance sheet of a broker-dealer are:

- Commercial Paper Outstanding
- Bank Loans
- Securities Sold Short
- Broker-Dealer Payables and Payables to Clearing Organizations
- Securities Sold Under Agreements to Repurchase
- Syndicate Payables
- Customer Payables
- Subordinated Liabilities
- Dividend, Principal, and Interest Payable
- Taxes Payable
- Other Account Payables

Commercial Paper

Many broker-dealers issue commercial paper to finance their day-to-day operations. They favor commercial because it is a short term, and highly liquid method of borrowing. Usually, credit-worthy broker-dealers can get very competitive rates on their short-term commercial paper.

Bank Loans

Broker-dealers obtain bank loans in order to finance firm and customer transactions. Firm and Customer excess margin securities (over 140% of the customer debit balance) are usually used as collateral for these loans.

Auditors should confirm outstanding bank loans and collateral and test to ensure that (i) the collateral is sufficient to secure the loan; and (ii) only customer excess margin securities are used to collateralize the loan.

Securities Sold Short

Securities sold short are positions that were sold but not owned by the broker-dealer. These positions include securities that are "covered" by call options or are "arbitraged" against a proprietary long position in a similar security.

Short sales are executed either because the broker-dealer expects the price of the underlying instrument to decline, or because he did not have the chance to purchase the security into inventory. Eventually, the position must be purchased into inventory and the short position must be eliminated. Profits or losses are earned on the difference between the sale price and the purchase price of the position.

Broker-Dealer Payables and Payables to Clearing Organizations

Balances in this category arise because of fails to receive, net payables to clearing broker-dealers, and net payables to clearing organizations.

Fails to Receive

A fail to receive results from the purchase of a security which the contra broker does not deliver to the firm by settlement date. The payable is created because the money due to the contra broker when the securities are delivered was never paid. The payable amount is the contract dollar value of the securities purchased. The firm has exposure if the market value of the securities not received increases and the contra broker does not deliver. The firm may have to purchase the securities from another broker-dealer at a higher price than the original transaction. The contra-transactions are usually fails to deliver to another broker-dealer.

Auditors should confirm fail to receive balances with the contra brokers. In addition, the aging of fails and the market value of the underlying securities should be reviewed and any problems or discrepancies discussed with management.

Net Payables to Clearing Broker-Dealers

Net payables to clearing broker-dealers are described in the Assets Section under "Broker-Dealer Receivables and Receivables from Clearing Organizations".

Net Payables to Clearing Organizations

Net payables to clearing broker-dealers are described in the Assets Section under "Broker-Dealer Receivables and Receivables from Clearing Organizations".

Securities Sold Under Agreements to Repurchase

Securities sold under agreements to repurchase represent securities used as collateral to obtain funds in a standard repurchase agreement. The securities should be marked-to-market every day to ensure that they adequately collateralize the funds received. Auditors should confirm any balances relating to the transaction and the terms of the agreements reached between the parties.

Syndicate Related Payables

Syndicate managers maintain the books for underwritings they manage and cut the checks for the net profits on the deal shortly after settlement date (90 days for equity deals, and 60 days for municipal deals). The managers should accrue the payables on their books until they are paid out to the syndicate members.

Customer Payables

Payables to customers arise from credit balances in their accounts due to deposited monies and the sale of securities. Auditors review these balances as part of the customer account confirmation process.

Subordinated Liabilities

Subordinated liabilities ("sub loans") are loans which are subordinated to the claims of general creditors as per a formal lending agreement.

Subordinated loans are a very common form of financing amongst broker-dealers. One reason why sub loans are popular is because they receive favorable treatment by the regulators in the calculation of Net Capital.

A secured demand note is a form of subordinated lending. The difference between a secured demand note and other forms of subordinated lending is that the demand note provides the borrower with securities or other collateral that the firm could use to borrow funds to finance their operations.

Auditors should ensure that subordinated loan agreements are approved by the appropriate regulatory bodies, and that they treated correctly in the computation of net capital. In addition, auditors should ensure that the value of the related collateral adequately supports the loan.

Dividend, Principal, and Interest Payable

Cash and stock dividend or principal and interest payables are usually due to other broker-dealers or customers that were long on record date. Payables may also be due because of short sales by the firm.

Auditors should ensure that the payable balances are being aged properly and reported for regulatory accounting purposes. Auditors should also review procedures for recording unclaimed dividends to determine the firm's compliance with state escheatment laws.

Taxes Payable

Corporations, including broker-dealers, must accrue for their estimated income taxes payable and pay them on a quarterly basis. Auditors should ensure that the accruals are being made and that the quarterly payments are being met.

OWNER'S EQUITY/STOCKHOLDER EQUITY

Owner's equity for proprietorships and partnerships is often identified as capital. Owner's equity for a corporation is usually identified as stockholder's equity or shareholder's equity.

Capital investments in a corporation by its owners at the inception of business and subsequently are called paid-in-capital. Paid-in-capital can be reported in two parts: (i) par value; and (ii) paid-in-capital in excess of par value.

Types of Ownership

Business can be organized in many forms. Business owners must decide whether their companies should be organized as sole proprietorships, partnerships, or corporations.

A proprietorship is a separate organization with a single owner. Sole proprietorships tend to be small retail businesses with fewer than 50 employees. From an accounting standpoint, each proprietorship is an individual entity that is separate and distinct from the proprietor.

A partnership is a special form of organization that joins two or more individuals together as co-owners.

Partnerships can be small or gigantic organizations. Many broker-dealers, such as Goldman Sachs, still operate as private partnerships. Again, from an accounting viewpoint, each partnership is an individual entity that is separate from the personal activities of each partner.

Corporations are organizations created by individual state laws. The owners are identified as stockholders or shareholders.

Although large publicly owned corporations have thousands of stockholders, many states require having only one stockholder for an entity to be a corporation; other states require at least two stockholders. Individuals form a corporation by applying to the state for approval of the company's "articles of incorporation". When approved, the corporation becomes a legal entity, an "artificial person", that conducts its business completely apart from its owners. The corporation is also an accounting entity.

The corporate form of organization has many advantages. The most notable feature is the limited liability of its owners, which means that corporate creditors ordinarily have claims against the corporate assets only. In other words, if the company falls into financial trouble, its creditors cannot look for repayment beyond the corporate entity. The owners' personal assets are not subject to lien. In contrast, sole proprietorships and partnerships have unlimited liability, which means creditors can look for repayment beyond the corporation's assets to the owner's personal assets.

FINANCIAL ANALYSIS OF BROKER-DEALER BALANCE SHEETS

The Statement of Financial Condition for Dewey & Howe, Inc., shown in Figure 5.1, is a typical balance sheet of a large full service broker-dealer.

Broker-dealer balance sheets are different from other financial statements in several ways. Some of the balance sheet items that are unique to broker-dealers are listed below:

Figure 5.1

STATEMENT OF FINANCIAL CONDITION FOR DEWEY & HOWE, INC.

December 31, 1989

ASSETS		
Cash		$1,000,000
Secs. Bought W/Agreements to Resell (reverse repo)		5,000,000
Fails to Deliver		2,000,000
Receivables from Customers		4,000,000
Securities Owned (at market)		5,000,000
Furniture & Fixtures (less depre.)		500,000
Other Assets		500,000
TOTAL	**$18,000,000**	
LIABILITIES:		
Drafts Payable		$600,000
Subordinated Loans		2,000,000
Secs. Sold W/Agreement to Repurchase (repos)		5,000,000
Fails to Receive		1,500,000
Payables to Customers		2,000,000
Securities sold but not yet purchased (at market)		1,500,000
Accounts Payable & Other Liabilities		300,000
TOTAL	**$12,900,000**	
STOCKHOLDERS EQUITY:		
Common Stock at Par of $4.90/share (1,000,000 shares offered)		$4,900,000
Paid-in-capital		100,000
Retained Earnings		100,000
Total Stockholder's Equity		$5,100,000
TOTAL LIABILITIES AND STOCKHOLDER'S EQUITY		**$18,000,000**

ASSETS

Cash and Securities

Broker-dealers usually have large amounts of liquid assets in cash and securities. The cash reserves are built up as a result of the need for large purchases of securities, and customer debits earned as a result of margin transactions. Securities balances may be large because of inventory needed for customer purchases, or investments in proprietary accounts.

In general, broker-dealers need to have sufficient liquid assets on its balance sheet to ensure that it has adequate Net Capital for regulatory purposes. Liquid assets, such as cash or marketable securities, receive full or close to full value for Net Capital purposes. Other types of assets, such as non-marketable securities or real estate investments, will be haircut for greater portions of their market value than liquid assets.

Reverse Repurchase Agreements

Reverse repurchase agreements ("reverse repos") are transactions exclusive to broker-dealers. Reverse repos are agreements to buy securities, usually government securities, with the agreement to sell them back to the contra-party at a designated period of time. The party that sells the securities in the agreements usually pays a stated rate of interest for the use of the funds. Reverse repos are in effect collateralized loans for short periods of time, ranging from one day to several months. The party that initially buys the securities (reverse repo) is lending funds to the contra-party, and thus books the transaction as an asset on its balance sheet.

If a broker-dealer has securities in inventory that will not be sold in the near future, reverse repos are an effective method of achieving a more competitive rate of return on the assets. By using reverse repos, the broker-dealer knows that it can achieve this return with the knowledge that the funds will be returned to him in a short period of time.

Customer Receivables

All businesses have receivables from customers. However, most of a broker-dealer's receivables arise from debit balances in customers' margin accounts. These debit balances are secured by the securities purchased, and the securities are marked-to-market every day to ensure that they adequately secure the account. The viability of customer receivables would usually be measured by the age of the balances. However, broker-dealers' receivables should also be reviewed to determine if they are adequately secured by the securities in the account.

LIABILITIES

Subordinated Loans

Broker-dealers use subordinated loans ("sub loans") as an integral part of the financing of their operations. Sub loans are usually for a defined period of time, and are usually made by parties with a close relationship to the broker-dealer or the principals of the broker-dealer, such as a parent company.

Basically, sub loans are popular with broker-dealers because they are subordinated to the claims of general creditors, and because they receive favorable Net Capital treatment if they are approved by NASD or the NYSE.

Short Sales

Short sales are also balance sheet liabilities that are exclusive to broker-dealers. Short sales are sales of securities not currently in the broker-dealers inventory. Short sales may be made to accommodate customer orders. Short sales are also executed when the firm believes the price of a security may decline.

Repurchase Agreements

As mentioned in the section on Assets, repurchase agreements are agreements to sell securities to a contra-broker with the agreement to repurchase the securities at a prearranged point in time. The firm that initially sells the securities pays a stated rate of interest for the use of the funds. Broker-dealers enter into repurchase agreements to help finance their operations with securities they may not currently need.

Securities Lending

The lending and borrowing of securities is usually used to meet the delivery needs of broker-dealers. Broker-dealers that are failing to receive certain securities can borrow them from another firm and make delivery.

Firms can also use securities lending to help finance firm operations. Because of higher interest rates with bank borrowing, securities lending is seen as a more efficient method for borrowing money.

CHAPTER 6: THE INCOME STATEMENT

DEFINITION OF INCOME

What is income and how should it be measured? Income can be viewed as the primary way of evaluating the economic performance of people, businesses, and economies as a whole. How it is measured depends on your role in examining income, e.g., corporate manager, tax accountant, or external auditor. This chapter will briefly explore the concept of income, how it is measured, and the specific balances created during the normal operations of a broker-dealer.

The Operating Cycle

Organizations are usually in business to satisfy a desire for a good or service. Whether the business is a for profit or not-for-profit organization, its business usually follows a pattern called a operating cycle. The operating cycle is the span of time during which financing is used to acquire inventory or services, which in turn is sold to customers, who in turn pay for their purchases with cash or a combination of cash and credit.

Broker-dealers provide their customers with a variety of services, including purchasing and selling securities for the benefit of retail and institutional customers; providing customers with research and insights on the many private and publicly traded securities in the marketplace; providing investment advice and tax strategies for investors; providing corporate financing advice to businesses of all sizes; and managing investment portfolios for private investors and institutional investors.

These services earn broker-dealers revenues through the fees they charge for the services, including: (i) mark-ups/mark-downs on securities prices for principal trades; (ii) commission charges for agency trades; (iii) investment bank fees for advisory services; (iv) investment banking fees for earned on new public offerings; and (v) fees for portfolio management or mutual fund management.

Review an example of the operating cycle through a customer purchase of 1000 shares of XYZ Corp. at $50 per share via an agency transaction, with a commission charge of $1,250:

BROKER-DEALER OPERATING CYCLE

(1) Firm receives order and finances $50,000.

(2) Firm purchases 50 shares of XYZ worth $50,000 for the benefit of the customer.

(3) The Firm now has an account receivable/customer debit equaling $51,250.

(4) The customer pays for the purchase with cash or cash & margin for $51,250.

Notes to the Operating Cycle

(1) The broker-dealer receives a customer's order for 1000 shares of XYZ. If does not have the securities in inventory, so it purchases them from another broker-dealer (the "contra-broker") via an agency transaction.

To pay for the order, the firm must take $50,000 from its bank account, or raise the $50,000 through various methods of financing:

(i) Bank loan. The firm can borrow money from a bank and pledge other securities as collateral;

(ii) Stock loan. The firm can loan another stock to a contra-broker and receive cash which it can use to purchase XYZ.

(iii) Reverse Repo. The firm can pledge government securities as collateral in return for the funds.

(2) The securities are delivered to the broker-dealer in exchange for the 1000 shares of XYZ. If the contra-broker does not deliver the securities by settlement date, then the firm will not pay for the securities, and it will have a fail to receive on its books (payable).

(3) A debit will be posted in the customer's account for $51,250

representing the total monies owed to the firm (customer debit/account receivable).

(4) The customer should pay for the transaction on settlement date by depositing the money in his brokerage account (customer credit).

Assuming the transaction was an initial purchase made on margin, then the customer will put up 50% of the purchase price and the broker-dealer will finance the other 50%.

The total deposit was $51,250 because: (i) the customer owed the firm $50,000 for the cost of the securities; and (ii) the additional $1,250 represents the commission charged to the customer for the service of purchasing the securities for the customer.

The $1,250 represents a commission of 2.5% on the principal value of the trade.

The Process of Income Determination

The process of income determination involves two steps: (i) identifying the revenues properly attributable to the period reported, and (ii) relating the corresponding costs/expenses with the revenues of the period either through direct association with the costs of the products sold or by assignment as expenses properly applicable as period costs.

Revenue Recognition

The first step in the process of profit recognition is the accrual of revenue. It is very important to recognize revenue as earned at the correct point in the operating cycle. The improper accrual of revenue will have undesirable effects:

1. Revenue may be recorded prematurely or late, in other words, assigned to the wrong fiscal period.

2. Revenue may be recorded before there is reasonable certainty that it will actually be realized. The result would be revenue booked in one period, then removed in another period. This would lead to unnecessary adjustments and fluctuations in the entity's income statement.

These two situations are not desirable and in order to minimize their occurrence, accountants have adopted strict and conservative rules regarding the recognition of revenues. The following criteria summarize the rules that have been established for the recognition of revenues. Recognition will only take place when the conditions have been met:

1. The activity undertaken to create revenue has been completed

2. In case of sales, the risk of ownership has been passed on to the buyer.

3. The revenue, along with the associated expenses, can be measured or estimated with substantial accuracy.

4. The revenue recognized should result in an increase in cash, receivables, or marketable securities. Under certain conditions, in an increase in inventory or other assets, or a decrease in liabilities.

5. The transaction giving rise to the income should be at arm's length with independent parties.

6. The transaction should not be subject to revocation.

While there are exceptions to these rules, they serve as excellent guidelines for determining revenue recognition.

REVENUE AND EXPENSE BALANCES OF BROKER-DEALERS

REVENUES

The most common revenues generated by broker-dealers on their income statements are:

- Commissions
- Market Making and Principal Trading
- Underwriting and Syndicate Fees
- Investment Banking and Advisory Fees
- Interest Income
- Investment Management Fees

Commissions

Commission revenues are generated when broker-dealers execute agency trades for their customers. An agency trade is when a broker-dealer purchases/sells a security for a customer directly from/to a contra-broker on the "Street" without running the security through their trading account. In other words, the transactions is really between the customer and the contra-broker, with the firm acting as and intermediary that brings the two parties together. Many firms will execute agency transactions in securities that they do not trade regularly.

The commission charge is usually based on a percentage of the principal amount of the trade. The NASD has a 5% maximum commission guideline for securities that trade over-the-counter.

Market Making and Principal Trading

Market making and principal trading income is earned through activity in a broker-dealer's trading and investment accounts.

A market maker is a broker-dealer who lists price quotations (bid and ask) for securities in published media such as the newspapers, NASDAQ, or with the National Quotation Bureau's Pink Sheets or Blue Sheets.

The purpose of quotations is the implied promise to buy or sell the security in question at the price that is listed. Broker-dealers who quote prices and buy and sell with the public at those prices are deemed market makers in those securities. The prices are quoted in form of bid and ask prices. The bid price is the price at which the broker-dealer will buy the security from another party. The ask price is the price at which the broker-dealer will sell the security to another party. The bid price is almost always lower that the ask price. In the rare event that the bid price is higher than the ask price, it is called a "locked market". No trades will take place in a locked market.

Revenues are earned on market making activity through the difference in the bid and ask price or the "spread". Principal trading activity is the regular buying and selling of securities to fill customer and firm trading orders via the firm's proprietary accounts. Profits are earned in principal trading activity in two ways: (i) trading profits; and (ii) investment profits.

Trading profits are earned through buying and selling securities and earning the spread, and through any appreciation in the security's price while it is in the trading account. Investment accounts are accounts specifically designated for broker-dealers to buy securities and hold them for dividends, interest, and long-term price appreciation. There are different tax implications for "trading profits" and "investment profits" and a tax accountant or tax guide should be consulted for further information.

Underwriting Fees

Broker-dealers earn underwriting and syndicate fees from activities relating to the selling of new securities issues. When a broker-dealer underwrites a new issue, the total revenue that can be earned is called the "gross spread". The gross spread is the difference between the price the investing public pays for the offering and the price the underwriter pays for the securities. The gross spread consists of two components: the underwriting fee and the selling concession. The underwriting fee is the amount the broker-dealer earn for bringing the issue to market.

Broker-dealers that manage a syndicate of underwriters earn a portion of the underwriting fee called the management fee. The selling concession is the amount the broker-dealer earns for placing the issue with institutions and individuals. The gross spread is negotiated between the underwriter and the issuing company. The factors that effect the size of the gross spread include: the size of the issue, the coupon or dividend rate, the size of the issuing company, the credit rating of the issue, and the liquidity of the issue.

Investment Banking and Advisory Fees

Many broker-dealers act as investment banks, which advise clients on new issues, mergers, and takeover activities.

Many times, the broker-dealer will help finance the activity through bridge loans or equity investments. For this advice, broker-dealers typically charge a fee which is a percentage of the total dollar value of the transaction.

Interest Income

Broker-dealers earn interest revenues from two sources: net cost-of-carry revenue and margin interest. Net cost-of-carry revenue is the interest earned on securities in the broker-dealers proprietary account minus the cost of financing the position. Margin interest is the interest charged customers for financing their securities purchases. The money loaned to customers is represented by the debit balance in the customer's margin account. Typically, customers are charged a point above the "broker call rate" on their debit balances.

Investment Management Fees

Many broker-dealers manage customer funds through investment advisory programs. In these programs, an in-house portfolio manager will tailor an investment strategy for clients for fee which is usually a percentage of the assets under management.

EXPENSES

The most common expenses that are generated during a broker-dealer's daily activities include:

- Compensation and Benefits
- Interest
- Communications
- Occupancy and Equipment
- Advertising
- Brokerage, Commission, and Clearing Fees
- Income Taxes

Since most of these expenses are typical to the average large company, I'll only discuss the expenses which are particular to a broker-dealer: Compensation and Benefits, Interest, and the Brokerage, Commission, and Clearance fees.

Compensation and Benefits

For most broker-dealers, compensation is the largest expense category. Wall Street's reputation for highly compensating its top performing traders and investment bankers is legendary. However, most of the compensation for the employees lies in their bonuses, not their salaries.

Many Wall Street "producers" are paid a small fraction of their compensation in weekly or bi-weekly salary checks, while the bulk of their compensation comes from quarterly or year-end bonus checks. Accruals should be made for estimated bonus compensation earned but not paid out.

Wall Street is not celebrated for the benefits it provides for employees. However, this may change as health care becomes a dominant issue on the national scene in the nineties and beyond.

Interest

Interest expenses are derived from various sources, such as: interest due on bank loans, commercial paper, and subordinated loans; interest payable on short sales; and interest payable on repurchase agreements.

Brokerage, Commission, and Clearance Fees

Brokerage and commission fees arise from such varied sources as: Regulatory and exchange fees, and order flow fees. Clearance fees arise from fees paid to the appropriate clearing corporations (NSCC, GSCC, etc.).

The Statement of Revenue and Expenses for Dewey & Howe shown in Figure 6.2 is an example of an income statement for a typical broker-dealer.

Figure 6.2

STATEMENT OF REVENUE AND EXPENSES FOR DEWEY & HOWE

For the year ending December 31, 1989.

REVENUE:	
Commissions	$1,000,000
Principal Trading	2,500,000
Underwriting and Selling Groups	1,750,000
Interest and Dividends	900,000
Investment Advisory Fees	500,000
TOTAL REVENUE:	**$ 6,650,000**
	EXPENSES:
Registered Representative Compensation	$950,000
General and Administrative	1,000,000
Floor Brokerage Fees	200,000
Clearance Fees	100,000
Interest Expense	350,000
Regulatory Fees and Expenses	100,000
Occupancy and Equipment	500,000
Communications	300,000
Research	200,000
TOTAL EXPENSES:	**$3,700,000**
NET INCOME BEFORE TAXES:	**$2,950,000**
INCOME TAXES (40%)	**$1,180,000**
NET INCOME AFTER TAXES:	**$1,770,000**

CLOSING THE REVENUE AND EXPENSE ACCOUNTS

The term "closing the books" refers to the final step taken at the end of the year to facilitate the recording of the next year's transactions. All balances in *temporary* stockholder's equity accounts are summarized and transferred to a *permanent* stockholder's equity account called **"Retained Income".** Closing entries transfer the revenues, expenses, and dividend balances from their respective accounts to the retained income account, leaving the current revenue, expense, and dividend accounts have zero balances.

Revenue, expense, and dividend accounts, which are subjected to yearly closings, are called temporary (or nominal) accounts. These accounts are subparts of ownership equity, and are created to provide a detailed explanation for changes in retained earnings from period to period. In contrast, the balance sheet accounts are known as the permanent (or real) accounts.

CHAPTER 7: PRIMARY AND SUBSIDIARY RECORDS

Regulatory guidelines (SEC Rule 17a-3) and accounting convention require broker-dealers to prepare records of transactions and dealings in securities for the accounts of the firm's customers as well as for its own risk and account. In addition, broker-dealers are required to prepare records of other financial transactions related to the business of the broker-dealer.

These requirements are intended to serve several basic purposes. First, it is expected that the broker-dealer maintain current books and records for the protection and convenience of its customers (prompt responses to inquiries and prompt resolution of claims).

Secondly, these requirements are intended to enable a broker-dealer to be aware of the extent of its compliance with the various rules and requirements, particularly the Net Capital Rule (SEC Rule 15c3- 1) and the Customer Protection Rule (SEC Rule 15c3-3). Third, a broker-dealer should have current books and records to enable it to fulfill its obligations and responsibilities to other broker-dealers with whom business is transacted. Finally, these records must be maintained if the broker-dealer is to have accurate consolidated financial statements at the end of its fiscal year.

DOUBLE ENTRY SYSTEM AND LEDGER ACCOUNTS

As mentioned earlier, the balance sheet equation for calculating equity helps ensure that ultimately, the total of all of a broker-dealer's accounts balance. However, that approach would not work for keeping record of the day-to-day activity of the average broker-dealer. In practice, ledgers must be used to track the multitude of transactions that affect each asset, liability, revenue, and expense account. A ledger contains a group of related accounts kept up-to-date in a systematic manner. Usually, firms will maintain a chart of accounts which details the name of each account used in the company and an assigned number. A chart of accounts is essential for tracking the opening and closing accounts and maintaining internal controls within the firm.

Ledgers may be kept in the form of a bound record book, a loose leaf sheet of papers, or a file on a computer disc or hard drive.

Ledger and account balances for broker-dealers are updated and maintained using the double-entry bookkeeping system (the same system used for commercial and not-for-profit entities). For every entry in an account there will be another entry that will offset it. The entries are represented by "debits" and "credits". A debit increases the assets or decreases the liabilities on the balance sheet; or increases the expenses or decreases the revenue on the income statement.

For example, the sale of a security to a customer with market value of $380,000 and mark-up fees of $20,000 will result in the ultimate receipt of cash, and a debit to the cash account (asset) of the balance sheet of $400,000. The payment of $30,000 in rent to the owner of the company's offices will result in a debit to the rent expense account of the income statement of $30,000.

However, these debits will be offset by credit entries, usually for the same amount, on the company's records. A credit increases the liabilities or decreases the assets on the balance sheet; or increases the revenue on the income statement.

For example, failing to receive securities with a market value of $100,000 from another firm will result in an increase the broker-dealer payable account (liability) through a credit to that account on the balance sheet of $100,000.

And that previous sale of securities to a customer will result in a credit to the inventory account (reduce assets) on the balance sheet of $380,000 and a credit to the principal trading revenue account (increase revenues) on the income statement of $20,000.

On paper, ledger accounts are commonly represented on "T accounts". They are called T accounts because they take the form of the capital letter "T". The vertical line in the T divides the account into its left and right sides. The left side of the T account represents debits and the right side of the T account represents credits. The title of the account is on the horizontal line. For example, review the format of the Cash account:

Cash	
Left side increases	Right side decreases

The following transaction would be shown in T accounts as follows:

Sale of customer's securities via an principal transaction with market value of $380,000 (10,000 shares at $38.00 per share) and mark-up fees of $20,000.

Cash	
(1) 380,000	
20,000	

Inventory	
	(2) 380,000

Trading Revenue	
	(3) 20,000

Customer's Account	
(4) 400,000	400,000

(1) The firm's cash account will be debited a total of $400,000 when the customer pays for his purchase; $380,000 for the market value of the securities and $20,000 for the mark-up charge.

(2) The firm's inventory account will be credited $380,000 in market value for the sale of the position to the customer.

(3) The firm earns $20,000 in trading revenue because of the mark-up on the customer's purchase.

(4) The customer's account is debited $400,000 on trade date for the purchase of the securities. On settlement date, when the funds are paid to complete the transaction, the customer's account is credited for $400,000.

The Recording Process

The recording process starts when the transaction is substantiated by source documents. These are supporting original records of any transaction. For broker-dealers, the source documents are usually the P&S blotters or the order tickets. Then, an analysis of the transaction is placed in a book of original entry, which is a formal chronological record of the effects of the entity's transactions on the balances in the firm's account. Books of original entry are more commonly known as "primary ledgers". Records which are derived from the primary ledgers are called subsidiary ledgers.

PRIMARY LEDGERS

The three primary ledgers are the trial balance, the general ledger, and the P&S blotter. The P&S blotter is the beginning of the recordation process. Its information regarding purchases and sales feeds most of transaction-related accounting information that gets booked to the general ledger. In turn, all of the different accounts on the general ledger, asset, liability, revenue, and expense accounts, are summarized and this information is used to compile the trial balance.

THE TRIAL BALANCE

The trial balance is a list of all accounts with their balances. It serves two purposes: (i) to help check on the accuracy of postings by proving whether the total debits equal the total credits; and (ii) to establish a convenient summary of balances in all accounts for the preparation of formal financial statements. It is the springboard for the preparation of the balance sheet and the income statement.

Broker-dealers are required to prepare a proof of money balances in all trial balance accounts at least once a month, and the preparation of a record of the computation of aggregate indebtedness and net capital as of the trial balance date currently at least once a month. Trial balances serve as a check upon the current status and accuracy of the ledger accounts which broker-dealers are required to maintain and keep current and will also keep members currently informed of their capital positions. Figure 7.1 is a sample of what a broker-dealer trial balance might look like:

Figure 7.1 A Trial Balance for Dewey & Howe, Inc.

DEWEY & HOWE, INC.
Adjusted Trial Balance
December 31, 1992

Cash	$1,000,000	
Secs. Bought W/Agreements to Resell	5,000,000	
Fails to Deliver	2,000,000	
Receivables from Customers	4,000,000	
Securities Owned (at market)	5,000,000	
Furniture & Fixtures (less depre.)	500,000	
Other Assets	500,000	
Drafts Payable		600,000
Loans Payable		2,000,000
Secs. Sold W/Agreement to Repurchase		5,000,000
Fails to Receive		1,500,000
Payables to Customers		2,000,000
Securities sold but not yet purchased (at market)		1,500,000
Accounts Payable & Other Liabilities		300,000
Paid-in-capital		4,330,000
Retained Earnings		-------
Commissions		1,000,000
Principal Trading		2,500,000
Underwriting and Selling Groups		1,750,000
Interest and Dividends		900,000
Investment Advisory Fees	500,000	
Registered Representative Compensation	950,000	
General and Administrative	1,000,000	
Floor Brokerage Fees	200,000	
Clearance Fees	100,000	
Interest Expense	350,000	
Regulatory Fees and Expenses	100,000	
Occupancy and Equipment	500,000	
Communications	300,000	
Research	200,000	
Income Tax Expenses	1,180,000	
TOTALS:	**$23,380,000**	**$23,380,000**

THE GENERAL LEDGER

The general ledger is the record that contains the group of accounts that supports the amounts shown in the trial balance and the major financial statements. Detailed below in Figure 7.2 is a sample of trial balance in T account form. Each T account represents a separate account in the general ledger. The general ledger for a typical broker-dealer will usually be saved on computer files using spreadsheet software or an accounting software package.

General Ledger T Account Entries for Dewey & Howe, Inc.

Transactions included in this illustration are:

1. An equity investment in the firm of $100,000

2. A loan from the bank of $50,000

3. The Firm purchased securities from another broker-dealer worth $75,000 and the contra-broker failed to deliver the securities.

4. The Firm bought securities from a customer X (agency transaction with no commission) worth $35,000 to deliver to a contra-broker. The customer did not deliver the securities by settlement date.

Figure 7.2: General Ledger T Accounts

Cash	
(1) 100,000	
(2) 50,000	

Paid-in-Capital	
(1) 100,000	

Loan Payable	
	(2) 50,000

Firm Inventory	
(3) 75,000	

Fail-to-Receive	
	(3) 75,000

Customer X Account Ledger	
	(4) 35,000

Firm Trading	
(4) 35,000	

The general ledger must be posted as frequently as may be necessary to determine compliance with the Net Capital Rule; but in any event not less than once per month. The general ledger must also be updated for daily marks-to-market in the firm's inventory, and collateral owned for secured loans, stock borrows, and repurchase agreements.

THE PURCHASE AND SALES BLOTTER (THE P&S BLOTTER)

The P&S blotter details every purchase and sale of securities made by the broker-dealer during its daily activity (see Figure 7.3 for a sample of a typical P&S blotter). The information on the P&S blotter includes:

- To whom or from whom securities are being sold or bought;
- Quantity;
- Name of the security;
- CUSIP number;
- Certificate number;
- Price;
- Interest (if any);
- Commission (if any);
- Total Transaction Amount
- Trade date;
- Settlement date;
- Customer account involved in the purchase or sale;
- Firm account involved in the transaction;
- Internal transaction number; and
- Time of purchase or sale.

Usually, large firms will have separate P&S blotters for each type of security that it traded.

The information in this blotter is origin of a Firm's accounting cycle and is used to update the firm's general ledger accounts and trial balance. The Purchase & Sales Blotter must reflect transactions as of trade date and should be prepared no later than the following business day.

Figure 7.3: Sample P&S Blotter

Johnston & Co.								
OTC Securities Purchase & Sales Blotter								
3/17/9X Trade Date								
CUSIP Number	Description	Quantity	Price	Transaction Account	Customer Account	Firm Amount	Settlement Date	Time
346823409	ACME Common	100	13	$1,300	ABX-45637	53421	3/24	14:59
564773908	XYZ Common	375	50	$18,750	333-99823	53421	3/24	14:30

The Customer Account Ledger

The Customer Account Ledger details all of the activity in a customer's account, including buys, sells, receipts of cash, deliveries of cash, adjustments, and any debits or credits. The ledger includes activity in both customer's cash and margin accounts. This ledger is essential a personal record for each individual customer.

The information on the customer ledger includes:

- Trade date and settlement date of any activity;
- Number of shares bought or sold, received or delivered;
- Price of shares bought or sold;
- Name and description of securities bought or sold, received or delivered;
- Commissions charged to the account for transactions;
- Interest and dividends received and charged;
- Net debits or credits for the account;
- Net long or short positions for the account.
- Long and short positions already in inventory

Customer accounts are updated for interim activity by the end of each month. The information included on Customer Account Ledgers is printed on customer confirmations and included on the customer's monthly statement.

Please refer to Figure 7.4 for an example of a Customer Account Ledger

Figure 7.4: Example of Entries on the Customer Account Ledger

Customer Account Ledger for Customer Z, Account Number 345-6789							
December 31, 199X							
Trade Date	Buy/Sell Receive/ Deliver	Quantity	Description	Price	Commission	Debit/ Long	Credit/ Short
4/16/9X	Buy	100	XYZ Common	15	50.00	1,550.00	
4/23/9X	Receive		Check				1,550.00
Portfolio Summary							
		100	XYZ Common	15			
		1000	ABC Common	4			
		300	ACME Common	50			
Net Market Value						$20,500	
Net Debit/Credit						$0	$0
Account Equity						$20,500	

Looking at Figure 7.4, Customer Z buys 100 shares of ABC common stock at $15 per share on 4/16/9X using his cash account. He pays the firm for his purchase on 4/23/9X. The firm executed his trade as an agency trade, and charges him a commission of $50. The customer already has 1000 shares of XYZ common stock and 300 shares of ACME common stock in his portfolio.

SUBSIDIARY LEDGERS

The subsidiary or secondary records are not records of original entry. These records are derived from the blotters of other records of original entry. The information that appears on these records is generally posted daily or at intervals required by the volume of business.

THE STOCK RECORD

The Stock Record provides a record and control of the quantities of each security for which the firm is accountable, identifying owners as well as locations of securities. The Stock Record reflects separately for each security all long and short positions (including securities in "safekeeping") carried by the broker-dealer either for his own account or for the account of his customers. The Stock Record shows the location for all securities that are long and the offsetting position to all securities short. The Stock Record is posted to reflect securities as of settlement date.

The Stock Record monitors the movement of securities within the firm by tracking the owners of securities positions and their location. An individual, broker-dealer, or other account that owns a security on the stock record is designated as being "long" the position. A location that is holding a securities position is designated as being "short". Every position on the Stock Record has a long side (owner) and a short side (location).

The total number of shares long must equal the total number of shares short for each security or the firm has a "stock record break". There are two types of stock record breaks: (i) long stock record breaks and (ii) short stock record breaks.

Long stock record breaks are situations where the firm has more shares on the short (location) side of the stock record than on the long (ownership) side of the stock record.

Short stock record breaks are when the firm has more shares on the long side of the stock record than on the short side. There are regulatory penalties for both long and short stock record breaks that are not resolved in a timely manner. The Net Capital Rule (SEC Rule 15c3-1) requires broker-dealers to take staggered deductions to their Net Capital of the market value of all short stock record breaks, with a maximum 100% deduction after 28 business days. The market value of short stock record breaks must be deducted from Net Capital if the underlying securities have been sold by the broker-dealer before they are adequately resolved, less any established reserves.

The Customer Protection Rule (SEC Rule 15c3-3) requires broker-dealers to add all short stock record breaks over 30 calendar days old to the credit side of the Customer Reserve Formula. This increases the likelihood that the broker-dealer may have to set aside funds in the Customer Reserve Account.

The typical long accounts listed on the Stock Record include:

- The firm's trading or investment accounts;
- Customers' accounts;
- Fail to Deliver
- Stock Borrowed

The typical short accounts listed on the Stock Record include:

- The Firm's vault or "box";
- Transfer Agent;
- Depository Trust Company (DTC) or an approved custodian bank;
- An omnibus account;
- An approved foreign depository, foreign bank, or foreign clearing agency;
- Domestic banks;
- Securities in transit;
- An affiliated company to the broker-dealer;
- Bank loan;
- Stock loan;
- Fail to Receive;
- Stock dividend receivables;
- Firm inventory account (short sales); and
- Customer accounts (short sales).

The Stock Record is maintained in security order (either alphabetically or in CUSIP number order) and the accounts listed above appear within each security.

Broker-dealers usually develop codes for the long and short accounts represented on the stock record. Usually, the codes for long accounts will be a different number sequence than for the short account codes (with the exception of firm and customer accounts).

Broker-dealers maintain two types of Stock Records: (i) the *Daily Stock Record*, and (ii) the *Main Stock Record*.

The Daily Stock Record details accounts with security movements **on any particular day**. The Daily Stock Record is an excellent tool for researching operational problems and determining exactly when a long position was liquidated or delivered. Various departments throughout the firm need this information to perform their daily responsibilities, including Dividends and Reorganization. The Main Stock Record shows **all accounts for which a position exists on a given day.**

The following types of information will be detailed on the typical Stock Record:

- What type of action is causing the security to move onto the Stock Record, such as a purchase or a delivery.
- The opening position;
- The actual movement;
- The closing position; and
- A memo field detailing additional useful information such as whether a position should be segregated, or whether a position is in safekeeping.

Figure 7.5 is a sample of a portion of a Daily Stock Record run:

Dewey & Howe, Inc.: Daily Stock Record Activity							
World Technologies Inc. CUSIP # 234965190							
December 23, 199X							
Account	**Price**	**Action**	**Opening Position**	**Debit**	**Credit**	**Closing Position**	**Memo**
Long							
ABJ-55523	22 5/8	N/A	100	100	0	200 Long	SEG.
DF1-90081	N/A	REC.	0	10,000	0	10,000 Long	SAFE.
23487	22 5/8	N/A	100,000	200,000	0	300,000 Long	N/A
Short							
067-71540	22	N/A	0	0	200	200 Short	N/A

The sample Daily Stock Record for Dewey & Howe Inc. (see Figure 7.5) shows all of the activity for World Technologies Inc. shares on December 23, 199X. The number after the name of the stock is the CUSIP number. The accounts are identified by code numbers. Most broker-dealers assign the branch office code as the first three numbers in a customer's account, followed by a five digit specific identification code for the branch. The five digit accounts (23487)

represent the broker-dealer's proprietary accounts, such as the Firm Trading Accounts. The accounts are listed in alphabetical order, then numerical order, with the customer accounts listed first, then the Firm accounts. The Price column details the closing market price of the security on the date of the Stock Record. In the Action column, REC means received and DEL means delivered. A debit on the Stock Record means that securities have been placed under the control of the broker-dealer for the benefit of the account that owns the securities. A credit on the Stock Record means that securities have been taken out of the control of the broker-dealer and delivered to another party. The Memo column details important messages about the customer's position; for instance, SEG. means the position must be segregated in accordance with the possession and control requirements of SEC Rule 15c3-3 (The Customer Protection Rule). SAFE. means the position is in safekeeping for the customer.

Figure 7.6 is a sample of a portion of a Main Stock Record run:

Dewey & Howe, Inc.: Main Stock Record Activity World Technologies Inc. CUSIP # 234965190 December 23, 199X							
Account	**Price**	**Action**	**Opening Position**	**Debit**	**Credit**	**Closing Position**	**Memo**
Long							
ABJ-55523	22 5/8	N/A	100	100	0	200 Long	SEG.
DF1-90081	N/A	REC.	0	10,000	0	10,000 Long	SAFE.
23487	22 5/8	N/A	100,000	200,000	0	300,000 Long	N/A
Short							
10000 (Vault)	N/A	N/A	N/A	N/A	50,000	50,000 Short	N/A
10001 (F/R)	N/A	N/A	N/A	N/A	200,000	200,000 Short	N/A
10002 (B/L)	N/A	N/A	N/A	N/A	25,000	25,000 Short	N/A
10003 (S/L)	N/A	N/A	N/A	N/A	25,000	25,000 Short	N/A
067-71540	22	N/A	0	0	200	200 Short	N/A
Total Long						**310,200**	
Total Short						**310,200**	

The Long positions are same as the ones described in the Daily Stock Record Run. On the Short side of the Stock Record, the Firm accounts are listed first, then the customer accounts. However, every broker-dealer may arrange their Stock Record differently, factoring in the type of business they engage in, and the volume of business. The Firm accounts are listed in numerical order, and the account numbers are assigned according to the allocation order suggested by the SEC for the Customer Protection Rule (Chapter 13).

The Vault is where physical securities are held while at the broker-dealer. The Vault is a secured area, and only authorized Operations personnel are allowed access. F/R represents Fails to

Receive. This means that the securities are located at the broker-dealer which the Firm is failing to receive from. You can determine who the Firm is by reviewing the Fail to Receive Ledger. B/L represents bank loan. The broker-dealer used these securities as collateral for a bank loan, and the securities are being held by the lending bank. S/L represents stock loan. The broker-dealer lent these securities to another party. These are being held by that party.

The Stock Record is an operation tool used to track securities which are under the broker-dealer's possession or control. While the Stock Record is not an accounting record in the traditional sense, it is vital to ensure that the broker-dealer's view of what securities it owns and what securities it's customers own are related to the true state of affairs. The integrity of the Stock Record is vital to any broker-dealer's business and it's reputation.

The Stock Record should be posted no later than the business day after settlement date or the date of the movement of securities. Stock Record differences are to be posted no later than seven business days after the date of discovery.

THE CASH RECEIPTS AND DISBURSEMENTS BLOTTER

The Cash Receipts and Disbursements Blotter details all inflows and outflows of cash to/from the firm every day. The information on the Cash Receipts and Disbursements Blotter includes:

- Amount of cash received or delivered;
- Whom delivered or received cash;
- Date cash was received or delivered;
- Account which received or delivered cash; and
- Check number or wire number involved in the receipt or delivery of cash.

The Cash Receipts and Disbursements Blotter must reflect transactions as of trade date and should be prepared no later than the following business day.

SECURITIES RECEIVED AND DELIVERED BLOTTER

The Securities Received and Delivered Blotter details all securities deliveries and receipts from the broker-dealer's vault area. The information on the blotter includes:

- The date of the receipt or delivery;
- The name of the security received or delivered;
- The CUSIP number;
- To whom the security was delivered or received from;
- The quantity of securities delivered or received; and
- The price of the securities received or delivered.

The Securities Received and Delivered Blotter must reflect transactions as of trade date and should be prepared no later than the following business day.

THE SECURITIES FAILED TO RECEIVE OR DELIVER LEDGERS

The Securities Failed to Receive or Deliver ledgers detail trades in which the contra-broker either fails to send the firm securities by settlement date (fail to receive) or the firm fails to send the contra-party securities by settlement date (fail to deliver). In the event that a customer fails to deliver securities or the broker-dealer fails to deliver securities to a customer, then can be regulatory ramifications for the broker-dealer in question. A broker-dealer's Net Capital will be reduced by the amount which the market value of fails to receive over 30 calendar days exceeds the contract value. Also, broker-dealers must increase the credits allocated to their Customer Reserve Formula computation for fails to receive over 30 calendar days. This increases the likelihood that they will have to deposit funds into the Customer Reserve Account.

A fail to receive is considered a payable from an accounting standpoint because once the contra-broker delivers the securities, the firm is obligated to pay for them. A fail to deliver is considered a receivable because once the firm delivers the securities the contra-broker is obligated to pay.

Securities regulations stipulate what actions can be taken by a broker-dealer when it is faced with an aged fail to receive.

Buy-ins are one method used by broker-dealers to deal with firms that refuse to deliver securities that they have promised to. For situations where the firm is failing to deliver securities, there are restrictions that will be placed on the firm's activities in that security until the fail to deliver is cleaned-up.

The information that is included on a fail to receive or deliver run includes:

- the fail date (the date delivery was due but not made);
- the number of shares or bonds;
- the name of the security;
- the purchase price;
- the broker-dealer from whom the delivery is due from or due to;
- the date the securities was received or delivered;
- the contract amount of the trade; and
- any additional notes regarding the failed transaction.

Fail ledgers must be posted no later than two days subsequent to settlement date.

SECURITIES BORROWED AND SECURITIES LOANED LEDGER

Broker-dealers keep track of securities borrowed to make deliveries for sales and securities lent to other broker-dealers through the Securities Borrowed and Securities Loaned Ledger.

The information included on the Securities Borrowed and Securities Loaned Ledger includes:

- the date of the borrowing or lending;

- the name of the broker-dealer from whom securities were borrowed or loaned;
- the number of shares or bonds;
- the name of the security;
- the price;
- the interest rate or premium on the security borrowed or loaned;
- the amount; and
- the date the securities were returned.

The Securities Borrowed and Securities Loaned Ledger should be posted no later than two days after the date of securities or monies movement.

THE MONIES BORROWED AND LOANED LEDGER

The Monies Borrowed and Loaned Ledger tracks all borrowings, regardless of whether customers' or firm's securities are pledged as collateral. The information on the Ledger includes:

- The name of the bank;
- the date of the loan;
- the interest rate;
- the amount of the loan;
- the terms of the loan;
- the date when the loan was paid;

In addition, any information regarding any collateral pledged should be kept on the Ledger, including:

- The number of shares or bonds
- The principal amount in the case of bonds;
- A description of the security; and

- The certificate numbers of the securities.

The Ledger should be updated for any substitutions of collateral.

The Monies Borrowed and Loaned Ledger should be posted no later than two days after the date of money movement.

DIVIDENDS AND INTEREST RECEIVED OR PAYABLE LEDGER

Broker-dealers are required to maintain a record of stocks and bonds that pay dividends and interest on securities (i) owned by the firm or (ii) carried by the broker-dealer for the account of customers but registered in the name of someone other than the customer.

The information on the Dividends and Interest Received or Payable Ledger should include:

- the name of the account or customer;
- the name of the security;
- the record date or beneficiary date;
- the ex-dividend or ex-interest date;
- the rate payable per share or bond; and
- the payable date.

The firm knows which customers should be paid and which should be charged based on the Stock Record. If a customer is long the position on record date or beneficiary date, then they are entitled to the dividend or interest payment. If the customer is short the position, then they will be charged the dividend or interest because they are not entitled to the payment. The amount the customer will receive or be charged equals the amount of shares or bonds they are long/short times the dividend or interest rate per share or bond.

The Dividend and Interest Received and Payable Ledger should be posted no later than two days after the date of securities or money movement.

SECURITIES IN TRANSFER LEDGER

The stock or bond certificates that a broker-dealer receives on purchases may often be in "street name" or in the names of individuals who have previously owned the securities. Some purchasers request to have the securities registered in their name. The securities must be sent to the issuing company's transfer agent to be changed to the name of the new owner. Broker-dealers must keep track of positions that are with the transfer agent via the Securities in Transfer Ledger. The information on the Ledger includes:

- the transfer number on the transfer receipt;
- the number of shares;
- the name of the security;
- the name in which it was registered;
- the new name;
- the date the item was sent out to transfer;
- the old certificate number;
- the new certificate number; and
- the date the item was received back from transfer.

The Securities in Transfer Ledger should be posted no later than two days after the date the item was sent to transfer.

PART IV: SYNDICATE ACCOUNTING

CHAPTER 8: CORPORATE FINANCE AND INVESTMENT BANKING ACTIVITIES

OVERVIEW

The world of corporate finance and underwritings is a network of institutions and communications channels through which two types of financial transactions take place: (1) Primary Markets and (2) Secondary Markets.

Primary markets are those in which capital is raised by business, government, and individuals for the financing of capital outlays.

Secondary markets are those in which financial securities already outstanding are exchanged among investors.

This chapter will focus on how the primary markets operate, with specific focus on the corporate primary markets. Secondary markets were already discussed in the first chapter.

The Primary Markets

The primary securities market includes all transactions that result in the accumulation of financial capital by firms, governments, or individuals to be used in consumption or real capital investment. The participants in this process are many and varied, but an important segment includes the money brokers who act as middlemen in the process of exchanging securities for funds. The brokers provide invaluable services. Their principal role is to assist in the pooling of funds by the creation security forms that will appeal to the ultimate target investor. There are two major categories of middlemen that perform the greatest portion of this task in the American economy: financial institutions and investment bankers.

Financial Institutions

Financial institutions such as banks, savings banks, credit unions, savings and loan associations, and some insurance companies take money from individual or business savers and distribute the funds to individuals and businesses who need funds to operate their households or firms. In the process, they take one form of security, a mortgage or business loan, and repackage it into a different security - a savings account, checking account, or certificate of deposit.

In other words, they have exchanged a relatively illiquid, indivisible instrument with unique risks into an instrument that is very liquid, and almost totally divisible, with fewer risks.

By intermediating this market, in other words, they have provided services to savers that increase the desirability of saving. This leads to a larger pool of loanable funds for use in the creation of productive facilities by other individuals and business firms.

Investment and Mortgage Bankers

Investment bankers and mortgage bankers perform many of the same services as regular financial institutions. However, the services provided differ according to the product being offered.

For example, a firm that needs long-term debt or equity capital would go to an investment banker like Merrill Lynch or Lehman Brothers to get advice on the cheapest and most advantageous method of raising the funds. The investment banker would perform two functions: (i) they advise the company on how much money can be raised, what it will cost, and with which kind of security; and (ii) performing all of the steps necessary for the distribution of the security to investors.

For performing these services, the investment banker is paid either through a fixed fee arrangement or through the spread between the remuneration it promises the company and the proceeds from the sale of the securities. Investment bankers provide the "pooling of funds" services of a financial intermediary, but does not issue deposit accounts.

Mortgage bankers provide the same sort of services as investment bankers except that security issuers are primarily a group of homeowners and the security purchasers are typically large investors. Savings and loans, insurance companies, and the Federal National Mortgage Association are examples of investors that hold the securities created through the mortgage banking function.

INVESTMENT BANKING

Investment banking is the first step in the process of underwriting newly offered securities. The objective of the investment banker is to raise capital for clients at the most advantageous rate possible.

The investment banking function is crucial to the underwriting process because it brings the issuer and the investing public together.

The duties of an investment banker includes:

- advising companies on money management issues;
- packaging and marketing corporate securities to the public;
- mergers and acquisitions advice;
- reviewing corporate financial statements and advising clients on their financial condition.

Investment bankers are contracted because it usually costs less to use them than for companies to issue securities directly to the investing public. Bankers have well-organized sales forces and contacts with other broker-dealers and the investing public. The services performed by investment bankers include the following areas:

Successful Sales

If an issuer attempted to distribute new offerings directly to the public, it cannot really be sure of a successful sale. Without the expertise and contacts in selling new issues, the company may not be able to sell all of its offering. This may have an adverse effect on the price of the offering and the amount of money obtained from the investing public. With the use of a skilled investment banker, the issuer can rest assured that it will sell all of its offering and receive all of the needed funds in a timely manner.

Advice on the Issue

Investment bankers are experts in securities offerings and the securities markets. The banker knows what types of securities are selling and can thus advise the issuing company on the best type to sell at that particular time. Investment bankers are also aware of the current yields on all types of securities, and therefore is positioned to advise the company on the face rate of interest or dividend rate that should be set on the securities. The investment banker is also aware of the right time to place a particular offering on the market.

Securities Find a Home

Investment bankers are skilled at placing offerings with investors that will hold on to the securities. Offerings that are placed with "shaky" investors may be dumped back onto the market at a moments notice without regard to the quality of the issuer.

Market Support

New offerings may decline in price shortly after being released for a variety of reasons. An untimely announcement or an initial lack of demand can potentially doom a new offering.

An investment banker will support the market price of a new issue by buying back shares from the market and continually marketing the offering. These efforts provide support for the offering and may prevent it from going into free-fall.

Financial Advice

Investment bankers continue to provide their clients with advice and guidance long after the offering is completed. For example, there may be further opportunities for additional offerings in the future, financial restructurings for the company, or investment advice that may be needed. Since the investment banker's reputation is affected by the performance of the securities he has sold, he will be interested in the future success of the company.

Private Placements

One important trend in recent years has been the reduction of the role of the investment banker in the sale of some securities.

Institutional investors, particularly life insurance companies, have been buying bonds directly from the issuing company. Bonds have also been privately placed with commercial banks and pension funds. One entire issue may be sold to one or to a small number of institutional buyers.

Common stocks are rarely sold through private placements. This is probably because certain financial institutions are either not permitted to buy them or are narrowly restricted in their purchases. More preferred stock than common stock issues have been privately placed.

If large institutional investors and the issuing company negotiate directly, the investment banker may have no role to play. Often, investment bankers will act as advisors and finders in private placement transactions. Bankers are experts in pricing new issues and vaulting companies. He also knows companies that need financing and institutions that want to invest.

In some cases, the investment banker is first approached by the investor, while in others the issuing company may call him in. When acting as go-between, the banker receives only an agent's or broker's fee for introducing the buyer and the seller. In this role, the investment banker has no risk exposure and the total effort required is substantially less.

Reasons for a Private Placement

The factors that suggest that a private placement may be a more favorable method of raising capital include:

- No Registration Cost

  The Securities Act of 1933 requires that security issues that are to be privately offered in interstate commerce must, with exceptions, be registered with the Securities and Exchange Commission (SEC). This process entails a considerable expense to the issuing company. Securities that are privately placed do not have to be registered.

- No Waiting Period

The Securities Act provides that no registered securities may be sold until the effective date of the registration statement. The effective date is usually 20 days after the statement is filed with the SEC. During this period the market may break and jeopardize the successful sale of the securities. When the issue is privately placed, there is no waiting period.

- Avoidance of Liability for Officers and Directors

The 1933 Act provides certain liability for officers and directors for any misstatement of material facts or omissions of material facts in the registration statement. Corporate officials could look at a private placement as a means of escaping such liability.

- Saving Bankers' Commissions

Companies avoid paying commissions altogether by issuing private placements.

- Good Investment for Institutional Investors

The assets of institutional investors have been rising rapidly over the years. These investors would have to compete with individual investors when attempting to purchase a public offering. With private placements, these investors can avoid competition and purchase high quality securities, sometimes at cheaper prices. Also, they may have the opportunity to purchase a larger amount of a private offering than a public offering.

Disadvantages to Private Placements

The disadvantages of issuing a private placement include:

- Inability to Buy Back Securities at a Discount

If securities are sold through regular channels, opportunities often arise later for a corporation to buy back its securities in the market at substantial discounts. If the securities are privately placed, the buyer will probably hold onto them until maturity, at which time the issuer will have to pay full value for the bonds.

- Future Financing may be More Difficult

If the issue is privately placed, no broad market is developed for the company's securities. In the future, the issuer may have problems selling additional securities to a broader group of investors.

TYPES OF INVESTMENT BANKING OFFERINGS

In our discussions we have assumed that the investment banker or groups of investment bankers will purchase the securities outright from the issuer and sell them to other investment bankers or investors. While this is the usual arrangement, there are actually three types of arrangements between bankers and issuers:

1. Firm Commitment

A firm commitment underwriting is when the investment banker pledges to buy all of the securities offered by the issuer and sell them to other broker-dealers and investors. If the investment banker cannot sell all of the offering, he will keep the securities in his own inventory. The issuing company will receive full payment for the offering when the securities are delivered to the investment banker. The full responsibility for selling the issue rests with banker and the issuer will not have to buy any of the offering back regardless of the performance of offering.

2. Stand-By Commitment

Under a stand-by commitment, the issuing company will sell its own securities and the investment banker or group of investment bankers agree to stand-by, take-up, and sell any part of the offering the issuing company has been unable to sell. Thus, the investment banker has a firm commitment to the extent of any of the securities cannot be sold by the issuer. This type of commitment is usually made when the company attempts to sell securities to its existing stockholders, or execute an exchange of new securities for existing securities.

3. Best-Efforts Commitment

Under the best efforts commitment, the investment banker does not guarantee to purchase any of the unsold portion of the offering. He agrees that he will use his best efforts to sell as many of the securities as possible. Thus, he is really only acting as agent in selling the company's securities. This type of arrangement is typically used in speculative common stock offerings where the successful sale of the securities is under doubt. Under this arrangement, the banker is only paid a commission on the securities he manages to sell.

REVIEW OF THE INVESTMENT BANKING PROCESS

DUTIES PRIOR TO REGISTRATION

The investment banking process begins with investment bankers contacting potential clients or being approached by potential clients. This process is known as "pounding the pavement".

Once a banker establishes contact with a potential issuer, they will investigate why the company needs additional capital, and what type of offering is appropriate for the client (e.g., equity, investment-grade debt, high yield debt, etc.). The information included in this analysis are:

- the existing capital structure of the company;
- the amount of money needed to be raised;
- the cost of the money;
- the purpose for which the money is needed;
- financial restrictions in the charter or by-laws of the company;
- the image and popularity of the company and its industry in the investment community;
- the investment grade of the offering;
- the quality of the management; and
- pending legislation or litigation involving the company and its industry.

If the investment bankers decide that an issue is worthy of underwriting, the deal is usually presented to an internal committee comprised of upper management personnel for approval. This committee will usually discuss the marketability of the offering and the potential public offering price.

Once the deal approved by management and the investment bankers decides what type offering will be best for the needs of their client, they will begin the process registering the deal with the Securities and Exchange Commission (SEC) as required by the Securities Act of 1933.

The Securities Act of 1933 requires every new offering of securities to be filed with the SEC via a registration statement. A registration statement sets forth all relevant information pertaining to the specific offering. Certain types of offerings are exempt from registration with the SEC. These offerings include:

- obligations or securities guaranteed by the U.S. government;
- obligations of, or guaranteed by, any state or municipality of that state;
- issues of domestic banks or trust companies (excluding bank holding companies);
- commercial paper or bankers' acceptances notices maturing within 270 days of issuance;
- issues of building and loan associations;
- securities of farmers' cooperative associations;
- securities of a common or contract carrier
- receivers' or trustees' certificates issued with court approval;
- issues of small business investment companies (SBIC);
- securities offered exclusively intrastate;
- issues of religious, educational, charitable, or non-profit institutions;

- ° insurance policies or mixed annuity contracts (variable annuities and variable life insurance policies are not exempted);
- ° offerings that qualify under Regulation A* of the Securities Act of 1933.

Regulation A*

Regulation A under the Securities Act of 1933 allows the filing of a limited registration statement.

The value of the securities offered by the issuer in the previous year cannot exceed $1,500,000. In addition, offerings by a person affiliated to the issuer cannot exceed $100,000. Regulation A requires an offering circular that details most of the same information that a prospectus would. However, it is still less expensive for a company to issue securities under Regulation A.

- ° offerings that qualify under Regulation D* of the Securities Act of 1933.

Regulation D*

SEC Rules 504 through 506, under the auspices of Regulation D, allows issuers to offer unregistered securities in specific quantities to a specific number or "type" of investor. These SEC Rules were specifically designed to facilitate the private placement of securities. These rules help issuers avoid the time, cost, and paperwork involved with a public offering.

SEC Rule 504

Any issuer who is a non-investment company (e.g., a mutual fund) or who is not subject to the public financial reporting requirements of the 1934 Act is eligible to issue securities without registering the offering. The issuer who met these requirements can publicly sell to any number of investors unregistered securities up to $500,000 during any 12 month period. In addition, there are no information disclosures under SEC Rule 504.

SEC Rule 505

An issuer who is not an investment company or is not eligible to issue securities under Regulation A can use SEC Rule 505 to offer unregistered securities up to $5 million in any 12 month period. The distribution cannot be made to more than 35 nonaccredited investors. There is no limit on the number of accredited investors.

Regulation D defines "accredited investors" as any of the following:

- Individuals with net worth over $1 million;
- Individuals with income in excess of $200,000 in each of the last two years, with reasonable expectation of having income in excess of $200,000 in the year of the purchase;
- Purchasers of at least $150,000 of the securities being offered, with the purchase price not exceeding 20% of the purchaser's net worth at the time of the sale;
- Corporate or partnership insiders;
- Financial institutions, such as banks and insurance companies;
- Private business development companies;
- Colleges or university endowment funds and other not-for-profit organizations with assets of $5 million or more; and
- Any entity owned by an accredited investor.

SEC Rule 506

Any issuer who is allowed to issue private placements under the Securities Act of 1933 can use SEC Rule 506 to issue nonregistered securities. Issuers can offer any amount of securities for any period of time to up to 35 nonaccredited investors. There is no limit on the number of accredited investors. The issuer must assure himself that these nonaccredited persons understand the merits and risks of the investment prior to purchase.

The SEC does not guarantee the adequacy or accuracy of any of the offerings registered under the Act. However, the investing public can find protection under the civil liability provisions of the 1993 Act. This law gives an investor the opportunity to bring suit for reimbursement for financial losses sustained from investing.

However, the purchasers must be prepared to prove that they lost money on their investment because of incomplete or distorted material information presented in the registration statement.

Omission of material facts and/or misrepresentation of fact are the two bases under which investors in a public offering can recoup their original investment.

REGISTRATION STATEMENTS

The registration of a new issue begins with the filing of a registration statement with the SEC. The registration statement includes all pertinent information and documents relative to that company and to the particular offering. The registration statement is prepared by the issuer in conjunction with the investment banker. The investment banker is experienced in what information should be included in the prospectus and how to present the information to ensure quick and easy processing by the SEC. The information in the registration statement includes:

- the name of the issuer.
- the name of the state under which the issuer is organized.
- the location of the issuer's headquarters.
- the names and addresses of the directors and senior management.
- the names and addresses of the underwriters.
- the names and addresses of persons owning 10% or more of any class of stock of the issuer.
- the amount of securities owned by the directors, senior management, underwriters, and 10% holders.
- a description of the issuer's business.
- a statement of the issuer's capitalization.
- the issuer's debt.

- how the issuer will use the funds received through this offering.
- compensation paid directly to the issuers. They will be named specifically when the compensation is over $25,000.
- the net proceeds to be derived from the offering.
- the public offering price
- compensation to be paid to the underwriters.
- itemized expenses incurred by the issuer in connection to the offering.
- the proceeds derived from any offerings sold by the issuer in the past two years and the details regarding that sale.
- any compensation paid to a promoter in the past two years.
- the names and addresses of any sellers of property or goodwill to be acquired with the proceeds of the offering.
- the names and addresses of the counsel that passed on the legality of the offering.
- a certified balance sheet of the issuer compiled within the last 90 days.
- a certified income statement of the issuer for the latest fiscal year and the last two years.
- certified financial statements of any issuer or business that will be purchased with the proceeds of the offering.
- a copy of the underwriting agreement.
- a copy of a law firm's written opinion attesting to the legality of the offering.
- a copy of the issuer's charter, bylaws, trust agreement, partnership agreement (if applicable), etc.
- a copy of the underlying agreement or indentures affecting any security offered by the issuer.

The SEC examines the registration statement for 20 days, trying to determine whether there are obvious omissions or misrepresentation of the material facts. If the SEC finds omissions or misrepresentations, it sends the corporation a deficiency letter explaining its position on the matter. The effective date of a registration statement is delayed or postponed indefinitely until that deficiency has been cleared-up. No securities can be sold to the public while the registration statement is pending.

If the SEC does not send out a deficiency letter, the registration automatically becomes effective on the 20th calendar day after filing. An earlier approval date can be obtained if it is requested by the underwriter and approved by the SEC. Frequent and reputable issuers of securities have been approved to issue their securities as soon as 48 hours after filing.

The Trust Indenture Act of 1939

The Trust Indenture Act of 1939 is an amendment to the Securities Act of 1939. It gives additional protection to investors in new offerings of corporate debt securities. Basically, the law states that issuers of debt subject to the law must appoint one or more trustees who will ensure that the terms of the indenture are kept by all parties to the agreement. The appointed trustees cannot have conflicting interests and reaffirm their qualifications to be trustees with SEC annually.

Many corporate debt issuers satisfy the Trust Indenture Act of 1939 by making a full disclosure in a formal registration statement which is submitted to the SEC. Debt offerings exempt from registration will comply with the 1939 Act by filing an indenture qualification statement with the SEC. This allows the offerings indenture to be registered with the SEC on effective date.

Regardless if whether a debt offering is registered with the SEC or not, the indenture must set forth the full terms and conditions under which the loan will be kept for its effective life. The facts include:

- the amount, frequency, and method by which interest will be paid;

- the maturity date and the means by which the principal will be repaid;
- redemption privileges reserved for use by the issuer or the debt instrument holder;
- convertible features;
- full description of the collateral securing the loan;
- the powers and responsibilities of trustees in the event of a default by the issuer on any portion of the indenture agreement;
- the responsibilities of the trustee;
- the rights of the bondholders; and
- the obligations of the issuer.

ACTIVITIES DURING THE 20 DAY COOLING-OFF PERIOD

During the 20 day period prior to effective date the issuer and the investment bankers work to finalize the public offering.

First the investment bankers and the issuing corporation will sign a preliminary agreement outlining whether the price the investment banker will pay the issuer for the offering how the investment banker will handle the securities; either through a "firm commitment", "best efforts" or "all-or-nothing basis".

Next the investment banker may desire to form a "syndicate" to underwrite and distribute the offering. A syndicate is a group of investment bankers that agree to put a designated amount of capital to underwrite an offering. A single investment banker with a deal may want to form a syndicate because it does not have the capital to underwrite the deal itself or does not want to risk the capital by itself. A investment banker with whom the deal originated will want to be the "syndicate manager" because they receive compensation above and beyond that of the other underwriters.

In exchange for the honor of being syndicate manager, the investment banker will (i) maintain the securities in its inventory, (ii) "maintain the books" or keep track of the profits/losses on the deal, and (iii) cut the checks for any profits or send out the bills for any losses experienced from the deal.

SEC Rule 10(b)-6

When an investment banker accepts an invitation to join a syndicate, it becomes subject to SEC Rule 10(b)-6. Section 10(b) of the Securities and Exchange Act of 1934 is one of the "anti-fraud" provisions of the Act. These provisions are generally prohibitions against "fraud", "deceit", or "manipulative or deceptive devices or contrivances" in the offer of securities. SEC Rule 10(b)-6 makes it unlawful for any underwriter or other person participating in a distribution to bid for or purchase any units of the security being distributed, with certain specified exceptions.

At this point, the investment bankers will also begin soliciting indications of purchase interest from institutional and select individual investors. This process consists solely of giving the potential investors some overall information regarding the issuer and does not involve any type commitment whatsoever.

SEC Rule 10(b)-7 (the Securities and Exchange Act of 1934) prohibits broker-dealers from soliciting orders or accepting unsolicited orders for new issuers prior to effective date. This step is designed to determine how much initial demand there is for the offering. This process is crucial in determining the public offering price ("POP").

Preliminary Prospectus

During solicitation of indications of interest, the investment banker will develop a "preliminary prospectus". It contains the most facts and information known about the issuer and the offering at that time. The preliminary prospectus will not have the final POP and other critical information.

The SEC has requested the setting of a maximum POP to give potential investors some idea of the value of the offering. The preliminary prospectus is the only permissible form of written communication between the investment bankers and investors prior to effective date.

Due Diligence Meeting

Prior to the effective date, a "due diligence meeting" must be held. The due diligence meeting is a meeting between the major participants in the underwriting to discuss the important aspects of the deal and to flesh out any unanswered questions.

The attendants of the due diligence meeting includes representatives of the issuer, the investment banker, the outside accountants (which review the financial information included in the prospectus), and the outside counsels for both the investment bankers and the issuer.

The topics discussed at the meeting includes: (i) review the information included in the registration statement; (ii) prepare the final prospectus; and (iii) begin negotiating the final underwriting agreement between the issuer and the investment banker.

The only item that will not be set at this meeting is the public offering price. This is because market conditions and interest rates will continue to fluctuate up until offering date. The POP is usually set just before offering date.

Road Show

During the period of time prior to effective date, usually after the syndicate is formed, a "road show" is developed to boost the marketing of the issue. During a road show, the investment bankers and sales personnel, along with representatives of the issuing company, visit various institutional investors in one or several cities to talk about the company. The main purpose of the road show is to introduce the company to investors and to generate interest in the offering.

Blue Sky

The managing underwriters outside counsel also works on "blue-skying" the issue prior to effective date. Blue-skying is actually the process of registering the offering with the states in which the offering will be sold. With the exception of some northeast and mid-

Atlantic states, almost every state requires that some affirmative action be taken to register securities before they can be sold in that state.

There are three ways to blue-sky an offering with a state: (i) notification, (ii) coordination; and (iii) qualification.

- Notification

  Securities may be registered by notifying the state of the pending offering only if they meet certain tests for stability and earnings coverage. The securities are registered by filing a statement demonstrating compliance with the statutory test, plus a description of the offering and the terms of the offering.

- Coordination

  Registration by coordination is similar to registration by notification except the only information required to be filed is a copy of the prospectus filed with the SEC.

- Qualification

  Registration by qualification may be required for those offerings which do not meet the requirements of the other methods. The issuer must file the same information it is required to file in a 1933 Securities Act registration statement. The registration does not become effective until it is approved by the state securities administrator.

Underwriting Agreement

The formal underwriting agreement between the issuer and the investment banker is usually signed just before effective date. The contract is then filed with SEC and becomes part of the registration statement. Underwriting agreements are usually signed under the terms of "severally but not jointly". This means that the underwriters limit their liability to the portion of the offering that they have purchased. Underwriters cannot be held liable for any portion of the offering that could not be sold by the other members of the syndicate. This stipulation is also known as "divided account".

With municipal bond underwritings however, you may sign the

agreement "severally and jointly". This means that all members of the underwriting team have full financial responsibility for any unsold bonds. This stipulation is also known as a united account.

AFTER THE DEAL IS DONE

Final Prospectus

A finalized prospectus must be delivered to each purchaser of new offering along with their customer confirmation. The prospectus is a condensed version of the registration statement filed with the SEC.

The prospectus is the only means of solicitation permitted by the SEC. The prospectus includes the final public offering price.

The Tombstone

The tombstone is an announcement that a security has been offered the public.

They are called tombstones because of the rectangular shape of the announcement and because they are usually very bland and unexciting. Tombstones are bland because they cannot be mistaken as an advertisement or solicitation for the offering. Securities laws prevent broker-dealers from selling an offering to the public without an accompanying prospectus. The information on the tombstone includes:

- the name of the issuer;
- the total principal value of the offering;
- for bonds and preferred stock: the interest rate, interest payable date(s), maturity date, and any parties which are guaranteeing the payment of principal or interest;
- a disclosure stating that the tombstone is not an offer to buy or sell the new issue, and a prospectus is available for that purpose;
- the public offering price;
- the effective date;
- a listing of the principal underwriters, with the syndicate

- manager at the top; and
- a disclosure that the securities may only be sold in states in which the offering is registered, in compliance with that state's blue sky laws.

Stabilizing the Aftermarket

If the market for an issue is not as strong as the underwriters expected, or an underwriting does not break syndicate, the issue may experience a sudden decline in price in the secondary market. If this decline occurred, it would shake investor confidence in the underwriter and in the issuer. For this reason, the SEC allows underwriters to maintain a "stabilizing bid" in the secondary market. SEC Rule 10(b)-7 permits an underwriter to make a stabilizing bid in an issue only to prevent or retard the decline of the issue in the open market. All purchasers of securities in which a stabilizing bid is maintained must receive notice of the existence of the stabilizing bid.

A stabilizing bid may be maintained for all or any portion of the underwriting. In addition, prompt notification of stabilizing bids must be filed with the SEC and the appropriate stock exchange or NASDAQ.

Dealing With Oversubscribed Offerings

There are also instances where an offering may have greater demand than the amount of securities available for sale. In the instance that an issue may do better in the secondary market than originally believed, the underwriter can sell the issue short, then cover the short position in one of two fashions: 1. Buy back the shares in the open market; or 2. Exercise the "Greenshoe Option".

Covering Short Positions in the Open Market

Covering short positions due to excess demand may cause the underwriter to incur a "short cover cost". The short cover cost is the difference between the price at which the issue was sold (the POP less the selling concession) and the price at which the short position was covered (the current price in the secondary market).

The current market price will tend to be higher because there is excess demand for the security.

The process of buying back the shares in the open market is referred to as stabilization if it happens between the time the issue is effective and the time the syndicate is terminated. After termination, the process of buying back is called short covering.

Exercising the Greenshoe Option

The Securities and Exchange Act of 1934 allows an issuer the option to grant underwriters up to a 15% overallotment on the original issue amount for up to 30 days after the offering date. This option is usually included in the underwriting agreement. The Greenshoe Option allows underwriters to cover short positions (and meet excess demand) without incurring stabilization/short covering costs, and earn management and underwriting fees. The Greenshoe Option increases each syndicate members' underwriting participation proportionately. The Option is usually exercised when there is strong demand for a new issue.

Example of How to Account for Stabilization/Short Covering Costs

Let's assume we Dewey & Howe underwrote 1,000,000 shares of Acme Inc. common stock. Acme's POP is $10 per share and the selling concession is $.50. Acme Inc. has developed a synthetic rubber that makes car tires last for 10 years without the need to change them. Due to excess demand by investors for Acme, Dewey decides to oversell the position to its syndicate members by 400,000 shares. In other words, Dewey has a short position of 400,000 shares of Acme Inc. in its inventory.

Because of the excess demand, the head trader for Dewey's Syndicate Desk decides that they should exercise the Greenshoe Option with Acme. Acme delivers 300,000 shares to Dewey, leaving Dewey with a short position of 100,000.

Meanwhile, in the aftermarket, Acme shares have gone up to $11 per share, based on the euphoria for its exciting new product. Dewey covers its 100,000 share short position in the marketplace for $1,100,000 (100,000 shares ***times*** $11 per share). Dewey sold the shares to the syndicate members at $9.50 per share ($10 POP ***less*** $.50 selling concession) or a total value of $950,000.

The total stabilization/short covering cost would be $1.50 per share, or $150,000 ($1,100,000 ***less*** $950,000). The full stabilization/short covering costs are shared by the syndicate members.

The NASD's Free-Riding and Withholding Interpretation

The NASD has always been concerned that its members make all new issues "bona fide" public distributions. In other words, every investor, large or small, well-connected or not so well-connected, who wishes to purchase a new issue, should have a reasonable chance to get it at the public offering price.

They are especially concerned about new issues which trade at a premium in the secondary market, which are known in the industry as "hot issues".

The failure to make an offering a bona fide public distribution when there is excessive demand can artificially raise the price in the secondary markets. This is a very important concern considering that underwriters have information about the offering (such as demand, company-specific information, etc.) that is not available to general investing public.

Therefore, the NASD deems failing to make an offering a bona fide public distribution "inconsistent with high standards of commercial honor and just and equitable principles of trade and leads to an impairment of public confidence in the investment banking and securities business".

Thus, in Article III, Section 1 of the NASD's Rules of Fair Practice, the Association issued the "Free-Riding and Withholding" Interpretation, which restricts the purchase of hot issues by certain parties ***for their own investment accounts.*** The term "free-riding and withholding" should not be confused with the term "free riding", which refers to improper purchases and sales in margin accounts.

The charts below (Figure 8.1 and 8.2) detail the restricted parties, the nature of the restrictions, and any exceptions.

Figure 8.1: Hot Issue Restriction List

HOT ISSUES RESTRICTION LIST	
POTENTIAL PURCHASER	**REQUIREMENT**
1. Underwriters	Restricted
2. Employees of Broker-Dealers	Restricted
3. Relatives of Employees of Broker- Dealers	Restricted unless all of the following conditions exist: ❑ The restricted person does not contribute to the support of the purchaser. ❑ The purchase is in accordance with their normal investment practice. ❑ The purchase is not disproportionate in size.
4. Finders or fiduciaries to the public offering (e.g., accountants, lawyers, financial advisors, etc.)	Restricted unless all of the following conditions exist: ❑ The purchase is in accordance with their normal investment practice. ❑ The purchase is not disproportionate in size.
5. Senior Officers of Banks, S&Ls, Insurance Companies, or Regulated Investment Advisory Firms.	Restricted unless all of the following conditions exist: ❑ The purchase is in accordance with their normal investment practice. ❑ The purchase is not disproportionate in size.
6. Broker-Dealers	Restricted unless the seller receives written assurance from the purchaser that the securities will not be sold to any restricted parties. The purchaser must also promise in writing that the securities will be sold at the public offering price, and without compensation.

Figure 8.2: Hot Issue Restriction List

HOT ISSUES RESTRICTION LIST	
POTENTIAL PURCHASER	**REQUIREMENT**
7. Domestic Banks, Trust Companies, or Conduit Accounts	Restricted unless the seller performs the following steps: ❑ Receives verbal assurance from the purchaser that the securities will not be sold to restricted persons. ❑ Records the name of the person who gave the verbal assurance on the order ticket, or other supporting documentation. ❑ The document must be initialed by a principal. ❑ Trading in the account is monitored by the principal.
8. Foreign Broker-Dealers or Banks Participating in the Syndicate or Selling Group	A paragraph in the underwriting agreement obligating the participant not to sell the securities to restricted persons.
9. Foreign Broker-Dealers or Banks **Not** Participating in the Syndicate or Selling Group	Restricted unless the seller performs the following steps: ❑ Receives verbal assurance from the purchaser that the securities will not be sold to restricted persons. ❑ Records the name of the person who gave the verbal assurance on the order ticket, or other supporting documentation. ❑ The document must be initialed by a principal. ❑ Trading in the account is monitored by the principal. **OR** ❑ File Form FR-1
10. Investment Partnerships and Corporations	Restricted unless the seller obtains the names and business connections of persons with a beneficial interest in the vehicle. **OR** Obtains the opinion of a lawyer stating that the account is not restricted.

SYNDICATE ACTIVITIES

The purchase of new offerings of securities by underwriters may involve investments of many millions of dollars. One investment banker may not have enough capital or may not be able to risk the capital needed for that level of financing. For these reasons, the banker may call in other investment bankers to help him finance the underwriting. The group of bankers are known as an underwriting syndicate or purchase group. In order to facilitate the sale of the securities, the purchase group may in turn form a special organization called the selling syndicate, or selling group, to whom the securities are sold.

The purchase agreement is the contract made between the issuer and the purchase group, with each member of the group separately contracting for its portion of the purchase directly with the issuer. However, all of the participants are included in the same purchase agreements.

Purchase agreements commonly include market out clauses which allow a member of the group to drop in the event of an occurrence before the offering of the securities. Such events can be, for instance, a declaration of war involving the United States, a closing of the stock exchanges, or a discovery of a false statement in the agreement, or an announcement relating to the company's financial condition.

The purchase group may be the only syndicate present in the distribution of the security, when it would then be known as the underwriting syndicate. This syndicate would then sell the securities through its own sales organization to institutions, to individual investors, and also to investment dealers.

When a syndicate group is set up, commonly the members of the purchase group also participate in the selling group. Then they can receive compensation for underwriting the issue and compensation for participating in the sale. This practice is known as "taking down" a part of the issue for sale by their own organization. The manager of the purchase group may set aside a portion of the issue for sale to institutional investors. The balance of the issue is "given up" for sale to the other members of the selling group.

Underwriter Compensation

The compensation received by investment bankers for underwriting and selling securities varies according to a number of different factors. However, generally speaking, the more risky the underwriting, the greater the compensation for the investment banker. For instance, the amount paid to the investment banker for a bond issue is less than the amount that would be paid for an equity issue of the same size from the same company. Also, the compensation is typically a lower percentage of the amount raised for a large issue than a small one.

The marketability of an issue plays a role in determining the fair compensation to an investment banker. For instance, an offering that can be sold in large blocks to institutional investors will result in lower compensation to the investment banker than a less marketable offering.

The method in which the investment banker obtained the privilege of underwriting a company's bonds also plays a role in their compensation. An issue obtained through a competitive bidding process will lead to lower compensation that one that was obtained through a negotiated process.

The market conditions at the time of the offering also plays a role in the investment banker's compensation.

Gross Spread

The difference between what the issuing company gets from the bankers for the securities and what the investors pay to the banker is called the "gross spread". The gross spread or spread represents the gross income from underwriting and selling. Out of this income the bankers would have to pay all of the expenses associated with the purchase and sale of the securities, and their other expenses.

In some instances, the spread is so small that a change in the market can wipe out the banker's profits altogether. For instance corporate bond offerings are notorious having extremely narrow spreads, and sometimes bankers must take a loss to underwrite bonds.

Bankers will take an occasional loss on a deal if it will mean continued goodwill and future business from a particular client.

A listing of the potential fees that must be paid from the gross spread include:

- SEC fees
- Exchange or NASDAQ listing fees
- Federal Reserve stamps

- State taxes and fees
- Trustees fees
- Engineering fees
- Accounting fees
- Printing and engraving fees
- Legal fees
- Travel and entertainment fees
- Other miscellaneous fees

The net of these fees from the gross spread represents compensation to the underwriter.

Price Stabilization

The price of securities trading in the secondary marketplace is determined by the relatively few securities that at any one time are being bought or sold in the market. When a new issue of securities is being sold, the effect of a relatively large quantity on the market at the same time is to depress the price. If the market price of securities already sold should weaken, it may jeopardize the sale of the remaining part of the new issue. In order to maintain the price of the securities the manager of the particular syndicate group is given permission to buy and sell the securities in the market. The agreement usually limits the amount from 5 to 10 percentage of the issue.

The manager may sell these repurchased securities in the market, or he may force the members of the syndicate group to take them up in proportion to their original participation in the group.

Although the manager mat attempt to maintain the price of the securities, if the market slips substantially he may have to keep lowering the price offered for the securities to maintain demand. The stabilization effort may be abandoned if the price slips into free fall.

Competitive Bidding

In private negotiations between the investment banker and the issuing company, the latter is more or less forced to take or leave the price for the securities offered by the banker. When there is competitive bidding for the issue, each banker knows that the other bankers are bidding on the issue and will tend to cut down on his spread and bid the highest price possible to get the issue. It can be argued that competitive bidding results in the lowest financing cost to the issuer. However, sales arranged through private negotiations can be set so that the bid price be contingent on market conditions at the time of the sale. This is a crucial advantage over competitive bidding, where the terms are set before the bankers are asked to submit their bids.

Smaller issuers may not be able to get several investment bankers to bid for their offerings. Also, when markets are unsettled, issuers may be leery of setting up competitive bidding and may instead want to enter into private, secure negotiations with one dependable investment banker.

CHAPTER 9: THE SYNDICATE ACCOUNTING PROCESS

OVERVIEW STEPS OF SYNDICATE PROCESSING

1. Once deal is priced, the syndicate manager must obtain the CUSIP number from Standard & Poors and enter the new security on firm's data base for processing by the firm's systems.

2. Specific trading accounts should be developed for the new offering.

3. New securities must be delivered to the syndicate manager and the manager pays the POP less the gross spread. The managing underwriter pays the issuer via clearing house funds (equity) or federal funds (same day funds) (debt). The managing underwriter gives the issuer either a check or a wire number (for Fed Funds) at the closing and will pick up the securities at issuer's agent bank.

4. The new securities are sold to underwriters and selling group members at POP less the selling concession. Underwriters and selling group members will pick up the securities from the managing underwriter and pay via check.

5. The syndicate and selling group members sell the new securities to institutional and retail customers at the public offering price. For institutional customers, the securities will usually be delivered to their agent bank, and payment will be made via check (equity offerings) or Fed Funds (debt offerings). For retail customers, the securities will be placed in the account at the Firm, and their accounts will be debited for payment.

6. If an offering is DTC eligible, the Firm will still take delivery of the securities from the issuer's agent bank. DTC will visit the managing underwriter, inspect the securities, then take the securities and place them on deposit for the benefit of the Firm.

ACCOUNTING FOR SYNDICATE ACTIVITIES

Syndicate accounting includes accounting for the various revenues, expenses, and accruals that are generated through syndicate activities. This section looks at syndicate accounting from the view of a syndicate manager. It is this perspective that encompasses all of the revenues and expenses that are booked by underwriters during a new public offering.

REVENUES

The primary source of revenues for an underwriter during a new offering is the "gross spread". The gross spread is the difference between the price the underwriter pays the issuer for the securities, and the price which the securities are sold to public (public offering price or POP). The gross spread is comprised of the following components:

- The Management Fee
- The Underwriting Fee
- The Selling Concession
- Reimbursement for Expenses

❑ The Management Fee

The management fee is what the syndicate manager earns for "keeping the books" (calculating the P&L) and housing the inventory for the syndicate group. The management fee may be split when an offering is co-managed.

❑ The Underwriting Fee

This fee is earned by every syndicate group member involved in the deal. The fee is compensation to the underwriters for risking their capital on the new offering. The underwriting fee, net of expenses, is usually distributed to the syndicate members by the lead manager after settlement date.

❑ The Selling Concession

The selling concession is usually the largest portion of the gross spread. The selling concession is earned by the underwriters and selling group members who distribute the offering to institutional and retail customers. Syndicate members usually purchase their share of the offering at the public offering price less the selling concession. The securities are then sold to investors at the public offering price.

REIMBURSEMENT OF EXPENSES

These are expenses generated in the preparation for a new issue that are generally paid by the issuer. However, because investment bankers are experienced in new offerings, they usually know the best outside vendors to use for certain underwriting-related products. Because of this, the investment bankers may arrange for the services, pay the vendors, then obtain reimbursement from the issuer through the gross spread.

Usually, the final gross spread is set right before offering date, so the syndicate members have a relatively good idea of what the total expenses will be. Any expenses that go beyond what is estimated in the gross spread must be shared by the syndicate group. However, the syndicate group may set aside a reserve for unallocated expenses, and include the reserve in the gross spread.

1. Issuer Expenses

The most common issuer expenses are as follows:

- Printing Fees

Red herring prospectuses, final prospectuses, registration statements, Blue Sky memorandums, underwriting agreements, and other documents must be printed in bulk quantities.

- Registration Fees

The SEC and other regulatory bodies require fees to register new issues and to register issues on the various exchanges.

- Blue Sky Fees

States require that issuers pay fees along with the registration application to allow the new offering to be purchased by residents.

- Accountant's Fees

Usually, an outside public accounting firm will be hired to attest to the fairness of the financial information included in the red herring and the final prospectus.

- Outside Counsel's Fees

An outside law firm will be hired to attest to the legality of the offering and assist with the Blue Sky registrations.

- Investment Banking Fees/Investment Advisory Fees

Investment banking fees are usually generated by the lead underwriter or co-managers who originally had or developed the client relationship. During the initial due diligence period, the investment banker(s) are traveling to issuer's headquarters, wining and dining the issuer, and analyzing the issuer's business to determine if an underwriting is feasible.

The investment banker records the time and expense spent on developing the deal in the form of a receivable for investment banking services. At some point in the future, the banker will be compensated for their efforts if they become the underwriter for the issue.

Usually, the expenses incurred during this process are included in the final determination of the gross spread. On occasion, an investment banker will spend time and resources on a deal that does not pan out, or the issuer may negotiate the bill to a lower amount. In this case, the investment banker will write-off all or some portion of the receivables to a uncollectible items account. Usually, the banker will have already set aside a reserve for such situations based on historical write-offs.

In any case, an underwriter cannot be compensated for a fee which was already paid by the issuer.

An example of a typical breakdown of the gross spread, on a per share basis, might look like the following:

Selling Concession	.50
Underwriting Fee	.10
Management Fee	.15
Expenses	.25
Gross Spread	**$1.00**
Price Paid to the Issuer	**$ 9.25**
Public Offering Price	**$10.25**

Let's review an example of a corporation (XYZ Corp.) issuing 1 million shares of stock under the terms stated above. The stock is being underwritten by a syndicate group lead managed by Gramm & Co. Securities Inc. is one of the underwriters and Rice, Stein, & Jones is one of the selling group members. Securities Inc. is underwriting 100,000 shares and Rice, Stein, & Jones will be allocated 25,000 shares to sell. However, Rice, Stein, & Jones is not part of the syndicate group and therefore will not earn the underwriting fee.

On settlement date, Gramm & Co. will pay XYZ Corp. $9,250,000 for 1,000,000 shares of XYZ common stock. XYZ will deliver those shares to Gramm & Co. on the same day.

Also on settlement date, Securities Inc. will deliver a check of $975,000 to Gramm & Co. to pay for its share of the offering. When Securities Inc. sells all of the 100,000 shares, it will earn a selling concession of $50,000 ($.50 x 100,000 shares). When all of the syndicate expenses are summarized, it will also earn an underwriting fee of $10,000 ($.10 x 100,000), less expenses.

Rice, Stein, & Jones will earn a selling concession of $12,500.

SEC Rules require that the final gross spread must be disclosed to all investors through the prospectus.

2. Syndicate Group Expenses

The expenses billed to syndicate are above and beyond the costs covered by the gross spread. Any costs which run above the amount covered by the gross spread will be shared by the underwriters proportionately, based on their takedown.

These syndicate fees usually include the following items:

- Certain legal fees;
- Advertising;
- Travel and entertainment;
- Closing expenses (e.g., the closing dinner, gifts, etc.);
- Losses on oversales;
- Telephone expenses;
- Postage;
- Communications;
- Computer and data processing expenses;
- Interest expense; and
- Miscellaneous expenses. Miscellaneous expenses can include items such as regulatory fees, CUSIP fees, ratings fees, insurance, DTC charges, and state fees.

DETERMINING THE FINAL SYNDICATE PROFIT OF LOSS

To calculate the final underwriting profit on a new offering, broker-dealers must include the following items:

- Net Syndicate P&L
- Selling Concession
- Mark-to-Market
- Cost-of-Carry
- Manager Bill and Delivers
- Designated Orders
- Hedging P&L

- <u>Net Syndicate P&L</u>

Some period after settlement date the syndicate manager will determine the final P&L for each syndicate member. Then the manager will either cut each member a check for their share of the net profit, or send a bill to each member for their share of the net loss.

The net P&L for each member is calculated by

(i) multiplying the underwriting fee per share by the number of shares underwritten. Syndicate managers will also take the total management fee (the management fee per share times the total shares offered;

(ii) adding up all of the designated syndicate expenses, dividing that number by the total shares offered (this gives you the syndicate expenses per share), and multiplying that number by the number of shares underwritten;

(iii) subtract the syndicate expenses from the underwriting revenue. Again, this number may result in a profit or loss, depending on several factors such as:

- Market conditions (stock market levels and interest rates);
- Demand for the offering;
- Significant world or economic events;
- Significant company events;
- Level of expenses;
- Level of the gross spread;

<u>NASD'S UNIFORM PRACTICE CODE SECTION 66</u>

Prior to 1985, a small group of elite investment banking firms acted as syndicate managers of new offerings. Second and third tier firms acted as either syndicate members or selling group members. The firms that acted as syndicate managers had the responsible calculating the P&L for each members' syndicate account and cutting a check or sending a bill to each member.

During the early to mid-eighties, the second and third tier firms began to complain to

the NASD that some syndicate managers were taking an inordinately long period of time to settle syndicate accounts.

Because of the complaints, the NASD began to survey the industry about the length of time needed to settle a syndicate account.

In October, 1985, the NASD enacted Uniform Practice Code Section 66 which required syndicate managers to settle syndicate accounts within 120 days. Later, the Uniform Practice Code Section ("UPC") 66 was amended to require syndicate managers to calculate and settle the syndicate accounts within 90 days of settlement date for corporate equity and debt underwritings (60 days for municipal syndicate underwritings).

Along with the final of the syndicate account, UPC 66 requires that syndicate managers provide the syndicate members with an itemized statement of the syndicate expenses, including the following categories of expenses: legal fees; advertising; travel and entertainment; closing expenses; loss on oversales; telephone, postage, and communications; co-manager's expenses; computer and data processing expenses; and miscellaneous expenses.

The total under miscellaneous expenses should not be disproportionately large in relation to the other expenses and should only include minor items that cannot be easily placed in another category. This is to prevent the padding of expenses by artificially "puffing-up" the miscellaneous or "other" expense category with items unrelated to the underwriting. Other major items not included in the above categories should be itemized separately.

SYNDICATE ACCOUNT SETTLEMENT STATEMENTS

Syndicate Managers will usually calculate the final expense total for the offering and send each syndicate member a statement of that calculation, as required by UPC 66. The typical Syndicate Account Expense Summary Statement might look like Figure 9.1.

Syndicate managers usually establish controls over the expense payment process to ensure that expenses are properly approved and documented.

These controls include:

- Establishing an accounts payable system to assign and record all expenses to a specific deal number, and to review the expenses charged by each investment banker.

❑

Figure 9.1: Syndicate Expense Statement

Syndicate Expense Statement For: Dewey & Howe	
Syndicate Offering: Acme Common Stock	
Public Offering Price: $10.25 per share	
Number of Shares Underwritten: 250,000 shares	
Underwriting Fee: $.15 per share	
Revenue:	
Underwriting Revenue	$37,500
Total Expenses:	
Legal Fees:	
Underwriters' Counsel:	$3,000
Blue Sky Survey & Fees:	500
Advertising:	2,000
Travel and Entertainment:	10,000
Printing:	1,500
Closing Expenses:	
Airline:	1,000
Hotel:	1,500
Food:	1,300
Loans:	
Day Loan:	500
Reserve for Unallocated Expenses:	450
Total Expenses:	**$21,750**
Enclosed please find a check for	**$37,500**

- ❑ Requiring all expense payments to be approved by a member of senior management.
- ❑ Requiring that the retention of all professional services (lawyers, accountants, etc.) for deals to be approved by senior management.
- ❑ Requiring supporting documentation (receipts, invoices, etc.) for all outside vendors services charged to deals.

❑ Selling Concessions

The selling concession earned by syndicate members and selling group members is usually the largest portion of the gross spread. The syndicate managers sell each syndicate member and selling group member their takedown at the public offering price less the selling concession. When the syndicate and selling group members sell the offering to the public at the POP, their net profit at that time will be the selling concession per share times the number of shares sold.

Each syndicate member must include the selling concession earned when calculating their total profits from the syndicate offering.

- Marking-to-Market

Once settlement date is reached and the deal is closed, new offerings will begin to trade in the secondary market.

In the secondary market, the price for the new issue will fluctuate based on demand, supply, and the overall state of the stock and bond markets. Broker-dealers must price their positions at the end of each day at the closing bid price. The closing price will be based on supply and demand on the market in which it trades.

- Cost of Carry

In order to obtain the large sums of money necessary to underwrite new issues, broker-dealers must borrow money from their banks, usually at the broker call rate. The interest rate charged by the banks is a real cost to underwriter, and must be taken into consideration when calculating the profitability of a underwriting.

For debt offerings, the cost of carry is offset by any interest earned on the position.

In low interest rate markets, the interest earned on the position may offset, or even surpass, the interest cost of financing the new issue. This leads to "negative" cost of carry, or interest income.

Most broker-dealers have systems to automatically calculate the cost of carry on any position in their inventory.

The formula for calculating the cost of carry is:

Annual interest rate to finance the position (usually the broker call rate)

Times

The number of days the position is held/360

Times

The market value of the position

Less (for debt offerings)

The interest earned on the position.

- Manager Bill and Delivers

An institutional customer may purchase shares of a new issue from several different members of a syndicate group.

However, they may not want to send checks to every member they purchase the shares from.

The customer may opt to have the syndicate manager to bill and deliver to them for the other syndicate members. In other words the managing underwriter will bill the institutional customer for payment, then deliver them the shares on behalf of the other syndicate members involved in the purchase.

When the syndicate manager calculates the P&L for syndicate members involved in the purchase, they will include the selling concession they earned on the transaction.

- Designated Orders

An institutional customer may purchase shares of a new issue from a syndicate manager, but may choose to have the selling concession go to another broker-dealer, perhaps in exchange for services previously rendered. When the manager settles the syndicate account, he will cut a check to the designated broker-dealer for selling concession on the number of shares chosen by the customer.

- Hedging P&L

If a new issue will not be completely sold out by settlement date, the managing underwriter may want to hedge the position in inventory until it sold. This is especially true for fixed-income offerings, which have a variety of products that can be used hedge potential losses. Hedging P&L must be accounted for and netted against the firm's final calculation of P&L for the underwriting.

PART V: BROKER-DEALER REGULATIONS

INTRODUCTION

Over the past ten years, Wall Street broker-dealers have been fined millions of dollars for violations of various SEC, NASD, and NYSE rules and regulations.

Probably more fines are paid for violations of securities industry laws than any other area of business outside of parking tickets and income taxes.

However, it has been proven over time that the securities industry needs to be heavily regulated because of the high potential for fraud and abuse. The securities markets are the places where the American dream is promulgated. Many small businesses and promising corporations use the securities markets to raise capital, expand production capacity, and increase research and development. And the American public has the opportunity to share in the American dream by investing their money in these promising corporations.

But to maintain the confidence of the average investor, the securities markets must be free of fraud and manipulative practices. And broker-dealers who facilitate these transactions must be well-managed, operationally efficient, and financially strong to ensure that investor's funds are safe and secure.

Public confidence in the securities markets is essential for our economy, and regulation is the only way to ensure public confidence!

A famous person once said, "Ignorance of the law is no excuse, but it's better than no alibi at all." Through this chapter of the book, we want to expose to some of the more important rules and regulations that relate to Stock Brokerage Accounting, and eliminate any ignorance, alibis and excuses!

The regulation of the brokerage industry essentially began with the stock market crash of 1929. Prior to the crash there was very little Federal regulation of the brokerage industry. Broker-dealers were subject only to the rules and regulations of the exchanges which they were members of.

Fraud, manipulative practices, and insider trading were rampant on Wall Street prior to the crash. The 1929 crash disclosed such a large amount of fraudulent activity that President Roosevelt and the Congress enacted several laws dealing specifically with securities regulation. These laws were the Securities Act of 1933 and the Securities and Exchange Act of 1934.

The Securities Act of 1933 regulates the public offering of securities. It prohibits offers or sales of securities which are not registered with the Federal government, subject to exceptions for certain kinds of securities and transactions. It also prohibits fraudulent or deceptive practices in any offer or sale of securities.

The Securities and Exchange Act of 1934 extended Federal regulations to trading practices regarding securities in the secondary market. The 1934 Act contains several provisions that regulate the activities of the different participants in the brokerage industry, including customers, broker-dealers, and registered representatives (stockbrokers). The 1934 Act established the Securities and Exchange Commission (SEC), and gave the SEC the responsibility of administering and enforcing the provisions of the 1933 and 1934 Acts. In addition, the 1934 Act:

- imposes financial disclosure and other requirements on publicly traded companies;
- prohibits various manipulative and/or deceptive devices or practices in the purchase or sale of securities;
- restricted the amount of credit that may be extended for the purchase of securities;
- requires broker-dealers to register with the SEC and self-monitor their activity; and
- provides for SEC regulation and supervision of any national securities exchanges or associations, clearing agencies, transfer agents, securities information processor (SIAC, NSCC, etc.).

The rules and guidelines of the SEC are also enforced by the stock exchanges (e.g., the New Stock Exchange, the American Stock Exchange, etc.) and the National Association of Securities Dealers (NASD). The Municipal Securities Rulemaking Board (MSRB) which was created in 1975, is the regulatory body for the municipal securities marketplace. Since the MSRB has no examining or enforcement authority, its rules are enforced by the SEC and the NASD.

The rules and regulations of the brokerage industry generally fall within three categories: financial and books and records; operational; and sales practice. We will focus on the financial and books and records regulations throughout most of our discussion, but we will also touch on several operational and sales practice rules as well.

CHAPTER 10: RECORDKEEPING

SEC RULE 17a-3 (AND MSRB RULE G-8):

SEC Rule 17a-3 requires that registered broker-dealers prepare records of transactions and dealings in securities for the accounts of the firm's customers as well as for its own risk and account. In addition, broker-dealers are required to prepare records of other financial transactions related to the business of the broker-dealer.

These requirements are intended to serve three basic regulatory purposes. First, it is expected that the broker-dealer maintain current books and records for the protection and convenience of its customers (prompt responses to inquiries and prompt resolution of claims). Secondly, these requirements are intended to enable a broker-dealer to be aware of the extent of its compliance with the various rules and requirements, particularly the net capital rule (SEC Rule 15c3-1) and the customer protection rule (SEC Rule 15c3-3). Third, a broker-dealer should have current books and records to enable it to fulfill its obligations and responsibilities to other broker-dealers with whom business is transacted.

Order Tickets and Confirmations

Subparagraphs (6) and (7a) of Rule 17a-3(a) require the preparation of a memorandum of each brokerage order and each principal transaction, and subparagraph (8) requires maintenance of copies of confirmations of transactions for the accounts of customers and partners. These are the basic source documents and transaction records of a broker-dealer. By their nature the memoranda of brokerage and principal transactions should be prepared at the time of the transactions, and the confirmations, which are prepared from the memoranda, should be prepared and mailed on the day of the transaction or the following business day.

Records of Original Entry

The blotters or other records of original entry described in subparagraph (1) of Rule 17a-3 itemize each day's transactions in a format that facilitates posting to the general and subsidiary ledgers.

Blotter records relating to securities transactions - e.g., daily purchase and sale blotters - should reflect all transactions as of the trade date and should be prepared no later than the following business day. Similarly, blotter records relating to securities movements and the receipt and disbursement of cash should reflect such transactions on the date they occur and should be prepared no later than the following business day.

General Ledgers

The ledgers prescribed in subparagraph (2) of Rule 17a-3 are the general records reflecting all asset, liability and capital accounts and all income and expense accounts and includes control accounts for subsidiary ledgers. The blotters and other records of original entry should be maintained not only on a daily basis as discussed above, but in a form which will facilitate posting of the general ledger as frequently as necessary to ascertain compliance with the net capital rule and the customers' reserve requirement. See Rule 15c3-3(e). For many broker-dealers, compliance with the customers' reserve requirement entails a weekly computation based on updated general ledger account balances.

A broker-dealer is required to be in compliance with the net capital rule at all times and the general ledger must be posted as frequently as may be necessary to make that determination. Compliance with this rule and the concern for frequent computations becomes particularly important in periods of sharp changes in security prices and increases in trading volume. Firms which are frequent participants in underwriting syndicates or which effect transactions in large blocks of stock may also find it necessary to post their ledger on a daily basis because of the need for making frequent net capital computations. If a broker-dealer effects only a limited number of transactions during an accounting period and it is clear from the nature of the business conducted that such transactions would have no material adverse effect on the broker-dealer's financial and operational condition, net capital or customer's protection requirements during the period it may be appropriate to post the general ledger on a monthly basis.

Customer's Ledger Accounts

Transactions involving the purchase and sale of securities should be posted to the customer's ledger accounts described in subparagraph (3) of Rule 17a-3 no later than the settlement date. Other customer transactions relating to securities movements and cash receipts and disbursements should be reflected as of the transaction date and should be posted to the accounts no later than the first business day following the transaction.

Subsidiary Ledgers

The subsidiary ledgers and other records* relating to securities in transfer, dividends and interest received, securities borrowed and securities loaned, and monies loaned required under subparagraphs (4)(A)-(D) should be posted no later than two business days subsequent to the date of the securities or money movements.

Transactions between brokers not completed on settlement date should be posted to the appropriate fail to deliver or fail to receive ledger (or other record) no later than the first business day following settlement date; resolution of fail transactions should be recorded no later than the first business day following resolution. A broker-dealer who maintains his accounts on the trade date basis of accounting and uses "fail" accounts to reflect transactions with other brokers should post transactions to the accounts no later than two business days subsequent to the transaction date.

In accordance with the provisions of Rule 17a-13(b)(5), long and short stock record differences shall be entered in an appropriate ledger account (subparagraph (4)(F)) no later than seven business days after the date of a required quarterly securities examination and verification. If counts are made on a cyclical basis in accordance with Rule 17a-13(c), and stock record difference shall be recorded within seven business days subsequent to examination and verification of a particular security.

*As used in subparagraph (4) and elsewhere in Rule 17a-3, the term, "other records" should be construed to include, where appropriate, copies of vouchers, confirmations, or similar documents which reflect the information required by the applicable subparagraph arranged in appropriate sequence and in permanent form, including similar records developed by the use of automatic data processing systems and produced or reproduced on microfilm.

Securities Position Record (Stock Record)

The securities record required by subparagraph (5) of Rule 17a-3(a) shall reflect the changes resulting from purchase and sale transactions either as broker or dealer as of clearance date, or settlement date, and should be recorded no later than the following business day. (The requirement for current maintenance of the securities record can be made by broker-dealers through preparation of a full securities record weekly, supplemented by a daily "takeoff" sheet summarizing and balancing each day's securities movements.) In addition, other changes in securities positions should be reflected on the date of the security movement or on the following business day as of the date of the movement. Long and short securities record differences shall be entered concurrently with their recording in the subsidiary ledger required by subparagraph (4)(F).

Transactions in Options

The record of puts, calls, spread, straddles, and other options described in subparagraph (10) should reflect transactions as of the date an option is written, guaranteed, traded or exercised and should be prepared no later than the business day following the transaction.

Trial Balances and Capital Computation

Subparagraph (11) requires the monthly preparation of a trial balance of all ledger accounts and a computation of aggregate indebtedness and net capital as of the trial balance date.

These records should be prepared no later than 10 business days after the end of the accounting period, except in those instances where the records must be prepared in a lesser period to satisfy any reporting requirements established by any self-regulatory authority of which the broker-dealer is a member. (Although not specifically referred to in Rule 17a-3, the weekly or monthly computation of the amount to be on deposit under the customers' reserve requirement rule must be made in sufficient time to enable the broker-dealer to make the required deposit no later than one hour after the opening of banking business on the second business day following the date on which the computation is based, as required by Rule 15c3-3(e)).

Other Records

The record of beneficial ownership of each cash or margin account (subparagraph (9) of Rule 17a-3) should be prepared before transactions are effected in an account. The employment questionnaire or application (subparagraph (12) of Rule 17a-3) should be prepared at or prior to the commencement of employment.

Time Lag in Transmission of Data

Under certain limited circumstances the accounting department of a broker-dealer may not be aware of a transaction until a few days after it occurs. Transactions such as receipts and disbursements in out-of-town branches or by correspondents should be recorded no later than the day after the transaction is reported to the accounting department, and dividend and interest claims from other brokers should be recorded no later than the day after the validity of the claim is established.

Service Bureaus

If a broker-dealer hires or engages an outside service bureau or their recordkeeping service to handle its records, the requirement to make and keep current the broker-dealer's books and records is in no way diminished and under such circumstances the broker-dealer is responsible to the same degree for maintaining current books and reports as if he were maintain them himself. Where a broker-dealer undertakes to have his books and records prepared and maintained by a service bureau or recordkeeping service, he should assure himself that the service will be provided in conformity with the Commission recordkeeping rules.

SEC RULE 17a-4 (AND MSRB RULE G-9)

SEC Rule 17a-4 stipulates the length of time broker-dealers are required to maintain its books and records.

The following records must be maintained for 6 years, the first two in an easily accessible place. Easily accessible means accessible within 24 hours.

- Purchase and Sales Blotter
- Receipts and Deliveries of Securities Blotter
- Receipts and Disbursements of Cash Blotter
- The General Ledger
- The Customer Ledgers
- The Stock Record
- Cash and Margin Account Records

The following records must be maintained for three years, the first two in an easily accessible place:

- Securities in Transfer Ledger
- Dividends and Interest Received Records
- Securities Borrowed and Loaned Records
- Monies Borrowed and Loaned Records
- Failed to Receive and Failed to Deliver Ledgers
- Long and Short Stock Record Differences
- Order Tickets
- Confirmations
- Comparisons
- Options Records
- The Trial Balance
- All Written Agreements
- Powers of Attorney

In addition, the employment application of all associated persons must be maintained until three years after the termination of the person's employment.

CHAPTER 11: MARGIN

PURPOSE OF THE MARGIN DEPARTMENT

The Margin Department handles the lending of funds to customers for the purchase of securities and customer account inquiries regarding cash and margin transactions.

The Margin Department employees also review, update, maintain, and service customer account records. The main reason for providing these services is to enforce lending procedures and policies, and to review the activities in the accounts.

Surveillance of customer accounts is required to ensure compliance with the regulations of the Federal Reserve Board (FRB), the New York Stock Exchange (NYSE), the National Association of Securities Dealers (NASD), other regulating agencies, and the broker-dealers' internal policies.

Margin Department Duties

The functions of the Margin Department are numerous, and can vary from firm to firm. Here we'll attempt to outline the duties we feel are the main responsibilities of the Margin Department. These responsibilities include:

- Customer account records should be current, including position and money balances.
- Issue margin calls (both initial and maintenance), and calls for additional cash or securities.
- Follow-up on the actual collection of cash and securities owed to the firm.
- Maintain records for customer accounts as required by the FRB, SEC, NYSE, and NASD.
- Establish systems and management reports that alert management to problems or violations of regulatory guidelines or firm policies.
- Handling inquiries and requests from customers, salesmen, traders, and management.
- Authorize withdrawals of cash and securities from customer

accounts.

Types of Customer Accounts

The two types of customer accounts are cash accounts and margin accounts. Usually, broker/dealers will use the same account number for each customer's cash and margin accounts, but with different check digits. (For instance, customer Sam Jones' cash account number might be XYZ-72345-1 (the number "1" is the type digit) while his margin account would be XYZ-72345-3. It is critical for margin employees to know which types of securities and transaction can occur in a customer's cash account versus his margin account.

If a client is paying in full for a security purchase, then the trade is on a "cash basis" and will be executed in their cash account. If the client is using credit or borrowing a portion of the purchase price from the firm, then the trade is on margin and should be executed in the margin account. Certain types of securities are eligible for purchase on margin, including listed common stocks, listed corporate bonds, and municipal bonds.

WHAT IS A MARGIN TRANSACTION

A margin transaction is a trade in which the broker-dealer lends the customer money to assist him in purchasing securities. The broker-dealer holds the securities purchased as collateral and charges interest on the loan. Broker-dealers usually borrow funds from a bank using the securities as collateral for the loan. The funds are borrowed from the bank at the "broker call rate".

The amount of funds that the customer must supply are dependant on three factors: (i) Federal regulations (**Regulation T**); (ii) exchange/NASD rules; and (iii) the broker-dealer's internal policies.

Why Trade on Margin?

Trading on margin provides investors with ***leverage***. In other words, the use of margin can provide a customer with a greater return on their investment dollars than a cash purchase.

For example, customer Sam Jones wants to purchase 100 shares of Acme Common Stock (assume it is NYSE listed), which is trading at $50 per share. If Mr. Jones purchases Acme in his cash account, he will pay $5,000, (assuming that there are no commissions on the trade). If the stock goes up to $60 per share in a year, Mr. Jones will have earned a return of $1,000, or 20%, on his investment.

If Mr. Jones purchased 100 shares at $50 per share by establishing a margin account, he would only have to invest 50% of the purchase price, or $2,500. His brokerage firm would lend him the other $2,500, plus interest. When Acme went up to $60 per share, Mr. Jones would again earn $1,000. However, the return on his investment would be 40%, excluding interest!

Using his margin account, Mr. Jones also could have purchased more shares of Acme with the same $5,000 he invested with his cash account. If Mr. Jones purchased $5,000 worth of Acme in his margin account, he would own 200 shares, twice the number he would own in a cash account.

These transactions we have illustrated are clear examples of how margin accounts gives investors leverage, and increases the purchasing power of their investment dollars.

REGULATION T

The Securities and Exchange Act of 1934 gave the Federal Reserve Board the responsibility and authority to regulate the extension of credit on the purchase and sale of securities. The FRB performs this responsibility through Regulation T. Regulation T covers both cash and margin account activity.

CASH ACCOUNTS

In a cash account, broker-dealers may effect for or with a customer any bona fide cash transaction in securities. The assumption is made that: (1) the broker-dealer will not be extending any credit to the customer; (2) the customer will deposit the full purchase price promptly (within 7 business days); and (3) the customer does not contemplate selling the security prior to making payment.

The NASD or the NYSE may grant extensions of time (known as "Reg T extensions) beyond seven business days if they are satisfied that: (1) the broker-dealer is acting in good faith in requesting the exception; (2) the request relates to a bona fide cash transaction; and (3) exceptional circumstances warrant the extension.

The NASD and the NYSE require broker-dealers to settle trades on settlement date (usually 5 business days from trade date) regardless of when the customer settles with the broker. An extension will usually give the broker-dealer an additional 7 days to settle the transaction.

If a customer purchases a security, and then for any reason sells it before full payment is made (known as "free-riding"), the broker-dealer may not, for 90 days calendar days from the date of sale, purchase a security for the customer unless full payment is received before the order is executed. However, if within 7 business days from the original purchase, the customer deposits the full purchase price and has not withdrawn the proceeds of sale before the full deposit is made, Regulation T provides that the 90 day restriction should be lifted.

If a broker-dealer purchases for or sells to a customer in a delivery versus payment transaction ("DVP" or "RVP" accounts), the broker-dealer shall have up to 35 calendar days to obtain payment if delivery of the security is delayed due to the mechanics of the transaction and is not related to the customer's ability to pay.

MARGIN ACCOUNTS

Federal Reserve Board Requirements

The FRB controls the margin requirement that customers are required to put up to finance a transaction. Currently, the FRB margin requirement is 50%. Thus, customer must deposit 50% of the total purchase price and the broker-dealer may lend him the balance (50%).

Any stock that trades on a national securities exchange is eligible to be purchased on margin. Stocks that trade in the over-the-counter (OTC) market must be approved for margin by the FRB. The FRB has compiled a list of approved OTC stocks. In addition, NASDAQ-NMS securities are eligible for margin. A newly issued security will not become eligible for margin until 30 days after the settlement date of the new issue. Certain securities, such as government and municipal securities, are referred to as exempt securities, are exempt from FRB margin requirements.

The FRB margin requirement is the percentage of the total purchase price which the investor must deposit. This deposit represents "equity" in the customer's account. The difference between the purchase price and the margin requirement is the debit balance. The broker-dealer borrows the debit balance from a bank at a rate known as the "broker call rate". The broker-dealer will charge the customer interest on the debit balance at a rate approximately a percentage point higher than the broker call rate. This rate is usually charged on a monthly basis.

The loan value of a margin account is the amount of credit that can be extended to the customer by the broker-dealer. The loan value is based upon the market value of the securities in the account. The loan value calculation for an initial margin purchase is the current market value of the securities times the loan value percentage (100% ***minus*** the FRB requirement).

Excess Equity and the Special Memorandum Account (SMA)

When the long market value of securities increase or the short market value of securities decrease, the equity in the account will increase. The equity in the account could exceed the FRB requirement in this situation. This excess would be journaled to a special account called the SMA. The excess or SMA can be withdrawn in cash by the customer. Once the customer withdraws cash, their debit balance will increase by the amount withdrawn.

Having a balance in the SMA creates "buying power" for the customer. Buying power is the amount of securities that a customer can buy using the SMA as the margin deposit. A customer's buying power equals the SMA balance divided by the FRB margin percentage requirement.

When a cash dividend is paid to a margin account, the customer is allowed to withdraw all of the dividend. Therefore, all of the dividend is credited to SMA. Once an account is credited with SMA, the SMA will not be reduced unless the customer withdraws it or uses the account's buying power.

Restricted Accounts

If the equity in an account falls below the initial margin requirement, the account becomes restricted. A restricted account can make additional purchases as long as the customer makes the required FRB deposit with that purchase. A purchase and sale of securities on the same day is permitted in a restricted account. This is known as a "same day substitution". If the amounts of the purchase and the sale are the same, then no additional deposit is required.

Frozen Accounts

The FRB stipulates that customers deposit the margin requirement within seven business days. If a customer cannot pay in the stipulated time period and an extension is not granted, the broker-dealer must freeze the account and sell a sufficient amount of securities to cover the margin requirement on the 8th day. When an account is frozen, it will remain frozen for 90 days. If the customer wants to purchase securities in a frozen account, they must deposit the full purchase price in the account before the order can be executed. If the customer wishes to sell securities in a frozen account, the broker-dealer must gain possession of the securities before executing the transaction. A frozen account means the customer has violated Regulation T.

Short Sales

An individual who sells short is selling securities that they do not own. The individual anticipates the market price of the securities falling, and hopes to profit from that fall by purchasing the securities at a lower price than the initial short sale price (sell high, buy low).

The broker-dealer will loan the customer the stock since they do not own it. Since the stock is borrowed, the customer is obligated to buy the securities, but there is not a required time period in which this must occur.

The FRB margin requirement for a short sale is 50% of the proceeds of the sale. When a customer sells short and makes the required margin deposit, they establish a credit balance in their account. The credit balance is the total of the proceeds of the short sale and the margin requirement on the value of the sale. The customer's equity is equal to the credit balance minus the current short market value of the securities sold.

Short selling power in a short account is calculated by dividing the SMA by the FRB margin percentage.

Combined Long and Short Accounts

When a customer has both purchased on margin and sold short, it is necessary to calculate the combined equity of the account. The combined equity equals: long market value (LMV) - short market value (SMV) - the debit balance (DR) + the credit balance (CR). The Regulation T excess is calculated as follows: Equity - 50% x LMV - 50% x SMV.

Regulation T Requirements Examples

Example #1:

Ms. Jones purchases 100 shares of XYZ for $7 per share. What is her initial margin requirement or Reg. T call?

Long Market Value = $700

Regulation T Margin Requirement = 50% of Market Value or $350.

Before Ms. Jones meets her initial margin requirement, her account will read as follows:

Ms. Jones' Account Activity				
Long Position	*Current Price*	*Market Value*	*Debit Balance*	*Equity*
100 XYZ	7	$700	$700	$0

At this point, there is no equity in her account. After Ms. Jones meets her Reg. T call, her account will read as follows:

Ms. Jones' Account Activity				
Long Position	***Current Price***	***Market Value***	***Debit Balance***	***Equity***
100 XYZ	7	$700	$350	$350

At this point, there would be $350 of equity in Ms. Jones account.

Example #2:

Assuming a Reg. T requirement of 50%, what would be Mr. Smith's Reg. T call if he purchased 200 shares of Company A at $50 per share?

Long Market Value = $1000.

Reg. T requirement = 50% of market value: 50% of $1000 = $500.

Assuming Mr. Smith met his Reg. T call, his account would read:

Ms. Smith's Account Activity				
Long Position	***Current Price***	***Market Value***	***Debit Balance***	***Equity***
200 Company A	50	$1000	$500	$500

Mr. Smith would have equity of $500.

Now, if the current price of the securities in Mr. Smith's account increased from $50 to $60, what would his account look like?

Ms. Smith's Account Activity				
Long Position	***Current Price***	***Market Value***	***Debit Balance***	***Equity***
200 Company A	60	$1200	$500	$700

Now Mr. Smith's equity has increased $200 and something else significant has occurred; Mr. Smith now has Reg. T excess!

Reg. T excess is the amount in Mr. Smith's margin account that may be used for additional purchases:

Reg. T excess is calculated by multiplying the Reg. T percentage requirement by the current market value of the securities in the account, and subtracting that amount form the equity in the account. For example:

50% of $1200 is $600. The equity in the account is $700, so the Reg. T excess is $100. This $100 can be used for the purchase of additional securities, it can be withdrawn, or a combination of the two. Usually, the Reg. T excess is placed in the SMA or Special Memorandum Account.

Let's assume that Mr. Smith wants to purchase 100 shares of ABC at $3 per share. There is $100 of Reg. T excess available for him to use on this purchase. Mr. Smith's Reg. T requirement (assuming 50%) would be:

Cost of Purchase = $300.

Reg. T requirement is 50% of cost or $150.

Any Reg. T excess is subtracted from the Reg. T requirement, therefore the Reg. T call will be:

50% of $300	= $150
Less Reg. T excess in Mr. Smith's account	= ($100)
Reg. T call due	= **$50**

After Mr. Smith deposits his Reg. T call, his account will read as follows:

Mr. Smith's Account Activity				
Long Position	*Current Price*	*Market Value*	*Debit Balance*	*Equity*
200 Company A	60	$1200	$500	$700
100 ABC	3	$300	$250	$50
TOTAL		$1500	$750	$750

Total Equity in Mr. Smith's account would be $750. Assuming that the Reg. T requirement is 50%, the Reg. T excess now in the account is $0.

NYSE/NASD REQUIREMENTS

Once a customer has deposited the initial FRB required margin, no additional FRB deposits are required if the market value declines or rises. The NYSE and the NASD have established requirements which cover additional deposits for movement in the prices of securities. The NYSE/NASD requires that customers establish a minimum equity on the initial transaction in a margin account. On a purchase the minimum is $2,000 or 100% of the purchase price, whichever is less. The initial transaction in a short account requires a minimum equity of $2,000 regardless of the total market value. Whenever the FRB requirement is larger than the NASD/NYSE requirement, the FRB requirement prevails. Broker-dealers have the right to set higher margin requirements, but never lower than what is required by the exchanges and the FRB.

The NYSE/NASD have also set up minimum margin requirements that would require customers to deposit additional cash or securities if their equity dropped below a specified percentage. The minimum margin to be maintained in the margin account of a customer is as follows:

(1) 25% of the market value of all securities long in the account, except for exempt securities;

(2) $2.50 per share or 100% of the market value, whichever is greater, of each stock short in the account with a market of less than $5.00 per share; and,

(3) $5.00 per share or 30% of the market value, whichever is greater, of each stock short in the account with a market value of $5.00 per share or above.

The maintenance requirement mandated by the NYSE is very similar to the margin rules of the NASD. NYSE Rule 431 requires that a minimum equity of $2,000 be established for all margin accounts. The maintenance margin requirement for long positions is 25% of the market value of the positions held. The maintenance requirement for short positions are:

- 100% of the market value or $2.50 per share for securities selling below $5.00 per share.

- 30% of the market value or $5.00 per share for securities selling above $5.00 per share.

Maintenance Margin Requirements (NASD and NYSE requirements) Examples

Example #1

Ms. Jones' first transaction in her margin account is a purchase of 100 shares of DEF Corp. at $100 per share, for a total cost of $10,000. She would have a Reg. T requirement (50% of cost) of $5,000. Her account would read like this:

Ms. Jones' Account Activity				
Long Position	*Current Price*	*Market Value*	*Debit Balance*	*Equity*
100 DEF Corp.	100	$10,000	$5,000	$5,000

At the time the transaction was made, the broker determined that $5,000 was needed to satisfy federal margin requirements. The margin calculations would normally have been taken two steps further at that time. The broker would normally compare the Regulation T call amount, in this case $5,000, to the following:

1. NYSE minimum equity requirement = $2,000
2. 25% of Market Value (.25 X 10,000) = $2,500

Since $5,000 is the larger of the two requirements, the Reg. T call satisfies all requirements in this situation. By depositing the $5,000, the customer satisfied Regulation T, NYSE minimum equity, and the NYSE initial maintenance requirement.

Example #2

If the market value of DEF declined from $100 to $60 per share, Ms. Jones account would read like this:

Ms. Jones' Account Activity				
Long Position	*Current Price*	*Market Value*	*Debit Balance*	*Equity*
100 DEF Corp.	60	$6,000	$5,000	$1,000

The NYSE minimum maintenance requirement here would not apply because the equity drop was due to a decline in market value, not a withdrawal of cash.

The NYSE maintenance requirement would be 25% of the market value, or $1,500. The equity in the account is $1,000, therefore Ms. Smith would be subject to a *Margin Call of $500*. Once the $500 is deposited, her account would read like this:

Ms. Jones' Account Activity				
Long Position	*Current Price*	*Market Value*	*Debit Balance*	*Equity*
100 DEF Corp.	60	$6,000	$4,500	$1,500

<u>You can meet a maintenance margin call by:</u>

1. Depositing cash
2. Depositing acceptable securities
3. Selling securities

<u>Example #3</u>

Mr. Smith wants to sell 500 shares of ABC short at $15 per share in his margin account for total proceeds of $7,500. The Reg. T requirement for short sales is 50% of net proceeds of the sale. Therefore, Mr. Smith would have to deposit $3,750. Before the deposit, his account would read as follows:

Mr. Smith's Account Activity				
Short Position	*Current Price*	*Market Value*	*Credit Balance*	*Equity*
500 ABC	15	$(7,500)	$7,500	$0

Once Mr. Smith makes his Reg. T requirement, his account will read as follows:

Mr. Smith's Account Activity				
Short Position	*Current Price*	*Market Value*	*Credit Balance*	*Equity*
500 ABC	15	$(7,500)	$11,250	$3,750

Suppose ABC increases in market value from $15 to $20 per share:

Mr. Smith's Account Activity				
Short Position	*Current Price*	*Market Value*	*Credit Balance*	*Equity*
500 ABC	20	$(10,000)	$11,250	$1,250

Smith's account would have a market value of ($10,000), and equity of $1,250. Thus Smith's account is in violation of the NYSE minimum maintenance requirement. Smith's NYSE margin requirement would be $3,000 (30% of $10,000) and Smith would have a margin call of $1,750. Once Smith met this margin call, his account would read as follows:

Mr. Smith's Account Activity				
Short Position	*Current Price*	*Market Value*	*Credit Balance*	*Equity*
500 ABC	20	$(10,000)	$13,000	$3,000

Example #4

Mr. Jones opens a margin account by purchasing 100 shares of SAM Corp. at $80 per share (total cost of $8,000) and 100 shares of TOMCO at $40 per share (total cost of $4,000). The transactions have total combined cost of $12,000. With the Reg. T margin requirement at 50%, Jones will be required to deposit $6,000 within 7 days of the trade.

Assuming Jones deposits the Reg. T requirement, his account will read as follows:

Mr. Jones' Account Activity					
Long Position	*Current Price*	*Market Value*	*Debit Balance*	*Credit Balance*	*Equity*
100 SAM.	80	$8,000	$4,000		
100 ROSSCO	40	$4,000	$2,000		
TOTALS		**$12,000**	**$6,000**	**$0**	**$6,000**

The equity in the account is $6,000, which is well in excess of the NYSE minimum equity requirement. The equity is also in excess of the minimum maintenance requirement of $3,000 (25% of the long market value).

Several days later, Jones sells 200 shares of ABC short at $12 per share for net proceeds of $2,400. Since there is no Reg. T excess on Jones' account, he will be required to deposit 50% of the proceeds, or $1,200. Assuming Mr. Jones makes the Reg. T deposit, his account will read as follows:

Mr. Jones' Account Activity						
Long Position	***Short Position***	***Current Price***	***Market Value***	***Debit Balance***	***Credit Balance***	***Equity***
100 SAM.		80	$8,000	$4,000		
100 ROSSCO		40	$4,000	$2,000		
	200 ABC	12	$(2,400)		**$3,600**	
TOTALS			**$9,600**	**$6,000**	**$3,600**	**$7,200**

The account's equity is calculated as follows: LMV + Cr - Dr - SMV

The account's equity amount is $7,200.

The NYSE maintenance margin requirement is calculated as follows:

25% of the LMV + 30% of the SMV

$3,000 + $720 = $3,720

Thus the account is compliance with the NYSE minimum maintenance requirement and its minimum equity requirement of $2,000.

OPENING A MARGIN ACCOUNT

Customers who wish to open margin accounts must complete a *margin agreement.* The margin agreement states that the customer must abide by the rules and regulations of the FRB, the NYSE, and the NASD. The required documents to open a margin account are:

- Margin New Account Form
- Joint Account Agreement (if a joint account)
- Voluntary Stock Loan Agreement
- Customer Hypothecation Agreement:
  - Customer agrees to the interest charges;
  - Gives the broker-dealer the right to collateralize the customer's stock; and
  - Gives the broker-dealer the right to liquidate securities with or without notice when a customer's account is under-margined.

SUMMARY OF MARGIN FORMULAS

Equity =

- LMV - DR + CR
- CR - SMV
- LMV - SMV - DR + CR

Regulation T Loan Value = Loan Value % **x** Long Market Value

Regulation T Excess =

1. Long Accounts

(a) Loan Value Method **=** LV **-** DR or **+** CR

(b) Equity **-** Reg. T Requirement

2. Short or Mixed Accounts

(a) Loan Value Method = 50% **x** LMV **-** 150% **x** SMV **-** DR

or

+ CR

(b) Margin Required Method **=** Equity **-** 50% **x** 50% **x** SMV

Maintenance Excess **=** Equity **-** Maintenance Requirement

Maintenance Call **=** Maintenance Requirement – Equity

11.7. MARGIN GLOSSARY

Trade Date	The day the trade is executed.
Settlement Date	The day the trade settles (clears) between the brokers.
Business Day	Any day the exchanges are open for business.
Balance	(from the customer's point of view) *Debit* = amount customer owes broker. *Credit* = amount broker owes customer.
Long Position	Represents a security position which belongs to the customer and held in the account by the broker-dealer.
Short	Represents a security position owed to the broker-dealer

Position	by the customer.
Payment Due Date	Funds are due promptly and in any event no later than seven business days after trade date.
Purchase	Any transaction in which a customer buys a security (or contract in an appropriate account) at a specific price.
Sale	The liquidation of a security held by a customer at a specific price.
Market Value	The total number of shares times price based on the previous night's closing price.
Equity	Net worth of the account; assets less liabilities.
Loan Value	Established by the Federal Reserve Board (FRB); The maximum amount the broker-dealer can lend the customer on his collateral. Currently 50% of long market value for acceptable equity securities. (Note: Options have no loan value).
Regulation T Excess	Additional loan value; the amount the loan value exceeds the debit (the amount loaned); commonly caused by favorable market action.
SMA Balance	Special Memorandum Account; a line of credit available to satisfy Regulation T requirements on new commitments. The SMA balance may also be used to issue a check to the customer.
Initial Regulation T Requirement	The minimum amount the customer must put up for a new commitment. It is the complement of the loan value percentage; currently 50% of the purchase cost for equity securities and 100% of purchase cost for options.
Regulation T Call	A call for additional margin due to a new commitment; due no later than seven business days from trade date; may be satisfied via deposit of cash or marginable securities.
Maintenance Requirement	The amount of equity required to be held in the account by the broker-dealer, stock exchanges, and the NASD. Regulatory requirements is currently 25% of the long market value.
Maintenance Excess	The amount the equity exceeds the maintenance requirement.
Maintenance Call	A call for additional maintenance margin; the amount the maintenance requirement exceeds the equity. Maintenance calls are due promptly and may be satisfied via the deposit of cash or marginable securities.

CHAPTER 12: THE NET CAPITAL RULE - SEC Rule 15c3-1

OVERVIEW

The Net Capital Rule is a uniform and comprehensive capital adequacy standard for the brokerage industry (including municipal securities dealers).

The purpose of the Rule is to ensure that broker-dealers have sufficient capital and liquid assets to ensure the protection of its customers, investors, creditors, and the industry in the event of insolvency or bankruptcy.

The Net Capital Rule involves a computation that is based on trade date accounting, and broker-dealers are required to ensure compliance with the Rule every day they are in business.

Essentially, the Net Capital computation is a reduction of a broker-dealer's GAAP net worth by a series of deductions and adjustments. In addition, broker-dealer's security inventory is marked-to-market, then reduced by a specified percentage based on the riskiness and liquidity of each category of security.

Once the computation is computed, this amount is compared to a "Net Capital Requirement", which is a specified amount of capital that a broker-dealer is required to have based on the type of securities business and the extent of securities business it engages in.

The Net Capital Rule ensures the government that broker-dealers have enough liquid capital to pay all of its obligations in case of bankruptcy. The essence of the Rule is that it takes a broker-dealer's net worth and either adds or subtracts adjustments based on the broker-dealers liquidity of the assets, the nature of its liabilities, and the riskiness of its security positions.

ADJUSTMENTS TO NET WORTH

The adjustments to net worth are as follows:

ADD TO NET WORTH:

1) Qualified subordinated loans

2) Unrealized profit and loses and deferred tax liabilities.

DEDUCTIONS FROM NET WORTH:

1) Non Allowable Assets (NAA):

Non allowable assets are basically assets which are not readily converted into cash. These NAA's include:

- **Fixed assets** (furniture, real estate, fixtures, exchange memberships, etc.) and **prepaid expenses** (insurance, goodwill).
- **Certain unsecured and partly secured receivables.** These include:
    1. unsecured and partly secured customer accounts (only the unsecured portion is deducted);
    2. the market value of stock loaned in excess of the collateral received;
    3. receivables arising from the mailing of securities in excess of $5,000 per shipment; and all mailings outstanding more than 7 business days;
- **Interest receivables, floor brokerage receivables, commissions receivable** from broker-dealers, **mutual fund concessions** and **management fee receivables from mutual funds** more than 30 days;
- **Dividend receivables** over 30 days older than payable date;
- **Good faith deposits from non-muni underwritings** over 11 business days from the settlement date of the underwriting with the issuer, and from muni underwriters, 60 days after settlement date.

2) Other Deductions:

- The amount by which the market value of securities **failed to receive** outstanding longer than 30 calendar days exceeds their contract value;

❑ For **fails to deliver** outstanding 5 business days or more (21 business days or more for municipal securities), deduct a haircut on the market value of the securities. The haircut should be increased by any excess the of the contract value of the fail to deliver over the market price. The haircut should be reduced by any amount which the market of the underlying security exceeds the contract price.

❑ 1% of the market value of **securities borrowed** collateralized by an irrevocable letter of credit.

❑ Short Security Differences:

% MV of short security difference	# of Days from discovery
25%	7
50%	14
75%	21
100%	28

❑ Long Security Differences:

The market value of any long security differences should be deducted if those securities were sold before the difference could be resolved.

❑ Any **open contractual commitments** (such as underwritings) must receive a haircut deduction on each net long position and net short position contemplated by any open contractual commitment in the proprietary account of any broker-dealer. Equity securities receive a 30% haircut (under the Aggregate Indebtedness method and the Alternative Method) unless the class and issue of the securities are listed on a national securities exchange or are designated as NASDAQ National Market System (NMS) securities. With exchange-listed and NASDAQ NMS securities, the haircut will be 15% of the greater of the long or short positions and 15% of the value of the lesser position that exceeds 25% of the greater position.

A broker-dealer that maintains in excess of $250,000 of excess net capital may add back up to $150,000 of any deduction computed under the open contractual commitment haircut deduction. Any deduction on open contractual commitments shall be reduced by any unrealized profit on the position, and increased by any unrealized losses.

3) Securities Haircuts

A "haircut" is a deduction on the market value of a securities position based on a percentage of the value. The haircut deduction is taken so that the broker-dealer's balance sheet presents a conservative picture of their net worth. In times of market pressure, such as a steep stock market decline, or financial difficulty, such as a bankruptcy, the broker-dealers' net capital will present a more accurate picture of its financial health. The haircut percentages are based on the relative riskiness and liquidity of the security in question. In other words, the riskier the position, the higher the haircut percentage.

Figure 12.1: U.S. and CANADIAN GOVERNMENT SECURITIES HAIRCUTS

Category	Maturity	Percentage
Category 1	Less than 3 months	0 %
" "	3 months but less than 6 months	1/2 of 1%
" "	6 months but less than 9 months	3/4 of 1%
" "	9 months but less than 12 months	1%
Category 2	1 year but less than 2 years to maturity	1 1/2%
" "	2 year but less than 3 years to maturity	2%
Category 3	3 years but less than 5 years to maturity	3%
" "	5 years but less than 10 years to maturity	4%
Category 4	10 years but less than 15 years to maturity	4 1/2%
" "	15 years but less than 20 years to maturity	5%
" "	20 years but less than 25 years to maturity	5 1/2%
" "	25 years or more	6%

The haircut for each category of government securities is computed as follows:

- compute the deduction for each net long or net short position in each sub-category;
- the deduction for the category is the net of the total deductions on the long positions and the aggregate deductions on the short positions in each category, plus 50% of the lesser

- ❑ of the total deductions on the long or short positions. However, the broker-dealer may elect to only deduct the applicable percentages of the market value of the net long or short positions in each sub-category.

Positions that are hedged by comparable government securities in another category may be excluded from haircut deductions, along with the hedge, if the two securities have maturity dates:

- ❑ Between 9 months and 15 months and within 3 months of one another;
- ❑ Between 2 years and 4 years and within 1 year of one another; or
- ❑ Between 8 years and 12 years and within 2 years of one another.

The net market of the two excluded positions will be haircut at the category of the security with the highest market value.

For government securities dealers that report to the Federal Reserve System, that transacts business directly with the Federal Reserve System, and that maintains at all times minimum Net Capital of at least $50,000,000 before haircuts, the haircut deductions on government securities (or an agency of the government), will be only 75% (or three-quarters) of the regular haircut deduction.

MUNICIPALS

For municipal securities, the haircut percentages listed below are applied to greater of the long or short positions.

Figure 12.2 Municipal Securities Haircuts for Positions that Mature in 2 Years or Less, and Do Not Trade Flat and Are Not in Default:

Maturity	Haircut Percentage
Less than 30 days to maturity	0%
30 days but less than 91 days	1/8 of 1%
91 days but less than 181 days	1/4 of 1%
181 days but less than 271 days	3/8 of 1%
271 days but less than 366 days	1/2 of 1%
366 days but less than 456 days	3/4 of 1%
456 days but less than 732 days	1%

Figure 12.3: Haircuts for Municipal Bond Positions More than 2 Years in Maturity Not Trading Flat or in Default

Maturity	Haircut Percentage
Less than 1 year	1%
1 year but less than 2 years	2%
2 years but less than 3 1/2 years	3%
3 1/2 years but less than 5 years	4%
5 years but less than 7 years	5%
7 years but less than 10 years	5 1/2%
10 years but less than 15	6%
15 years but less than 20 years	6 1/2%
20 years or greater	7%

CANADIAN DEBT OBLIGATIONS

Canadian debt haircuts are the same as U.S. government debt haircuts.

MUTUAL FUNDS

Money Market Funds:

2% of the market value of the greater of the long or short positions.

U.S. Governments, Canadian Governments, and Muni Bonds Funds:

7% of the market value of the greater of the long or short positions.

U.S. Governments, Canadian Governments, Municipal Bonds, and Non-Convertible Debt Funds:

9% of the market value of the greater of the long or short positions.

COMMERCIAL PAPER, BANKERS ACCEPTANCES, and CD'S

The haircut percentages for these securities are applied to the greater of the long or short positions:

Figure 12.4

Maturities	Haircut Percentages
Less than 30 days	0%
30 days but less than 91 days	1/8 of 1%
91 days but not less than 181	1/4 of 1%
181 but not less than 271	3/8 of 1%
271 but not less than 1 year	1/2 of 1%

The haircuts for securities greater than 1 year of maturity shall be the same as those for U.S. government securities.

INVESTMENT GRADE NON-CONVERTIBLE DEBT

(having fixed interest rate, fixed maturity, not trading flat or in default, and having been rated in one of the 4 highest rating categories)

Figure 12.5

Maturities	Haircut Percentages
Less than 1 year	2%
1 year but less than 2 years	3%
2 years but less than 3 years	5%
3 years but less than 5	6%
5 years but less than 10	7%
10 years but less than 15	7 1/2%
15 years but less than 20	8%
20 years but less than 25	8 1/2%
25 years or more	9%

Nonconvertible positions may be excluded from the above percentages if the position is hedged by U.S. government or government agency securities; or nonconvertible debt securities having a fixed interest rate and a fixed maturity date and which do not trade flat or in default and are rated in one of the four highest rating categories by at least two of the nationally recognized rating agencies; and have the following maturity dates:

1. Less than five years and within 6 months of each other;
2. Between 5 years and 10 years and within 9 months of each other;
3. Between 10 years and 15 years and within 2 years of each other; or
4. 15 years or more and within 10 years of each other.

If the non-convertible debt position is hedged with U.S. government or government agency securities, the hedging securities are excluded from any haircuts, and the hedged position will be haircut as follows:

Figure 12.6

Maturities	Haircut Percentages
Less than 5 years	1 1/2%
5 years but less than 10	2 1/2%
10 years but less than 15	2 3/4%
15 years or more	3%

For positions hedged or offset by other nonconvertible debt securities, the hedged position will be haircut as follows:

Figure 12.7

Maturity	Haircut Percentage
Less than 5 years	1 3/4%
5 years but less than 10	3%
10 years but less than 15	3 1/4%
15 years or more	3 1/2%

INVESTMENT GRADE CONVERTIBLE DEBT

If the market value is over par value, then the haircut is 15% of the greater of the long or short positions and 15% of the value of the lesser position that exceeds 25% of the greater position. If the market value is less than the par value, then use the haircut schedule on investment grade nonconvertible debt.

INVESTMENT GRADE PREFERRED STOCK

10% of the market value of the greater of the long or short position.

RISK ARBITRAGE POSITIONS

30% of the long or equivalent short position, whichever has the greatest market value.

ALL OTHER SECURITIES

15% of the greater of the long or short positions and 15% of the value of the lesser position that exceeds 25% of the greater position.

OTC SECURITIES NOT TRADED ON NASDAQ

If the security has two independent market makers, the haircut will be 40%. If it has less market makers, the haircut is 100%.

UNDUE CONCENTRATION

Any single class of securities or money market instruments (except securities classified under 15c3-1(c)(2)(vi)(J), such as exchange-listed or NASDAQ-NMS securities) that are in the broker-dealer's account long or short for more than 11 business days, and have a market value in excess of 10% of the net capital before haircuts, then 50% of the regular haircut on that position shall be taken on the portion that exceeds 10% of the net capital before haircuts.

For securities classified under 15c3-1(c)(2)(vi)(J), the deduction will be 15% of the value of the position in excess of 10% of net capital before haircuts.

These deductions will be taken provided that the additional deduction in the case of equity securities is taken in excess of $10,000 or 500 shares, whichever is greater, or $25,000 in the case of debt securities.

NET CAPITAL REQUIREMENTS

The Securities and Exchange Commission ("SEC") published

amendments to the Net Capital Rule in December 1992 which raised the absolute minimum net capital required of certain broker-dealers. The increases to the new net capital levels are incremented over three six month periods.

There are two methods for determining the minimum Net Capital required to be held by a broker-dealer: (i) the *Aggregate Indebtedness Standard*; and (ii) the *Alternative Standard*. Each standard has minimum Net Capital requirements which depend on the type of business performed by a broker-dealer.

THE AGGREGATE INDEBTEDNESS STANDARD

Broker-dealers are required to have Net Capital of at least 6.66% of their aggregate indebtedness. For the first year of operation, they must have Net Capital of at least 12 1/2% of their aggregate indebtedness.

Aggregate indebtedness is the total money liabilities of a broker-dealer arising in connection with any transaction the broker-dealer engages in. Aggregate indebtedness items include monies borrowed, monies payable against securities loaned, fails to receive, customer's free-credit balances, and customer credit balances in accounts having short positions.

There are several liabilities which are *excluded* from aggregate indebtedness categorization. These items include:

- Any indebtedness which is adequately collateralized by securities which are carried long by the broker-dealer.
- Amounts payable against securities loaned if the securities are carried long by the broker-dealer and have not been sold.
- Amounts payable against securities failed to receive which are carried long by the broker-dealer and have not been sold.

- Eighty-five percent (85%) of amounts payable to a registered investment company related to fail-to-deliver receivables of the same quantity arising out of purchases may be excluded.
- Eighty-five percent (85%) of amounts payable against securities loaned for which the broker or dealer has receivables related to securities of the same class and issue and quantity that are securities borrowed by the broker-dealer may be excluded.
- Amounts on deposit in the Customer Reserve Bank Account.
- Fixed liabilities secured by assets acquired for use in the ordinary course of business; the assets must be the sole recourse of the lender in the event of default.
- Subordinated loans.
- Deferred tax liabilities (unrealized profits).

Minimum Net Capital Requirements Under the Aggregate Indebtedness Standard

The minimum Net Capital requirements for the Alternative Standard vary based on the level of business a broker-dealer engages in. As stated earlier, the SEC amended the Rule and the increases were staggered over six month intervals:

1. Broker-Dealers That Engage in a General Securities Business and Do Not Hold Customer Funds or Securities (Reference: 15c3-1(a)(1)(i)): $250,000

Most full service broker-dealers fall within this category.

2. Clearing Firms that Receive Customer Funds and Securities, but Do Not Maintain Custody of the Assets After Settlement Date (Reference 15c3-1(a)(2)(ii) and (a)(8)): $100,000

These broker-dealers are usually exempt from the Customer Protection Rule (SEC Rule 15c3-3) under the (k)(2)(i) exemption.

3. Broker-Dealers Who:

- **Write Over-the-Counter (Not Listed on any Exchange or NASDAQ) Options (Reference: 15c3-1(a)(2)(iii)(A)): $100,000**
- **Execute Ten or More Transactions in Any One Calendar Year for its Own Investment Account (Reference 15c3-1(a)(2)(iii)(B)): $100,000**

4. Introducing Firm who Receives but Does Not Hold Customer or other Broker-Dealer Funds or Securities (Reference: 15c3-1(a)(2)(iv): $50,000

These broker-dealers are allowed to participate in underwritings in which other members of the dealer group take-on the underwriting commitment. In other words, these broker-dealers are allowed to participate in new offerings as selling group members, not as underwriters.

5. Introducing Firms that Do Not Receive Customer Securities: $5,000

6. Broker-Dealers who Only Sell Redeemable Mutual Funds and Certain Other Share Accounts (Reference 15c3-1(c)(2)(v)):

- **Wire House Basis: $25,000**
- **Subscription Basis: $5,000**

Additional Requirements for Over-the-Counter ("OTC") Market Makers

OTC market makers must also comply with the following Net Capital requirements:

- They must maintain Net Capital of $2,500 for each security they make a market in that trades above $5 per share.

- They must maintain Net Capital of $1,000 for each security they make a market in that trades at $5 or less per share.

THE ALTERNATIVE STANDARD

Broker-dealers that have excessively large aggregate indebtedness are allowed to compute their Net Capital requirement using what is known as the *Alternative Net Capital Standard* (paragraph 15c3-1(a)(1)(ii)). With this method, the requirement is either $250,000 ($150,000 for certain municipal securities dealers) or 2% of your aggregate debit items which is computed under the Customer Protection Rule, whichever is greater. The Net Capital Rule amendment requires that broker-dealers notify their designated examining authority, in writing, of the selection of the alternative standard, or if they wish to discontinue using it. The Rule previously required broker-dealer to notify the regional office of the SEC. If you are exempt from the Customer Protection Rule you cannot compute Net Capital using the alternative method.

Once a broker-dealer elects to use the alternative method, its haircut calculations change:

Risk arbitrage positions and non-convertible debt securities which have a market value below par or are not investment grade, have the following haircut calculation:

15% of the market value of the long positions. To the extent that the market value of the short position exceeds 25% of the long positions, there is a 30% deduction on the excess.

OTC Derivatives Dealers

OTC derivative dealers may apply to the SEC to compute their capital charges for market and credit risk pursuant to SEC Rule 15c3-1 Appendix F instead of the regular securities haircut charges.

In order to receive this special treatment, the OTC derivatives dealer must meet the following hurdles with the Securities & Exchange Commission:

1. Methods for Computing Market Risk Charges

The OTC derivatives dealer must provide a description of all statistical models used for pricing OTC derivative instruments and for computing value-at-risk ("VAR"), a description of the applicant's controls over these models, and a statement regarding whether the firm has developed its own internal VAR models.

If the model incorporates empirical correlations, the derivatives dealer must detail the process for measuring the correlations and describe the quantitative and qualitative aspects of the model.

The OTC derivatives dealer must indicate if it intends to use an alternative method for computing its market risk charge for equity instruments, and if applicable, a description of how its own theoretical pricing model contains the minimum pricing factors required by this rule (detailed below). The derivatives dealer must also describe any category of securities having no ready market or any category of debt securities having which are below investment grade for which the OTC derivatives dealer wishes to use an alternative method for computing this charge and a description of how those charges would be determined.

2. Internal Risk Management Control Systems

The OTC derivatives dealer must provide a comprehensive description of its internal risk management control systems and how the systems adhere to SEC Rule 15c3-4.

3. Amendments to the VAR Model

The derivatives dealer must file an application with the SEC when it wants to make a material adjustment to its VAR model. The adjustment cannot be implemented until after the SEC approves the adjustment.

4. Market Risk

The OTC derivatives dealer using Appendix F must compute a capital charge for market risk. The charge will be the sum of the sub-components:

1. Value-at-Risk

The dealer will deduct from its net worth the VAR amount of its eligible OTC derivative instruments, multiplied by the appropriate multiplication factor detailed below.

2. Equities

The net worth deduction can be the amount computed according to Appendix A. In this computation, the dealer can use its own theoretical pricing model, provided it use the minimum pricing factors detailed in Appendix A.

3. Non-marketable Securities

A VAR model cannot be used to determine the charge for non-marketable securities or below-investment grade securities unless specifically approved by the SEC.

4. Residual Securities

For any positions not included in the OTC derivative charge, the market risk charge must be determined by the regular haircut charge in the net capital rule (15c3-1(c)(2)(vi).

5. Credit Risk

The capital charge for an OTC derivative dealer's eligible OTC derivative instruments is as follows:

1. For insolvent, bankrupt institutions, or institutions whose senior, unsecured long-term debt is in default:

The charge is the net replacement value of the account of the counterparty. This includes the effect of legally enforceable netting agreements and the application of liquid collateral.

2. For all other counterparties:

The net replacement value of the counterparties account multiplied by eight, then multiplied by the Counterparty Factor. The Counterparty Factors is as follows:

Counterparty Factors:

1. 20% for counterparties with senior, unsecured long-term debt or commercial in the two highest rating categories by a nationally recognized statistical rating organization ("NRSRO").

2. 50% for counterparties with ratings for senior unsecured long-term debt in the third and fourth highest rating categories by an NRSRO.

3. 100% for counterparties with ratings for senior unsecured long-term debt below the four highest rating categories.

3. Concentration Charge

If the net replacement value in the account of a counterparty exceeds 25% of the OTC derivative dealers tentative net capital, the charge is as follows:

1. For counterparties with ratings for senior unsecured long-term debt or commercial paper in the two highest rating categories by an NRSRO, 5% of the amount of the net replacement value in excess of 25% of the OTC derivative dealer's tentative net capital.

2. For counterparties with ratings for senior unsecured long-term debt or commercial paper in the third and fourth highest rating categories by an NRSRO, 20% of the amount of the net replacement value in excess of 25% of the OTC derivative dealers tentative net capital.

3. For counterparties with ratings for senior unsecured long-term debt below the four highest rating categories, 50% of the amount of the net replacement value in excess of 25% of the OTC derivatives dealers tentative net capital.

4. Non-rated OTC Derivatives Dealers

Counterparties that are not rated by an NRSRO may be rated by the OTC derivatives dealer, or an affiliated bank or broker-dealer. The rating procedures and categories must be approved by the SEC.

5. VAR Models

An OTC derivatives dealer's VAR model must meet the following qualitative requirements:

a. The VAR model must be integrated into the firm's daily risk management process;

b. The dealer must conduct stress tests of the VAR model and develop procedures to take action as a result of the tests;

c. The dealer must conduct reviews of the VAR model. The model must also be subject to annual reviews by the independent public accountants.

d. The dealer must conduct backtesting of the VAR model.

The VAR model must also meet the following quantitative requirements:

a. The VAR measures must be calculated on a daily basis using a 99 percent, one-tailed confidence level with a price change equivalent to a ten-business day movement in rates and prices.

b. The effective historical observation period for VAR measures must be at least one year, and the weighted average time lag of the individual observations cannot be less than six months. Historical data sets must be updated at least every three months and reassessed whenever market prices or volatilities are subject to large changes.

c. The VAR measures must include the risks arising from the non-linear price characteristics of options positions and the sensitivity of the market value of the positions to changes in the volatility of the underlying rates or prices. An OTC derivatives dealer must measure the volatility of options positions by different maturities.

d. The VAR measures may incorporate empirical correlations within and across risk categories, provided that the OTC derivatives dealer has described its process for measuring correlations in its application to use this capital treatment with the SEC and it has been approved. If the VAR model does not incorporate empirical correlations across risk categories, the dealer must add the separate VAR measures for the four major risk categories in Appendix F of the Net Capital Rule to determine its aggregate VAR measure.

e. The VAR model must use risk factors sufficient to measure the market risk inherent in all covered positions. The risk factors must include interest rate risk, equity price risk, foreign exchange rate risks, and commodity price risk. For material exposures in major currencies and markets, the model must capture spread risk and incorporate enough segments of the yield curve to capture differences in volatility and imperfect correlation of rates along the yield curve.

NET CAPITAL COMPUTATION EXAMPLES

We have prepared two examples (the Aggregate Indebtedness method and the Alternative method) of Net Capital computations using the trial balance of Acme Securities Inc.:

Figure 12.8:

Acme Securities Inc.
Summary Trial Balance
December 31, 1993

	DEBIT	***CREDIT***
Cash - First National	500,000	
Cash - State Bank	375,000	
Cash - N.Y. Bank (Special Reserve)	250,000	
Customer Receivables	400,000	
Fails to deliver (Firm related)	350,000	
Fails to deliver (customer related)	300,000	
NSCC clearing deposit	200,000	
Securities inventory (stocks)	175,000	
Securities inventory (corporate bonds)	100,000	
Securities inventory (municipal bonds)	75,000	
Furniture & Fixtures (net of depreciation)	100,000	
Prepaid Insurance	5,000	
Customer payables		300,000
Fails to receive (Firm related)		200,000
Fails to receive (customer related)		200,000
Bank loans (Firm related)		350,000
Bank loans (customer related)		600,000
Accrued expenses payable		100,000
Subordinated liabilities		200,000
Capital stock		300,000
Paid in capital		200,000
Retained earnings (opening balance)		100,000
Profits		280,000
	2,830,000	2,830,000
	========	========

Notes on Trial Balance:

1. The equities are all exchange listed securities
2. The corporate bonds all have 7 years in maturity left.
3. The municipal bonds all have 10 years in maturity left.
4. All positions are long.

Example 1: The Aggregate Indebtedness Method

Acme Securities Inc.
Net Capital Computation
December, 31 1993

Total Ownership Equity:	$880,000
Add: Approved Subordinated Loans:	$200,000
Total Capital and Approved Subordinated Liabilities:	**$1,080,000**
Deduct: Non Allowable Assets	
Furniture and Fixtures	$100,000
Clearing Deposits	$200,000
Prepaid Insurance	$ 5,000
Total Non Allowable Assets:	$305,000
Tentative Net Capital:	**$775,000**
Less Haircuts on Securities:	
Equities:	$175,000 x 15% = $26,250
Corporate Bonds	$100,000 x 7% = $7,000
Municipal Bonds	$ 75,000 x 6% = $4,500
Total Haircuts:	$37,750
NET CAPITAL:	**$737,250**

Acme Securities Inc.
Computation of Aggregate Indebtedness
December 31, 1993

Customer Payables	$300,000
Customer Fail to Receive	$200,000
Accrued Expenses Payable	$100,000
Customer Bank Loans	$600,000
Total Aggregate Indebtedness	**$1,200,000**

Acme Securities Inc.
Computation of Minimum Net Capital Requirement (A.I. method)
December 31, 1993

The requirement is the greater of:	$100,000 or
6 2/3% of Aggregate Indebtedness =	$80,000
Net Capital:	$737,250
Less the Minimum Requirement:	($100,000)
EXCESS NET CAPITAL:	**$637,250**

Example 2: The Alternative Method

Acme Securities Inc.
Computation of Net Capital
December 31, 1993

Tentative Net Capital (Same as A.I. method)	$775,000
Less Haircuts on Securities: (Same as A.I. method)	
Equities:	$175,000 x 15% = $26,250
Corporate Bonds	$100,000 x 7% = $7,000
Municipal Bonds	$ 75,000 x 6% = $4,500
Total Haircuts:	$37,750
	=======
NET CAPITAL:	**$737,250**
	========

Acme Securities Inc.
Computation of Minimum Net Capital Requirement
December 31, 1993

The requirement is the greater of 2% of the aggregate debit items in SEC Rule 15c3-3, or $250,000.

Aggregate Debit Items (Per 15c3-3):

Customer Receivables	$400,000
Customer fails to Deliver	$300,000
Total Aggregate Debit Items:	$700,000
	========

2% of $700,000 = $14,000

Therefore, the Net Capital requirement is	$250,000
Net Capital	$737,250
Minimum Requirement	($250,000)
EXCESS NET CAPITAL	**$487,250**
	========

CHAPTER 13: THE CUSTOMER PROTECTION RULE (SEC RULE 15c3-3)

The securities industry experienced an operational crises in the late 1960s and early 1970s. During that crises, broker-dealers lost control of their books and records and did not have in their possession many of the securities that they were supposed to be holding as custodians for their customers. In response to the operational crises, the SEC enacted Rule 15c3-3, better known as the Customer Protection Rule.

Before exploring the various provisions of the Rule, we should first review what the Rule defines as a "customer". According to the Rule, a customer means any person from whom or on whose behalf a broker-dealer has received funds or securities for the account of that person. The term customer shall not include general partners or directors or principal officers of the broker-dealer or any other person to the extent that the person has a claim for property or funds which by contract, agreement, or understanding, or by operation of law, is part of the capital of the broker-dealer or is subordinated to the claims of creditors of the broker-dealer. The term customer shall apply to a broker-dealer to the extent that the broker-dealer that maintains an omnibus account for customers in accordance with Regulation T.

There are two major components of the Customer Protection Rule: (i) *Possession and Control*; and (ii) The *Customer Reserve Formula.*

POSSESSION AND CONTROL

SEC Rule 15c3-3 requires that broker-dealers **promptly obtain and maintain physical possession and control of all fully-paid and excess margin securities.** Excess margin securities are securities in each customer's account that are in excess of 140% of the net debit balance in each customer's account.

In order to ensure that broker-dealers do not use customer fully-paid or excess margin securities, these securities must be physically segregated from all other securities. The segregation process is initiated by the Margin Department. First, the Margin

Department determines which securities are excess margin

securities and which securities are customer fully-paid securities. Next, Margin will issue segregation instructions to the Cashier's Department and the Stock Record Department. The Stock Record Department will note the segregation instructions on the Stock Record because the Stock Record is used to determine if all fully-paid and excess margin securities are in the possession and control of the broker-dealer.

The locations that are considered to be acceptable possession and control locations are as follows:

- **The Box**
- **Transfer (within 40 days)**
- **DTC or a SEC approved custodian bank**
- **An omnibus account**
- **A SEC approved foreign depository, foreign bank, or foreign clearing agency**
- **Domestic banks**
- **In transit**
- **Held by an affiliated company**

Securities positions which are borrowed or are under a repurchase agreement are exempt from possession and control requirements.

<u>Excess and Deficit Positions</u>

In order to determine which, if any, securities are required to be in possession and control of the broker-dealer, positions are classified as being in "excess" or in "deficit" of the 15c3-3 possession and control requirements.

If customers' fully-paid and excess margin positions in a particular security are greater than the amount of securities in good control locations, then the security is considered to be in "excess". If it is established that a position is in excess of the possession and control requirements, then the broker-dealer need not take any further action.

If customers' fully-paid and excess margin securities in a particular position are less than the amount of securities in a good control location, then the security is considered to be in "deficit".

A deficit in a given security required for possession or control may be eliminated changing the selection of securities in margin accounts representing collateral for the debit balance. This allows broker-dealers to change the securities which represent the excess margin securities, and therefore which securities prompt action must be taken for (recall of collateral, recall of securities loaned, buy-ins, etc.).

Broker-dealers must determine whether customer fully-paid or excess margin securities are in excess or deficit positions every day, by the close of the next business day. However, inactive margin accounts may be computed on a weekly basis.

Allocation of Deficit Positions

If the position is in deficit of the requirement, then the broker-dealer is required to allocate the location of the position in deficit.

The allocation priority recommended by the SEC is as follows:

- Bank loans
- Stock loans
- Fail-to-receive over 30 calendar days
- Stock dividends receivable over 45 calendar days

Bank Loan

Securities pledged as collateral for a bank loan should be recalled no later than one business day after the discovery of the deficit. The broker-dealer must obtain physical possession or control of the securities within two business days of the date of issuance of the recall instructions.

Securities Loaned

Securities loaned should be recalled no later than one business day after the day of discovery. The broker-dealer must obtain physical possession or control of the securities within five business days following the date of issuance of recall instructions.

Securities Failed to Receive Over 30 Calendar Days

Broker-dealers must take prompt steps to obtain physical possession or control of securities failed to receive over 30 calendar days by the business day following the day of discovery. The securities can be bought-in, or other steps can be taken.

Security Dividend or Stock Splits Receivables

Securities receivable as a stock dividend, stock split, or other similar distributions for more than 45 calendar days must be obtained into the physical possession or control of the broker-dealer by the business day following the day of discovery. The securities can be bought-in, or other steps can be taken.

Same Day Turnarounds

The same day receipt and redelivery (turnaround) of a security that is received as a result of the settlement of a trade is permitted even if the same security is required to satisfy possession and control requirements, provided that the turnaround does not create or increase a deficit. Same day turnarounds do not include securities received as the result of a recall from bank loans or securities loaned, from safekeeping, or from any good control location.

Specific Identification Method

Broker-dealers can also allocate deficit positions by the "specific identification method". With this method, the broker-dealer would have to know the actual transaction that caused the deficit, then take action to close the deficit. Most broker-dealers have too much activity to use the specific identification method on a manual basis. However, many firms use computer programs to assist them in allocating deficit positions. If a firm uses the specific identification method, then it does not have to use the allocation hierarchy recommended by the SEC.

Detailed below is an example of how broker-dealers determine the possession and control requirements for the securities held by their customers:

Possession and Control Example

Suppose Mr. Jones' brokerage account at Acme Securities held the following positions as of 5/17:

ACME SECURITIES INC.			
Mr. Walter Jones and Mrs. Janet Jones Joint Account			
Positions	***Price***	***Market Value***	***Debit Balance***
100 ABC	7	$700	$250
200 DEF	25	$5,000	$1,750
500 TOM	15	$7,500	$2,000
TOTAL		**$13,200**	**$4,000**

140% of Mr. Jones' debit balance is $5,600 (140% of $4,000). Jones' positions have a market value of $13,200. Jones has excess margin securities of $7,600. Any security in his account totaling this amount must be segregated. If the margin clerk chose TOM as the excess margin securities, then all 500 shares of TOM in Mr. Jones' account must be segregated.

The Stock Record for TOM reads as follows:

TOM				
Long (Ownership)				
Account	**5/14**	**5/15**	**5/16**	**5/17**
Mr. Jones	500	500	500	500
Trading Account	50	50	50	50
Fail to Deliver	50	50	0	0
Total	**600**	**600**	**550**	**550**

TOM				
Short (Location)				
Account	**5/14**	**5/15**	**5/16**	**5/17**
Box	300	300	300	0
Fail to Receive	50	50	0	0
DTC	250	250	250	0
Bank Loan	0	0	0	550
Total	**600**	**600**	**550**	**550**

On 5/17 Mr. Jones' excess margin securities are not in the possession and control of the broker-dealer. The deficit was discovered on 5/18. The broker-dealer must take timely action to obtain those securities or become in violation of the possession and control requirements of SEC Rule 15c3-3.

Based on a review of the stock record, it appears that the deficit was caused by the use of TOM as collateral for a bank loan. The broker-dealer must recall the securities and obtain physical possession and control of the securities within 3 days (which is 5/23, assuming 5/19 was Saturday and 5/20 was Sunday).

If the Cashier Department recalled the bank loan, and obtain possession of the securities by 5/23, the stock record would look as follows:

TOM				
Long (Ownership)				
Account	**5/18**	**5/21**	**5/22**	**5/23**
Mr. Jones	500	500	500	500
Trading Account	50	50	50	50
Fail to Deliver	0	0	0	0
Total	**550**	**550**	**550**	**550**

TOM				
Short (Location)				
Account	**5/18**	**5/21**	**5/22**	**5/23**
Box	0	0	0	500
Fail to Receive	0	0	0	0
DTC	0	0	0	0
Bank Loan	550	550	550	50
Total	**550**	**550**	**550**	**550**

Completion of Sell Orders on Behalf of Customers

If a broker-dealer executes a customer's sell order (other than a short sale) and the broker-dealer has not obtained possession of the securities from the customer within ten business days after settlement date, the broker-dealer must close the transaction by purchasing the same quantity of a similar security. However, this section of the Rule does not apply to exempted securities.

Buy-In of Short Security Differences

Broker-dealers are required to buy-in all short security differences noted on the stock record within 45 calendar days after its discovery as a result of the count, verification, and comparison of securities in accordance with SEC Rule 17a-13.

Extensions of Time

If the stock exchanges or the NASD is satisfied that a broker-dealer is making a good-faith effort in complying with the provisions of SEC Rule 15c3-3, then they may entitled to extensions of time on which they have to take action on several provisions of the Rule, including:

- Fails to Receive over 30 days;
- Stock Dividends Receivables over 45 days;
- Buy-Ins of Short Security Differences; and
- Buy-Ins of Customers who Fail to Deliver on Sell Transactions

CUSTOMER RESERVE FORMULA

SEC Rule 15c3-3 requires every broker-dealer to maintain a "Special Reserve Bank Account for the Exclusive Benefit of Customers" ("Reserve Account") at a bank when deposits are required to be held. The Reserve Account must be separate from any other bank account, cannot be subject to any liens, and cannot be pledged as collateral.

Broker-dealers must maintain in the account cash or qualified securities in amounts calculated in a "Formula for Determination of the Reserve Requirement for Brokers and Dealers" ("Formula"), which is specified in the Rule. (see Figure 13.1)

The computation to determine the Reserve requirement must be made weekly, as of the close of the last business day of the week. The actual deposit should be made no later than one hour after the opening of banking business on the second following business day.

However, a broker-dealer may make monthly computations if it meets the following criteria: (i) it's aggregate indebtedness must not exceed 800% of its net capital; (ii) its aggregate customer funds as computed in the prior Reserve computation does not exceed $1,000,000. If the computation is made monthly, then it should be calculated as of the last business day of the month, and the broker-dealer should deposit 105% of the required amount no later than one hour after the opening of banking business on the second following business day.

If a broker-dealer is computing its Reserve requirement on a monthly basis, and its aggregate indebtedness exceeds 800% of its net capital, then it is required to compute its requirement weekly for four consecutive weeks. If its aggregate indebtedness does not exceed 800% of its net capital during the four week period, then it may return to calculating the requirement on a monthly basis.

Exemptions to the Customer Protection Rule

Paragraph (k)(1) of the Rule specifies that a broker-dealer must meet all of the following conditions to be exempt from SEC Rule 15c3-3:

- Its dealer transaction (as principal for its own account) must be limited to the purchase, sale, and redemption of mutual funds and interests in insurance company separate accounts;
- Its transactions as broker (agent) are limited to the sale and redemption of mutual funds and interests in insurance company separate accounts; the sale of securities of customers to obtain funds for immediate reinvestment in a mutual; and the solicitation of share accounts for savings and loan associations insured by an instrumentality of the United States government.
- It promptly transmits all funds and delivers all securities received in connection with its activities as a broker-dealer, and does not otherwise hold funds or securities for, or owe money to, customers.

Paragraph (k)(2) of the Rule exempts customers from the Rule if they abide by one of the following restrictions:

1. The broker-dealer cannot carry any margin accounts, promptly transmit all customer funds and deliver all securities received in connection with its activities as a broker-dealer, does not otherwise hold funds or securities for, or owe money or securities to, customers, and executes all financial transactions between itself and customers through one or more bank accounts, designated as "Special Account for the Exclusive Benefit of Customers of (name of the broker-dealer).

OR

2. The firm, as an introducing broker-dealer, clears all transactions with and for customers on a fully disclosed basis with a clearing broker-dealer, and promptly transmits all customer funds and securities to the clearing broker-dealer which carries all of the accounts of the customers and maintains such books and records in accordance with SEC Rules 17a-3 and 17a-4.

Figure 13.1a: FORMULA FOR DETERMINING THE RESERVE REQUIREMENT FOR BROKER-DEALERS

Debits	***Credits***
1. Free credit balances and other credit balances in customers' security accounts. (See Note A)	$XXX
2. Monies borrowed collateralized by securities carried for the account of customers. (See Note B)	XXX
3. Monies payable against customers' securities loaned. (See Note C)	XXX
4. Customers' securities failed to receive. (See Note D)	XXX
5. Credit balances in firm accounts which are attributable to principal sales to customers.	XXX
6. Market value of stock dividends, stock splits and similar distributions receivable outstanding over 30 calendar days.	XXX
7. Market value of short security count difference over 30 calendar days.	XXX

8. Market value of short securities and credits (not to be offset by longs or by debits) in all suspense accounts over 30 calendar days.	XXX
9. Market value of securities which are in transfer in excess of 40 calendar days and have not been confirmed to be in transfer by the transfer agent or the issuer during the 40 days.	XXX
10. Debit balances in customers' cash and margin accounts excluding unsecured accounts and accounts and accounts doubtful of collection. (See Note E)	$XXX

Figure 13.1b: FORMULA FOR DETERMINING THE RESERVE REQUIREMENT FOR BROKER-DEALERS

Debits	***Credits***
11. Securities borrowed to effectuate short sales by customers and securities borrowed to make delivery on customers' securities failed to deliver.	XXX
12. Failed to deliver of customers' securities not older than 30 calendar days.	XXX
13. Margin required and on deposit with the Options Clearing Corporation for all option contracts written or purchased in customer accounts. (See Note F)	XXX
TOTAL $XXX	**$XXX**
Excess of total credits (sum of items 1-9) over total debits (sum of items 10-13) required to be on deposit in the Reserve Bank Account. If the computation is made monthly, the deposit cannot be less than 105% of the excess of the total credits over the total debits.	**$XXX**

NOTES TO THE FORMULA

Note A

Item 1 shall include all outstanding drafts payable to customers which have been applied against free credit balances or other credit balances and shall also include checks drawn in excess of bank balances per the records of the broker-dealer.

Note B

Item 2 shall include the amount of letters of credit obtained by a member of the Options Clearing Corporation which are collateralized by customers' securities, to the extent of the member's margin requirement at the Options Clearing Corp.

Note C

Item 3 shall include in addition to monies payable against customers' securities loaned the amount by which the market value of securities loaned exceeds the collateral value received from lending the securities.

Note D

Item 4 shall include in addition to customers' securities failed to receive the amount by which the market value of the securities failed to receive and outstanding more than 30 calendar days exceeds their contract value.

Note E

1. Debit balances in margin accounts shall be reduced by the amount by which a specific security (other than a exempted security) which is collateral for margin accounts exceeds in aggregate value 15% of all securities which collateralize all margin accounts receivable; provided, however, the required reduction shall not be in excess of the amounts of the debit balance required to be excluded because of this concentration rule. A specified security is deemed to be collateral for a margin account only to the extent that it represents not more than 140% of the customer debit balance in a margin account.

2. Debit balances in special omnibus accounts, maintained in compliance with the requirements of Regulation T, or similar accounts carried on behalf of another broker-dealer, shall be reduced by any deficits in such accounts, (or if a credit, such credit shall be increased) less any calls for margin, mark to market, or other required deposits which are outstanding 5 business days or less.

3. Debit balances in customers' cash and margin accounts included in the formula under item 10 shall be reduced by an amount equal to 1% of their aggregate value.

4. Debit balances in cash and margin accounts of household members and other persons related to principals of a broker-dealer and debit balances in cash and margin accounts of affiliated persons of a broker-dealer shall be excluded from the Reserve Formula, unless the broker-dealer can demonstrate that such debit balances are directly related to credit items in the formula.

5. Debit balances in margin accounts (other than omnibus accounts) shall be reduced by the amount by which any single customer's debit balance exceeds 25% (to the extent such amount is greater than $50,000) of the broker-dealer's tentative net capital, unless the broker-dealer can demonstrate that the debit balance is directly related to credits in the formula. Related accounts are deemed to be one account for the purposes of this item.

A broker-dealer may request that the registered national securities exchange or the registered national securities association (the NASD) having responsibility for examining it, give it a full or partial exemption from this provision. The debit balance may be included in the Reserve Formula computation five business days from the day the request is made.

6. Debit balances of joint accounts, custodian accounts, participation in hedge funds or limited partnerships or similar type accounts or arrangements of a person who is not considered a customer by definition of SEC Rule 15c3-3, should be handled in the following manner: if the percentage ownership of the non-customer is less than 5% then the entire debit balance can be included in the formula; if the percentage ownership is between 5% and 50% then the portion of the debit attributable to the non-customer shall be excluded from the formula unless the broker-dealer can demonstrate that the debit balances are directly related to credit items in the formula; if the ownership is greater than 50%, then the entire

debit balance should be excluded from the formula unless the broker-dealer can demonstrate that the debits are directly related to credit items in the formula.

Note F

Item 13 should include the amount of margin deposited with the Options Clearing Corp. to the extent that such margin is represented by cash, proprietary qualified securities and letters of credit collateralized by customers' securities.

Example of the Customer Reserve Formula

Using the summary trial balance of Acme Securities Inc. (Figure 13.2) we have prepared a customer reserve computation for a broker-dealer using the aggregate indebtedness method for the Net Capital Rule.

Acme Securities Inc. would have to deposit $424,200 in cash or U.S. government securities in the Special Reserve Bank Account by the second business day following the date of computation.

Figure 13.2

Acme Securities Inc.
Customer Reserve Formula Computation
December 31, 199X

		Debits	Credits
Item 1	Free credits and other credits (Payables to customers)	300,000	
Item 2	Customer bank loans	600,000	
Item 3	Customer stock loans	0	
Item 4	Customer fails to receive	200,000	
Item 5	Firm short sales to customers	0	
Item 6	Market value of stock dividend receivables over 30 days	0	
Item 7	Market value of short security count differences over 30 days	0	
Item 8	Market value of short securities and credits in suspense greater than 30 days	0	
Item 9	Market value of unconfirmed items in transfer over 30 days		0
Item 10	Debits in customer balances		400,000
Item 11	Customer stock borrows		0
Item 12	Customer fail to deliver		300,000
		1,100,000	**700,000**
Less 1% of customer debits			4,000
		1,100,000	**696,000**
Excess credits over debits		**$ 404,000**	
Customer Reserve Deposit: 105% of $ 404,000 =		**$ 424,200**	

CHAPTER 14: MISCELLANEOUS SEC REGULATIONS

SEC RULE 17a-5: PERIODIC STATEMENTS OF FINANCIAL CONDITION

In 1975 the SEC prescribed a new and streamlined financial and operational reporting system utilizing a document known as the FOCUS report, which stands for Financial and Operational Combined Uniform Single Report. The Focus system is the key to the SEC's reporting requirements for broker-dealers for the purposes of surveillance of financial health and viability. SEC Rule 17a-5 also sets requirements for the filing of annual audit reports and the mailing of customer statements.

1. FOCUS Reporting

Every broker-dealer who clears transactions or carries customer accounts is required to file a Focus Part I report within 10 business days after the end of each month. The Focus Part I is a breakdown of the broker-dealers balance sheet by various financial and operational criteria. The Focus Part I also includes a computation of the firm's.

Every broker-dealer who clears transactions or carries customer accounts is required to file a Focus Part II report within 17 business days after the end of the calendar quarter and within 17 business days after the date selected for the annual audit of financial statements where said date is other than a calendar quarter.

Every broker-dealer who does not clear transactions or carry customer accounts is required to file a Focus Part IIA report within 17 business days after the end of each calendar quarter and within 17 business days after the date selected for the annual audit of financial statements where said date is other than the end of the calendar quarter.

The Focus Part II report includes a statement of financial condition, an income statement, a computation of the net capital rule and customer protection rule requirements, and various operational information.

The Focus reports must be filed with: the NASD if the broker-dealer is a sole member of the NASD; or one of the national securities exchanges (NYSE) if the broker-dealer is a member of a national securities exchange. If the broker-dealer is not a member of the NASD or a national securities exchange, then the Focus report is filed with the SEC.

The Focus reports are considered to be confidential and unavailable to the general public.

2. <u>Annual Filing of Audited Financial Statements</u>

Every broker-dealer is required to file annually, on a calendar year or fiscal basis, a financial report which should be audited by an independent public accountant. This financial report must be as of the same date every year unless a change is approved by the SEC.

The annual audited report shall contain a Statement of Financial Condition (in a format consistent with the totals reported on the Focus Report Part II(A); a Statement of Income; a Statement of Changes in Financial Condition, a Statement of Changes in Stockholders' or Partners' or Sole Proprietors' Equity; and a Statement of Changes in Liabilities Subordinated to the General Claims of Creditors.

Supporting schedules shall include, from the Focus Part II(A), a Computation of Net Capital under Rule 15c3-1, a Computation for Determination of the Reserve Requirements under Rule 15c3-3, and Information Relating to the Possession or Control Requirements under Rule 15c3-3, and shall be filed with the audited report.

A reconciliation of the differences between the Rule 15c3-1 and 15c3-3 computations on the Focus Part II(A) report, the annual audited financial statements will be included the audited report if there are any material differences. If no material differences exist, this must be stated in the report. The annual audited report shall not be filed more than 60 days after the date of the financial statements.

Copies of the audited financial statements must be filed with the SEC and any self-regulatory organizations to which the broker-dealer is a member.

3. Customer Statements

Customers must receive a statement of the broker-dealers financial condition, the net capital computation, and any material inadequacies within 105 days of the date of the audited financial statement.

Customers must also receive the same information mentioned above as of 6 months of the date of the audited statements and must be furnished no later than 65 days after the date as of which the statements were prepared.

SEC RULE 17a-8: REPORTING OF CURRENCY AND FOREIGN TRANSACTIONS

Mandates every registered broker-dealer to comply with the Currency and Foreign Transactions Reporting Act of 1970.

- Transactions over $10,000 must be reported.
- Transactions in which currency is paid or received from a foreign country.
- Accounts for the broker-dealer held in foreign countries must be reported.

SEC RULE 17a-11: TELEGRAPHIC NOTICE TO THE SEC

If a broker-dealer's Net Capital or Debt-Equity ratio falls below the required amounts, they must file telegraphic notice with the SEC within 24 hours.

If a broker dealer fails to maintain current books and records as per 17a-3, they are required to file telegraphic notice with the SEC within 48 hours.

17a-13: QUARTERLY SECURITY COUNTS

Fully clearing broker-dealers are exempt from this rule. Once each calendar quarter, broker-dealers are responsible for:

1) Physically examine and count all securities held.

2) Account for all securities in transfer, transit, pledged, loaned, borrowed, deposited, failed to receive, failed to deliver, subject to repurchase or reverse repurchase agreements or otherwise subject to its control but are not necessarily in their possession by examination and comparison of the supporting detail records with the appropriate ledger accounts.

3) Verify all securities in the aforementioned account when the securities have been in these account for over 30 days.

4) Compare the actual count and verification results to the records.

5) Any unresolved differences must be recorded on the books and records of the broker-dealer within 7 business days after the count.

6) The examination, count, and verification must be performed by someone not whose regular duties do not include protection of the securities involved, or making or recording of the corresponding records.

15c3-4 INTERNAL RISK MANAGEMENT CONTROL SYSTEMS FOR OTC DERIVATIVE DEALERS

Every OTC derivatives dealer must establish, document, and maintain a system of internal risk management controls to assist it in managing the risks associated with its business activities, including market, credit, leverage, liquidity, legal, and operational risks.

In addition, the OTC derivatives dealer must consider the following when adopting its internal control system guidelines, policies, and procedures:

1. The ownership and governance structure of the OTC derivatives dealer;

2. The composition of the governing body of the OTC derivatives dealer;

3. The management philosophy of the OTC derivatives dealer;

4. The scope and nature of established risk management guidelines;

5. The scope and nature of the permissible OTC derivative activities;

6. The sophistication and experience of relevant trading, risk management, and internal audit personnel;

7. The sophistication and functionality of information and reporting systems; and

8. The scope and frequency of monitoring, reporting, and auditing activities.

An OTC derivatives dealer's internal risk management control system must include the following elements:

1. A risk control unit that reports directly to senior management and is independent from business trading units;

2. Separation of duties between personnel responsible for entering into a transaction and those responsible for recording the transaction in the books and records of the dealer;

3. Periodic reviews and annual reviews of the OTC derivatives dealer risk management systems;

4. Definitions of risk, risk monitoring, and risk management; and

5. Written guidelines, approved by the OTC derivative dealer's governing body that include and discuss the following:

   a. Quantitative guidelines for managing the dealer's risk exposure;

   b. Risk management exposure reporting;

   c. The procedures and timing for management's review of the risk management system, guidelines, and processes;

   d. Independence of the risk management function;

e. The authority and resources of the risk management function;

f. Response when risk management guidelines are exceeded;

g. Procedures to address the risk when an OTC derivatives contract is unenforceable;

h. Documentation of OTC derivatives transactions;

i. Authorizing procedures for employees executing OTC derivatives transactions;

Management must periodically review the OTC derivative dealer's business activities for consistency with risk management guidelines, including the following:

1. The risks arising from OTC derivative activity are consistent with prescribed guidelines;

2. Risk exposure guidelines are appropriate for the business unit;

3. Information necessary to perform risk monitoring and risk management is available on a timely basis and information systems are able to capture, monitor, analyze, and report data;

4. Procedures for management to take action when guidelines are exceeded;

5. Procedures are in place to monitor and address the risks that a contract will be unenforceable;

6. Procedures are in place to identify and address any deficiencies in the operating systems and to contain the extent of losses arising from unidentified deficiencies;

7. Procedures are in place to authorize specified employees to commit the dealer to particular types of transactions, to specify quantitative limits on such authority, and to provide for the oversight of their exercise of such authority.

8. Procedures are in place to provide for adequate documentation of the principal terms of OTC derivatives transactions and other relevant information regarding those transactions;

9. Personnel resources with appropriate expertise are committed to implementing the risk monitoring and risk management systems and processes; and

10. Procedures are in place for the periodic internal and external review of the risk monitoring and risk management functions.

GLOSSARY

A Lowercase: used in newspaper stock transaction tables after dividend to designate that extra cash dividends were paid during the previous year. Uppercase: used in the newspaper reports of a corporation's earnings to designate that the principal market place for the corporation's securities is the American Stock Exchange.

ABOVE PAR A stock or bond whose market price is higher than its face value.

ABOVE THE MARKET A sell order identified as being higher in price than the market's current price for that security.

ABSORPTION POINT The point at which the market no longer can accept securities without making price concessions.

ACCEPTANCE Agreement to buy or sell a particular security by a specific date for a specific price.

ACCOUNT Any bookkeeping record of a client's transactions, including credit or debit balances, either in cash or securities. Also, an investment syndicate's books that indicate contractual relationships, securities currently or previously owned, and the financial balance between a syndicate participant and the syndicate.

ACCOUNT BALANCE The difference between debits and credits in an account. If debits are higher than credits, the account has a negative balance.

ACCOUNT DAY The day stock or commodity exchanges must be settled between exchange members.

ACCOUNT STATEMENT A periodic report giving the status of a client's transactions, debits and credits.

ACCOUNTING CYCLE Accounting activities that occur during a specific period of time. The period starts and ends with the account balance, all its credits, debits, and any other transactions recorded during the cycle.

ACCOUNTING PERIOD A time span for keeping taxpayers' records. Most businesses operate on the calendar year. A fiscal year is established if the accounting period does not end in December.

ACCOUNTING PROCESSES The classification of accounting procedures and controls through which changes in financial status and condition are recorded.

ACCOUNTING RATE OF RETURN Any income during a specific period of time divided by the amount of money invested during that period.

ACCOUNTS RECEIVABLE Money owed, but not yet collected, for goods or services.

ACCRETION The carrying value of a bond bought at an original discount is adjusted upwards over time approaching the bond's face value. The Internal Revenue Service clearly and precisely defines its provisions for this upward adjustment.

ACCRETION ACCOUNT A record of the increase between the price of a bond purchased at discount and the bond's face value.

ACCRUAL BASIS An accounting system through which revenues are recorded when they are earned and expenditures recorded when they result in liabilities for benefits received. This differs from cash accounting under which an entry is made only when cash is paid or received.

ACCRUED INCOME Income which is earned, but not received.

ACCRUED INTEREST (1) Liabilities which arise from expenses incurred, but not yet paid. (2) The amount of interest that the buyer owes the seller on transactions involving fixed income securities, such as most bonds and notes.

ACCUMULATION absorbing an excess supply of stock, thereby increasing the demand for it. Accumulation generally occurs after a stock's price drops and stabilizes, thus increasing demand. Accumulating shares of a security over a stretch of time avoids attracting attention.

ACCUMULATION AREA Price range in which investors buy stock.

ACTIVE BOX The place where collateral for securing a broker's loan or a customer's margin position is held, or where securities are held for safekeeping either for a dealer or a dealer's customer.

ACTIVE MARKET Term used to describe either a marketplace or the buying and selling of an individual security that is marked by frequent transactions, reasonable volume and, relatively narrow spreads between the bids-offers that successive transactions are made at moderate price changes. The term is relative; what is active for security A may be inactive for security B.

ACTIVITY The trading volume of a stock, or group of stocks, on a particular exchange.

ACTUAL A physical commodity, as opposed to a futures contract, that is present and ready for delivery or storage. It is sold on a cash market. Delivery is rarely taken. Rather, the customer pays a fee to store the commodity.

ACTUAL CASH VALUE The theoretical value of a contract when it is redeemed, as opposed to its market value.

ACTUALLY OUTSTANDING Stocks and bonds that a corporation has issued, but not re-acquired.

ACQ Abbreviation used on the consolidated tape for a transaction that represents an exchange acquisition (i.e., a block trade initiated by a buyer with all transaction costs paid by a purchaser). Such transactions are infrequent.

ADD BY SELLER Form submitted by the selling firm (two days after trade date) to compare trades not previously submitted to National Securities Clearing Corporation (NSCC).

ADDED TRADE CONTRACT The last in a series of contract reports rendered by NSCC. It contains the totals of previously compared trades from regular way contract, supplemental contract sheets, and the trades compared through QT, DK, and CHC processing.

ADEQUATELY COLLATERALIZED Indebtedness for which the difference between the amount of the indebtedness and the market value of the collateral is sufficient to make the loan acceptable as a fully secured loan to banks regularly making comparable loans to brokers or dealers in the community.

ADJUSTED BASIS Base price from which to calculate capital gains or losses when a stock or bond is sold. The price is adjusted to compensate for stock splits and transactions costs that have occurred since the stock's original purchase.

ADR See American Depository Receipt.

ADVANCE REFUNDING The exchanging of fixed-income securities before they are due for another issue. This allows the issuer to issue the new bonds at lower rates.

ADVANCING MARKET Widespread increase in market prices, with indications that the market will remain on the upswing.

ADVISORY FUNDS Money a client deposits with his or her bank which the institution then invests at its own discretion.

ADVISORY PROCESSING Procedure by which the opposing firm's version of a trade is accepted by the named firm. Advisory notices accompany regular way contract reports received from the NSCC.

ADVISORY SERVICE An agency investors use to obtain market information and investment advice.

AGAINST THE BOX Sale of borrowed shares of stock in which an investor's position is long. Sellers may sell "against the box" in order to avoid ownership, disclosure, or to benefit from tax considerations.

AGED FAIL Contract between two brokers that is not settled by the agreed upon date. The opening balance no longer can be considered an asset, and the buying broker must adjust his or her capital accordingly.

AGENCY SECURITY	A US government-issued security that was not issued by the Treasury Department and may be backed by the full faith and credit of the United States depending on the issuing agency.
AGENCY TRANSACTION	A trade in which the firm operates as a broker, that is, it executes trades as an agent and charges a commission for the service.
AGENT	(1) A person who buys and sells for the account and risk of another. Generally, an agent takes no financial risk and charges a commission for his services. (2) In state securities law, any person who represents an issuer or a broker-dealer in the purchase or sale of securities to, or for, a person domiciled in that state.
AGENT BANK	Bank that act as an intermediary between customer and broker.
AGGREGATE INDEBTEDNESS	Total amount of money or shares a broker or dealer owes to customers.
AGGRESSIVE GROWTH	Stressing riskiness and profit potential over quality and security. This approach is a philosophy that may be applied to the direction of an individual company or an investment outlook.
AGGRESSIVE PORTFOLIO	Collection of securities purchased for short-term profit potential rather than defensive quality and income.
AIR POCKET STOCK	When stock prices take a dramatic nose dive and shareholders rush to sell. The action is compared to a plunging aircraft that has hit an air pocket.
ALL OR ANY PART	Brokers may execute any part or all of an order in a discretionary account within a client's price limit.
ALL OR NONE OFFERING	A new security that is offered publicly with the requirement that the entire issue must be sold by a certain date or all offers will be canceled.
ALL OR NONE ORDER	A request to buy or sell a security in which all of the security must be involved in the transaction, or all of it will be canceled. For example, an investor may place an order with a broker to purchase 1,000 shares of XYZ stock at $50 per share. If only 500 shares are available at that price the order will not be completed.
ALTERNATIVE ORDER	A buy or sell order that allows several alternatives to be used to fill the order. When part of the order is executed, the unused alternatives will be canceled. For example, an investor may be willing to purchase 20,000 shares of stock at $26 1/2, but he or she may only post an initial bid of 5,000 shares at 26 1/4. The broker may be given some discretion in this matter.

AMERICAN BOARD OF TRADE Provides spot and deferred markets, and offers investors stock market information.

AMERICAN DEPOSITORY RECEIPT A share of stock that is issued by an American bank and that is backed by foreign securities on deposit.

AMERICAN MUNICIPAL BOND ASSURANCE CORPORATION (AMBAC) Insures the payment of principal and interest on new municipal bonds. AMBAC-insured bonds carry the highest bond rating.

AMERICAN OPTION Any option an investor can exercise before its maturity.

AMERICAN STOCK EXCHANGE (AMEX) The second largest stock exchange in the United States. Otherwise known as AMEX, the exchange is located at 86 Trinity Place in downtown Manhattan. The AMEX tends to specialize in securities of slightly smaller capitalization.

AMORTIZATION An accounting term indicating the apportionment of an incurred expense over the life of the asset. For example, if a three-year magazine subscription (an expense) is paid in year one, it should be "amortized" (or spread out) over the three-year life of the subscription (the asset).

AMORTIZATION OF PREMIUM Any premium paid for a bond above its par value or call price is amortized over the life of the bond.

AMORTIZED LOSSES Losses may occur when interest-bearing instruments are sold prior to maturity during a time when interest rates are fluctuating.

AMOUNT AT INTEREST The amount of principal deposited to earn interest.

AN ACTUAL A security that underlies an option or the security that satisfies a contract when it is delivered.

AND INTEREST The buyer of an outstanding bond must pay the seller any interest that has built up between the last interest payment and the settlement date.

ANNUALIZED PERCENT Translating a partial year's figures into an annual rate.

ANNUAL REPORT A formal presentation of the corporation's financial statements that is sent to its registered stockholders. If shares are registered in the nominee's name (in care of the brokerage firm), the proxy department has to obtain copies of the report and mail them to the beneficial owners (clients).

ANNUALIZED RETURN Based upon interest, dividends, and unrealized appreciation, this is the value that an investment has achieved over a 12-month period.

ANNUAL YIELD	The amount of money an investment earns in interest or dividends each year.
ANNUITY	Periodic payments, usually in equal amounts, made over a specified period of time, such as interest payments on bonds.
ANNUITY BOND	A security with no date of maturity that pays interest for an indefinite length of time.
ARBITRAGE	The buying and selling of stocks, foreign exchange, precious metals, bonds or other commodities from one market to be sold at a profit to a separate but related market. An arbitrage opportunity arises when two companies plan to merge or when one security is convertible into another.
ARM'S LENGTH TRANSACTION	A contract in which the parties act as though they are independent of each other.
AROUND	The number of points on either side of par. For example, when quoting a premium or discount, a three-three around would mean three points on either side of par.
ARREARAGE	Cumulative preferred shares' unpaid dividends (see preferred stock).
ARREARS	Any past due amount.
AS OF	A term used to describe any trade processed not on the actual trade date, but "as of" the actual trade date.
ASK	The specific price accompanying an offer to sell.
ASKED PRICE	The lowest price at which a dealer will sell a security.
AS PRINCIPAL	A brokerage firm which is buying or selling securities for or from its own account. In such cases, commissions are not charged.
ASSET	Everything owned by a corporation or individual, from buildings and equipment to intangible assets such as patents and reputation.
ASSET AND LIABILITY STATEMENT	A balance sheet.
ASSOCIATE MEMBER	A person with limited membership rights at the American Stock Exchange.
ASSOCIATE SPECIALIST	An exchange member who assists the market specialist.
AT A DISCOUNT	A security that sells for a price that is below its par value.
AT A PREMIUM	A security that sells for a price that is above its par value.
AT BEST	A customer order to buy a security at the best rate possible.

AT MARKET	A customer order to buy or sell securities immediately at the best price available.
AT OR BETTER	A customer order to buy a security at or below a specified price, or to sell a security at or above a specified price.
AT PAR	A security that sells at its par value.
AT SIGHT	A securities payment that is due immediately upon presentation or demand.
AT THE CLOSE	A customer order that is to be completed at the best price possible when the market closes for the day.
AT THE MONEY	A put or call option with an exercise price equal to the underlying security's current market value.
AT THE OPENING	A customer order that is to be completed at the best price possible when the trading for the security opens. The order is canceled if not executed immediately.
AUTEX SYSTEM	A computer network that relates which brokers want to buy or sell large blocks of stock.
AUTHORIZED STOCK	The maximum amount of stock a corporation may issue. The fixed amount is stated in the company's certificate of incorporation.
AUTOMATED BOND SYSTEM	A New York Stock Exchange computer network that lists all orders for non-convertible bonds.
AUTOMATED CLEARING HOUSE	A firm set up with computers and used by member financial institutions to combine, sort, and distribute payment orders.
AUTOMATED CUSTOMER ACCOUNT TRANSFER SERVICE	Members of the National Securities Clearing Corporation can transfer customer accounts through a computer.
AUTOMATED PRICING AND REPORTING SYSTEM	The New York Stock Exchange computer network used to process and assign prices to certain odd-lot orders.
AUTOMATIC REINVESTMENT	A system that enables investors to buy new shares with income dividends or other money earned from the stock market.
AVERAGE	Buying or selling of securities in order to obtain a better overall price.
AVERAGE DOWN	Buying shares at a lower price in order to reduce a stock's average price.
AVERAGE EQUITY	A trading account's average daily balance. It is used to ensure that margin requirements are met.

AVERAGES A single value given to a specific set of market information and used to reflect the market's current strengths or weaknesses. The most widely followed is the Dow Jones Industrial Average.

AVERAGE UP Buying additional shares of stock at a price higher than the original cost to lower the stock's average cost basis. The stock is perceived as a good investment even at higher prices.

AWARD A borrower accepts a competitive bid for a security by notifying the high bidder.

AWAY FROM ME A market-maker's quote. The best bid or offer price is someone else's.

AWAY FROM THE MARKET A limit order bid is lower or the offer price is higher than the stock's current market price.

B Used lowercase in stock tables to signify that dollar dividend is annual plus payment of stock dividend.

BABY BOND A bond with a face value of less than the usual $1,000. $100 and $500 are common face values of baby bonds.

BACK-END LOAD Investment products that do not have initial sales charges sometimes have a redemption fee. Such charges often are lowered over time. For example, 5% in the first year, 4% in the second year, etc.

BACKING AWAY A market maker in a specific security fails to honor a firm bid for the minimum quantity. Backing away is considered unethical under the National Association of Securities Dealers guidelines.

BACK OFFICE The operational department of a bank or brokerage house. The department is not directly involved in selling or trading, but is responsible for accounting, compliance with government regulations, and inter branch communications.

BACK UP The reversal of a stock market trend. The change may be up or down.

BAD DELIVERY A securities certificate that is delivered in less than acceptable form as a result of damage or improper signature.

BAIL OUT Selling securities arbitrarily while in a panic without first considering the potential loss. The term also applies to a financially strong company coming to the rescue of a weaker company.

BALANCE Subtraction of debits from credits in a given account.

BALANCE ORDER The net balance instructions, issued by a clearing corporation, to receive or deliver securities. The instructions give all the information needed by the member firm to clear its transactions on a given settlement date.

BALANCED MUTUAL FUND A fund that buys both growth and income securities in an effort to get the highest returns with the least amount of risk.

BALANCE SHEET Financial accounting of a company's assets, liabilities, equity, and net worth as of a specific date.

BALANCE SHEET EQUATION Liabilities added to stockholders' equity equals a company's total assets.

BALLOON INTEREST Feature of serial bond issue in which earlier years' coupons are lower than coupon interest rates for later serial maturities.

BALLOON MATURITY Feature of serial bond issues in which dollar amounts of earlier maturities are smaller than dollar amounts of later maturities.

BALLOONING Manipulating stock prices so they increase far beyond the stocks' real values.

BAN See bond anticipation note.

BANKED COST A dealer who previously charged less than regulations permitted can add those undercharges to current margins to make up for the loss of commissions.

BANKING SYNDICATE A group of banks that have banded together to underwrite and sell a specific issue of securities.

BANK QUALITY Any bond with a top investment grade rating of AAA, AA, A or BBB, with AAA being the highest quality rating. Bonds with these ratings are suitable for purchase by institutions such as bank trust departments. Also known as investment grade.

BANK SECURITIES Capital debentures, preferred stock, or common stock issued by a commercial bank.

BAR CHART A market chart that illustrates stocks' highs, lows, closing information, and other index and volume changes that occurred during a specific time period.

BARGAIN A security that represents good relative value when the underlying company's assets and earning power are considered.

BAROMETER A compilation of market information that simulates overall market trends.

BAROMETER STOCK A widely followed issue that is used as a yardstick to predict future market conditions.

BARRON'S CONFIDENCE INDEX Weekly index prepared by the publishers of Barron's. The index compares yields of higher-grade to lower-grade corporate bonds. As yields on lower-grade bonds fall, it shows that investors are more confident about the economy. Used for an insight into possible market sentiment about equity securities.

BASE A stock pattern that indicates a long-term, tight price range that usually follows a market decline.

BASEBUILDING A long term, lateral price trend, which sometimes is considered necessary after a long decline in the stock market before prices can start going up again.

BASE MARKET VALUE The average price of a group of securities over a specific period.

BASIC Acronym for Banking and Securities Industry Committee. Promotes standardization of securities operations and of certificate processing systems.

BASIC YIELD The annual rate of return on a no-risk investment.

BASIS The original cost plus transaction costs and adjustments for splits, in the case of equity. The Internal Revenue Service requires that this figure be used to calculate capital gains and losses.

BASIS BOOK A reference manual of the Financial Publishing Company of Boston that contains such information as coupon interest rates and the time remaining until maturity of many bond issues. The book enables investors to calculate the dollar prices and yields of various securities.

BASIS POINT One one-hundredth of one percent. For example, an addition of 40 basis points to yield of 7.50% would increase the yield to 7.90%. Basis points normally are used when quoting yields on bonds or notes.

BASIS PRICE The figure upon which a stockholder calculates all capital gains or losses when selling his or her securities.

BASIS QUOTE The difference between the cash price and the futures price of a commodity.

BASIS TRADING Large investors establish underlying stock and index futures positions. If index futures look cheap, these investors buy futures and sell their stock. When stocks look cheap, the opposite takes place.

BASIS VALUE A security's value as an investment, and a bond's value at maturity.

BD FORM A document containing names of principals, capital compliance, and financial information about a broker-dealer firm. All broker-dealers are required to file this form with the Securities and Exchange Commission.

BEAR A person who expects the stock market to fall or the economy to slow down.

BEARDING A large order for securities is split into several smaller orders that will be executed by several brokers. Bearding keeps private the intentions of the large investors so he or she will not drive up the price of securities before the buy is complete.

BEARER Any person who holds a negotiable instrument.

BEARER BOND A bond issued and payable to anyone with physical possession, as opposed to a bond issued and registered in the owner's name.

BEARER FORM A security the issuing company hasn't registered on its books that, therefore, is payable to whomever holds it.

BEARER INSTRUMENT Any instrument (security) in bearer form.

BEAR MARKET A long-term decline in security prices.

BEAR SQUEEZE Institutions sometimes know bears have sold securities short before prices go up, resulting in a bear panic. High bid prices force the bears to cover their shorts and take losses.

BEAR TRAP A stock price that drops, after which many people sell, but then surges back up again.

BEATING THE GUN Accepting orders for a new stock before the security's registration becomes effective. The Securities and Exchange Commission prohibits this practice.

BEDBUG LETTER A letter the Securities and Exchange Commission sends to a company after the company files a preliminary registration statement for permission to sell stocks. The term got its name from the Securities and Exchange Commission's desire to get the bugs out of the registration statement before the company can begin to issue securities.

BELL A ringing or buzzing that signals the opening and closing of major stock exchanges each day.

BELL WETHER A specific stock, such as Xerox or IBM, that serves as a general indicator of the direction of the overall market. See benchmark.

BELOW PAR Selling for a price that is less than the security's face value.

BELOW THE MARKET A bid that is lower than the highest bid for a specific security.

BENCHMARK A quantitative gauge in the securities market (see Bell wether).

BENEFICIAL OWNER A person who benefits from owning a security, even though the security's title actually is in the name of a bank or broker. The classic example is stock held in "street name" by a broker for a client.

BEST EFFORTS UNDERWRITING An offering of new stock in which the underwriter makes a "best effort" to place the issue but is not responsible for unsold portions.

BETA A measure of risk; the higher the beta, the higher the risk. Beta represents the average percentage change in the price of a stock compared to the percentage change of the market index.

BID AND ASKED The highest price an investor will pay for a security (bid), or the lowest price someone will sell a security (asked).

BID-ASKED SPREAD The difference between the best buying price and the best selling price for any given security.

BIDDING UP The bid price for a security moves higher and higher as demand for the security increases.

BID IN COMPETITION An investor with a block of securities to sell approaches several dealers, then sells the securities to the one dealer with the highest bid. The dealer may inventory the stock in an effort to attract future business from the investor.

BID PRICE The highest price an investor will pay for a given security.

BID WANTED An investor, through a broker, announces that he or she wants to sell a security and is ready to accept bids.

BID WILL IMPROVE Traders tell a seller who requests a market picture that the trader can pay more than the bid represents, but first the seller must offer a counter-proposal. Often the buyer and the seller will split the bid-ask spread.

BIG BOARD The nickname for the New York Stock Exchange (NYSE), the oldest and largest stock exchange in the United States. Historically, the companies listed on the Big Board are bigger and more established than those listed on the American Stock Exchange.

BILL DISCOUNTED Interest is deducted from the face amount at the time of purchase and the face amount is paid at maturity. The classic example is the US Treasury Bill.

BILL OF EXCHANGE A short-term debt, the collateral for which is either a commodity or another product in the midst of transit.

BILL STRIP The US Treasury Department auctions Treasury bills of different maturities at the same average price.

BLACK MARKET Any illegal securities trading.

BLANKET CERTIFICATION FORM NASD form FR-1. Given by foreign brokers or dealers who purchase new-issue securities, which begin trading at an immediate premium, for their customers from NASD members. The form states that the foreign broker understands the NASD rules on hot issues and will abide by them.

BLANKET FIDELITY BOND The brokerage insurance that protects firms from incidents of fraudulent trading, forgery, and loss of securities. Dealers are required to maintain this coverage by the Securities and Exchange Commission's regulations.

BLIND BROKERING One person acts as an intermediary between a borrower and lender; sometimes one of the parties remains anonymous.

BLIND ENTRY An incomplete bookkeeping entry with only account credits and debits listed without any further financial information.

BLOCK AUTOMATION SYSTEM A communications computer at the New York Stock Exchange used when institutional investors trade large blocks of securities. The computer allows investors to identify buyers and sellers quickly.

BLOCKED A trader is told that his or her blocks cannot be crossed at the trader's price either because the spread is too tight or because another dealer is offering a deal as good or better.

BLOCK HOUSE A brokerage firm that specializes in trading in blocks of stocks.

BLOCK OF STOCK A trading unit of stock - 10,000 shares or more.

BLOCK ORDER An order to buy or sell $1 million or more worth of bonds or 10,000 or more shares.

BLOCK TRADING The acquisition or disposition of large quantities (10,000 shares or more) or "blocks" of stock by a broker or dealer in order to facilitate the execution of buy and sell orders of customers, usually institutions. Often a broker or dealer absorbs a portion of the order for its own account and risk in order to avoid market disruption.

BLOOD BATH Occurs when the stock market plummets and investors lose tremendous amounts of money - at least on paper.

BLOTTER A record of original entry. A written manuscript of broker or dealer activity for any given day, including purchases, sales, cash receipts and disbursements, and securities received and delivered. A blotter usually carries trades and customer account numbers, segregated by point of execution.

BLOTTER CODE A system by which trades are identified by type and place of execution. The code enables firms to balance customer-street-side trades.

BLOW OUT An offering of securities that is almost immediately sold out.

BLOWING OFF The peaking of stock prices after a lengthy advance and heavy trading. A buying climax.

BLUE CHIP A term used to describe the common stocks of corporations with the strongest reputations.

BLUE LIST BOOK A financial list published daily that reports which bonds are for sale, their prices, and their yields. The list includes bonds for sale by more than 700 dealers.

BLUE SKY LAW Securities must be registered according to the laws of each particular state before they can be sold in that state. Those stocks which do not follow a particular state's registration laws become restricted. The nickname came from a judge who once said a certain stock had as much value as a patch of blue sky.

BOARD OF ARBITRATION A committee of three to five people who decide the outcome of disputes between stock exchange members as well as non-member brokerage firms. An arbitration board may also be used to work out disagreements between clients and brokers. Those involved in the dispute first must agree to settle their fight with the board. The board's decision is binding.

BOND A long term debt security, issued by a corporation or government, with a stated interest rate and fixed due dates when interest and principal must be paid. Specific features are written into each bond's indenture, including whether the interest and principal will be paid to the person in whose name the security is registered, or if it will be payable to anyone presenting it, in which case it is considered a bearer bond.

THE BOND BUYER A newspaper published daily that lists indexes and statistics from fixed-income markets.

BOND BUYER'S INDEX Published in The Bond Buyer, this index contains gauges to judge the yields from municipal bonds and to help predict future trends.

BOND DISCOUNT The negative difference between a bond's market or purchase price and its par value.

BOND FUND Mutual fund invested in fixed-income instruments.

BOND HOLDER Anyone who owns a bond, whether it is in registered or bearer form.

BOND HOUSE A firm that deals in securities, but concentrates its business on bonds.

BOND POWER A certificate that accompanies a bond when it is transferred from one owner to another. The certificate appoints an attorney-in-fact, the seller's broker, who will complete the ownership transfer in the corporation's records.

BOND PREMIUM The positive difference between a bond's market or purchase price and its par value.

BOND QUOTATION While corporate bonds carry face values in dollar amounts, they are quoted in points based on the dollar amounts. One point represents $10, with minimum variations of one-eighth of a point. US Treasury Bonds are quoted in 32nds of a point.

BOND RATING A rank of quality ranging from AAA to D (default) given to a bond based on its value as a sound investment. The rating is based on such things as the issuer's reputation and its record in paying interest.

BOOK A written record of either anticipated interest for a proposed underwriting, or the activities of underwriting account members.

BOOK CREDIT Financial commitments that are not backed by any securities, but show up in ledger accounts.

BOOK ENTRY SECURITIES Securities, such stocks held in "street name," that are recorded in a customer's account, but are not accompanied by a certificate. The trend is toward a certificate-less society.

BOOKKEEPING EQUATION A one-line balance sheet summary, expressed as assets minus liabilities equals shareholders' equity.

BOOK VALUE The original cost of an asset minus depreciation. In corporate terms, book value equals the net asset value.

BOOK VALUE PER SHARE From total assets subtract all liabilities and the par value of stock and divide by the number of outstanding shares of common stock. This figure represents the break-up value per share if a company were liquidated.

BORROWED STOCK A broker borrows shares of a security to complete a client's short sale.

BORROWING POWER OF SECURITIES The amount of money an investor can borrow from his or her broker to buy securities based on the value of assets in their account. The brokerage firm lists each customer's borrowing power on his or her monthly statement.

BOTTOM The price level at which a security is not expected to drop below before it starts to go up again.

BOTTOM OUT The point at which a stock price has dropped so far that demand exceeds supply and the price begins to rise again.

BOUTIQUE A small brokerage firm that specializes in a limited number of securities with a select number of customers.

BOX A "short" position in the stock record representing securities on hand in the possession of the broker or dealer. A place where securities are kept such as a vault, and file cabinet. "Boxes" are also identified as "safekeeping box," "segregation box," "name-of box," and active box.

BOX COUNT An actual count of the securities in the box either in connection with an audit or with periodic checking.

BREADTH OF THE MARKET The number of stocks involved in a market move compared to the total number listed. If two-thirds of all stocks rose in price on a given day, investors say the breadth was good for an advancing day.

BREAK An abrupt, unexpected reversal in market prices.

BREAKAWAY GAP Price movements with highs and lows that do not overlap the previous day's movement and begin a new trend. For example, a positive trend may be forthcoming if today's price is higher than yesterday's high price.

BREAKOUT The price of a security increases above its previous high point, or falls below its previous low point. In a breakout, the security is expected to continue in the same direction for some time.

BROAD MARKET When securities trading is unusually heavy.

BROAD TAPE Wire service stock reports that provide a wider range of information than the ticker tape which merely shows prices and sizes of trades.

BROKER The intermediary between a buyer and a seller of securities. The broker, who usually charges a commission, must be registered with the exchange in which he or she is trading.

BROKER'S CALL RATE The rate that banks charge brokerage firms for the financing of margin accounts and inventory positions.

BROKER LOAN Short-term secured loan made to a broker from a commercial to finance customer security positions.

BROKERAGE ACCOUNT A broker will keep records of all transactions in which his or her clients ever have been involved. The customer will receive statements disclosing monthly transactions, current positions, and cash balances.

BROKERAGE HOUSE A firm that buys and sells securities for customers.

BROKER-DEALER A firm that not only handles transactions for customers, but also buys securities for its own account and then sells those securities to customers for a profit.

BROKER LOAN RATE	The interest rate brokers pay when they borrow money to pay for their customers' positions in the securities market.
BROKER'S FREE CREDIT BALANCE	The New York Stock Exchange provides a monthly report of the amount of money each firm has sitting idle in its brokerage account.
BROKER'S MARKET	Describes heavy trading by brokers in their own accounts, but little interest by individual investors.
BROKER'S TICKET	A record of a broker's executed buy and sell orders, including all information pertinent to the orders, such as names, dates and prices.
BROKER'S TRANSFER ACCOUNT	An account kept by the transfer clerk of a broker or dealer giving details of securities transferred for the account of other brokers or dealers. The account arises when delivery is made by transfer as directed (TAD) instead of by delivery of the actual certificates.
BROKER'S TRANSACTION SERVICES INCORPORATED	Sells trade processing and reporting services to brokers.
BUCKETING	A broker who executes a customer's order in his or her own account rather than on the open market because the broker believes he or she will profit from a balancing transaction later. The Securities and Exchange Commission prohibits bucketing.
BUCKET SHOP	A brokerage house will confirm a customer's order at a specific price without executing the order on an exchange in hopes of obtaining a better price. The firm would then pocket the difference between the two prices. Such practices are prohibited by the Securities and Exchange Commission.
BUCKING THE TREND	Doing the opposite of the rest of the market. For example, buying long when the market is going down, or selling short when the market is on an upswing.
BULGE	A short, quick price rise in an entire market or an individual stock.
BULK SEGREGATION	Securities owned by individuals, but not registered in their names and keep separate from securities owned by the broker-dealer.
BULL	Someone who expects the securities price, or the economy in general, to improve.
BULLET	Borrowed money or a borrowed security that must be repaid in one lump sum at the end of its term, instead of having smaller payments that are due regularly.
BULL MARKET	A long-term rise in security prices.

BUNCHING Putting together a lot of small orders to be executed at the same time, instead of spending time on them individually.

BUOYANT Securities that are rising in price.

BUSINESS DAY Any day the brokerage community and stock exchanges are open for trading. There are several days during the year where banks are closed but stock trading continues.

BUY AND HOLD The accumulation of a security for long-term appreciation and/or income rather than short-term profits.

BUY AT BEST In the purchase of a large block of over-the-counter securities, the dealer-broker is instructed to buy at the best price available, but all securities need not be purchased at the same price.

BUYERS' MARKET Supply exceeds demand, so prices are attractive.

BUY IN A selling broker fails to deliver on time, so the buying broker must obtain the securities from someone else.

BUYING CLIMAX A quick surge in the price of a security or the overall market, which prompts investors to purchase more. Soon, there is no one to whom they can sell the higher priced stock, which creates a vacuum and a sudden drop in the stock's price.

BUYING OUTRIGHT The opposite of buying on margin - buying a security by paying 100 percent cash.

BUYING POWER The amount of money a person has available to spend on securities; this hinges on the level of assets the person has in his or her brokerage account and how much is on margin.

BUYING RANGE If market prices are dropping an advisor determines the point at which he or she believes prices may start to increase again. Based on that information, the advisor recommends when an investor should start buying stock.

BUY-IN PROCEDURE If a broker or dealer does not deliver a promised security to a purchaser, the purchaser can notify the agent, and within two days can buy the security on the open market and charge the delinquent agent with any losses incurred.

BUY MINUS An order to buy stock at a price lower than the current market value. Normally, an investor will try to make such a deal when the stock's price is dropping.

BUY ON BID An investor buys a listed stock from an odd-lot trader who is selling at bid price, instead of waiting to buy from the odd-lot trader after a round-lot sale.

BUY ON THE OFFER An investor buys an odd-lot stock at the lowest asking price plus the odd-lot differential so that he or she does not have to wait for a round-lot sale to determine the odd-lot price.

BUY ORDER A client orders his or her broker to buy a specific amount of stock at a particular price.

BUY SIGNAL A chart indicator that, because of market movements, shows a buyer that it's a good time to purchase stock or other securities.

BUY STOP ORDER A client orders his or her broker to buy a security that is increasing in value after it has hit a certain price, then to buy at the best price available.

BUY THE BOOK A client orders his or her broker to buy all shares of a specific security that are available at the offer price.

BUY TICKET An investment department document that tells the order department to buy a specific security. The ticket states the date, time, size, and price of the security purchased.

CA Abbreviation often used in bond tables and in offering sheets for callable.

CAGE The term given to the area of the broker's or dealer's office where the cashier, stock clerk, loan clerk, transfer clerk, blotter clerk, and others have, as part of their duties, responsibility for the receiving and delivering of securities.

CALENDAR A list of securities that will be offered publicly for sale. Separate calendars are issued for new stock issues, corporate bonds, and municipal bonds.

CALL (1) The action whereby a company elects to redeem a security prior to its maturity date. (2) An option to buy a stated number of shares of a security at a stated price on or before a specified date.

CALL OPTION The right to purchase 100 shares of a specific stock at a specific price within a given time in exchange for a premium. The buyer will profit if the stock's market value rises above the sum of the striking price and the amount paid for the call at the time of expiration. Options are traded on several exchanges. The premium can provide extra income for the seller (writer) of the option.

CALLABLE A securities feature that allows the issuer to retire the issue when desired. Should the issue be called, the issuer usually pays a premium.

CANCEL Instruction to void a prior order to buy or sell, or price, or amount. The instruction may or may not be accompanied by new instruction.

CAP The highest interest rate a securities issuer will pay on a bond issue, or the highest price at which a securities underwriter will sell a new stock.

CAPITAL A company's net assets, including retained earnings.

CAPITAL ACCOUNT A business owner's account that indicates his or her equity.

CAPITAL GAIN In capital assets, the difference between the sale price and the cost less depreciation. In financial assets, the difference between the sale price and the purchase price adjusted for splits and transaction costs. In brokerage, a trading profit. Trading gains that occur in six months or less are short-term capital gains; those that occur in periods longer than six months are long-term capital gains. Short-term and long-term capital gains are treated differently for tax purposes.

CAPITAL ISSUES Permanent and fixed securities, such as common and preferred stock.

CAPITAL LOSS A trading loss. Losses are long- or short-term as are gains. See capital gains.

CAPITAL MARKETS A market in which capital funds, such as equity and debt, are traded.

CAPITAL RISK A person may not be able to recover all of his original investment when the investment is liquidated. This is in direct contrast to insured investments, such as certificates of deposit, wherein principal is guaranteed.

CAPITAL STOCK The source of a corporation's equity capital, indicating stocks that represent ownership. Capital stock usually refers to common, not preferred, stock.

CAPITAL SURPLUS The amount by which a security's balance sheet value exceeds its par value.

CAPITALIZATION The total dollar value of all common stock, preferred stock, and bonds issued by a corporation.

CAPITALIZE To categorize a specific asset cost as a long-term investment instead of charging it to current operations.

CAP ORDER A large buy or sell order giving the exchange specialist permission to use his or her own discretion in executing the deal. While this practice is formally prohibited by the exchanges, it still is used in some instances for expediency.

CARRY The act of holding stocks for a customer.

CARRY INCOME OR LOSS The difference between the interest income and the financing cost of an investment portfolio purchased on margin.

CARRYING BROKER The broker or dealer who holds a customer's account.

CARRYING CHARGE The amount of money a broker charges to carry securities for a client on credit. It also refers to the amount of money a person must spend to carry, store, and insure commodities.

CARRYING MARKET When distant positions hold a premium over nearby positions, with the premium high enough to pay for carrying charges.

CASH Any negotiable currency in spendable form.

CASH ACCOUNT A brokerage firm account in which all transactions are completed in cash. All securities purchased must be paid for in full by the fifth business day but no later than the seventh business day after trade.

CASH BASIS Money is credited to a person's account only as it is received. The alternative is a method whereby money is credited to an account when it is accrued.

CASH BASIS ACCOUNTING An accounting technique in which the basis for recording transactions is the receipt and payment of cash. It is the date on which cash changes hands, not the date on which goods and services are rendered.

CASH BOOK An accounting record with both cash receipts and cash disbursements. The cash book's balance should correspond with the cash balance on the general ledger.

CASH BUDGET The amount of cash a company expects to receive and disburse over a given period of not more than one year.

CASH BUYING Buying securities and commodities to be delivered immediately.

CASH DELIVERY Securities are traded and delivered in the same day.

CASH DIVIDEND Dividends that corporations pay, on a per-share basis, to stockholders from their earnings.

CASH EQUIVALENTS Investments with a high level of liquidity.

CASH FLOW A company adds the annual depreciation charge for fixed assets to its earnings after interest, taxes, and preferred dividends.

CASH FLOW BOND A fully amortizing debt instrument with a fixed coupon rate and a fixed payment schedule, having an average life equal to or less than its securing collateral.

CASH FORWARD SALE A commodity is sold with the actual delivery taking place at a later date.

CASH ITEMS A company's bank deposits, government bonds, etc., that are listed on its financial statement as cash equivalents.

CASH MANAGEMENT BILL A short-term money market instrument the US Treasury issues to pay for its short-term financial obligations.

CASH MARKET	The ownership of a security or commodity is transferred and payment is made when the security or commodity is delivered.
CASH ON DELIVERY	Used typically on buy orders entered by institutional investors, many of whom are prohibited from delivering cash unless an asset is received in its place.
CASH POSITION	The percentage of a company's total net assets that is available in cash.
CASH PRICE	The amount it would cost to buy a specific quantity of a commodity to be delivered immediately.
CASH SALE	A trade that settles on trade date and that is used in equities at the end of the year for tax purposes.
CASH TRADE	A security transaction in which settlement with payment and delivery on the security occur on the same day as the trade.
CASHIER'S DEPARTMENT	A division of the operations department of a broker or dealer that handles securities and money that are received or delivered by the broker or dealer.
CEASE AND DESIST ORDER	Used by the Securities and Exchange Commission to stop people it believes are violating federal trading laws.
CENTRAL CERTIFICATE SERVICE	To reduce the physical movement of stock certificates, subscribers of this service can deliver securities to each other through a bookkeeping computer.
CERTIFICATE	A document verifying security ownership. A certificate includes such information as the issuer's name and the terms under which the security was issued.
CERTIFICATED SECURITIES	The number of shares of a particular commodity that are certified and ready to be delivered on a futures contract.
CERTIFICATELESS TRADING	Trading securities that do not have certificates of ownership issued to the holder. The holder can prove ownership by requesting a nonnegotiable certificate issued in the name of the broker who originally executed the transaction.
CERTIFICATE OF ACCRUAL ON TREASURY SECURITIES (CATS)	A US Treasury bond that is sold at a deep discount from its face value. Although it pays no interest, it is redeemable for the full face value when it matures.
CERTIFICATE OF DEPOSIT (CD)	A short-term debt instrument issued by banks. CDs of larger denominations are negotiable and can be traded in the secondary market.
CHANGES IN STOCKHOLDERS' EQUITY	A section in a company's annual report that shows the stockholders' equity, which is the difference between their assets and their liabilities.

CHARTIST A technical analyst who maps out stock, bond, and commodity patterns, looks for recurring patterns, and then recommends which securities should be purchased.

CHARTIST'S LIABILITY The risk of buying or selling short a security when the transaction is based solely on a chartist's recommendation.

CHART OF ACCOUNTS A list that shows the names of accounts and the order in which they appear on a company's ledger.

CHEAP Used to describe a stock price as low compared to its present value. "Underpriced" is used when a stock price is low compared to its potential future value.

CHECKING THE MARKET Surveying market-makers to find out what the best bid is for a specific security.

CHERRY PICKING Choosing the best stock while ignoring the less valuable.

CHICAGO BOARD OF TRADE (CBOT) The largest exchange in the United States for trading futures contracts. The Chicago Board Options Exchange is a subsidiary of the Chicago Board of Trade.

CHICAGO BOARD OPTIONS EXCHANGE (CBOE) The largest market in the United States for trading put and call options.

CHINESE MARKET Investors are willing to pay more than the lowest offer for a stock, or sell for less than the highest bid, but only if a large number of the securities are included in the deal.

CHINESE WALL An intangible barrier between the trading side of a broker-dealer firm and the finance and research side that prevents broker-dealers from taking advantage of the finance department's inside information.

CHUMMING A person artificially inflates the stock market's volume to attract more orders in one competitive security issue.

CHURNING Excessive trading in a customer's account in an effort to increase the broker's commissions. The customer will usually be worse off or in no better condition. Although difficult to prove, churning is illegal under the Securities and Exchange Commission's rules.

CIRCLE An indication of how much interest will be expressed in a new security while the security is still in the registration process. Company representatives make lists of potential buyers, then circle the names of those who express an interest.

CLASS Categorization of securities with similar features. For example, puts are one class and calls are another. Also bonds are one class of security, and stocks are another.

CLASSIFIED STOCK Equity securities are separated into groups such as Class A or Class B. The difference between the two will be determined by the provisions of the charter and bylaws. Differences can distinguish privileges in voting power, dividends, and liquidation procedures.

CLEAN If a block positioner can match buy and sell orders without taking the security into his or her inventory thus taking a risk, the transaction is said to be "clean." (Also called "natural") A clean balance sheet will be free of debt.

CLEAR Verifying the details of a security's trade before its settlement.

CLEARANCE The act of clearing securities between buyers and sellers; receipt or delivery securities against payment.

CLEARED When the purchaser of a security pays for and receives the security.

CLEARING AGREEMENT A document in which one broker-dealer agrees to execute and settle another broker-dealer's transaction for a fee.

CLEARING CORPORATION A central receive and distribution center operated for its members, who are made up of various brokerage firms. Many offer automated systems that expedite comparison procedures. Among these are National Securities Clearing Corporation (NSCC) and Options Clearing Corporation (OCC).

CLEARING HOUSE A central location where deals between member firms are matched, executed and settled.

CLEARING HOUSE COMPARISON (CHC) A form used to submit trades to NSCC that have missed the normal entry methods. Such trades enter the system on the third business day of the trade cycle.

CLEARING MEMBER An exchange member who is granted membership in a clearing house.

CLEARING ORGANIZATION Usually a broker or dealer which clears the transaction of another broker or dealer.

CLEARING THE MARKET Changing the price of a securities transaction to the satisfaction of the buyer and seller.

CLIMAX A time of heavy trading after a long rise or drop in market prices. The climax signals the top or bottom, so prices usually change directions following it.

CLOSE The final 30 seconds of trading on the stock exchange floor, designated by a bell that rings continuously for the 30 seconds.

CLOSE A POSITION Eliminating an investment from a portfolio, usually by selling if a long position exists or by buying in the case of a short security position.

CLOSED ACCOUNT	A brokerage account that the customer or broker has terminated. Although the brokerage house by law retains transaction records, all securities and money involved are sent to the customer.
CLOSED TRADE	A transaction closed when a security that was paid for earlier is sold.
CLOSE PRICES	When the difference between bid and ask prices are fractional.
CLOSE TO THE MONEY	A put or call contract with a striking price that is close to the current market value of the underlying security.
CLOSING QUOTE	The final bid or offer on a security before the exchange closes for the day.
CLOSING TRANSACTION	One securities deal that cancels another securities deal, both of which carry the same terms.
CMO	See collateralized mortgage obligation.
CMV	Frequently used abbreviation for current market value in ledger displays of margin accounts.
COD TRANSACTION	A broker buys a security for a client's account and delivers the security to the client's agent, who then pays for the purchase. Also known as "delivery against cost" and "delivery versus payment."
COEFFICIENT OF DETERMINATION	A gauge that determines the amount of market-imposed risk on a specific security.
COLD CALL	A broker or agent of a broker calls a potential investor for the first time in an effort either to sell a security or to set up a meeting in which a security will be discussed.
COLLAPSE	Either the sudden drop in a stock's price or the failure of a business venture.
COLLATERAL	An asset pledged to support a loan.
COLLATERALIZE	To put up an asset as pledge that a loan will be repaid. For example, to collateralize a margin loan by the deposit of stock with the broker.
COLLATERALIZED MORTGAGE OBLIGATION (CMO)	A security which pools together mortgages and separates them into short-, medium-, and long-term positions. This system provides interest and principal in a more predictable manner.
COMEX	A commodity exchange located at 4 World Trade Center, New York.
COMBINATION ORDER	In listed options trading, an order to simultaneously buy or sell a put and a call, each having the same underlying security but different series designations.
COMMERCIAL PAPER	A short-term debt instrument issued by corporations. Its rate of interest is set at issuance and can be realized only if held to maturity.

COMING TO ME Over-the-counter traders who give a price quote that is not their own. While the price does represent another dealer's market, id does not necessarily reflect the over-the-counter trader's final offer.

COMMINGLING Mixing an investor's securities with those owned by a company in the company's proprietary accounts.

COMMISSION Fees charged by a firm for executing trades.

COMMISSION BROKER An agent, usually a floor broker who executes the public's trades for a commission.

COMMITMENT FEE A person planning to issue securities gives money to investors to motivate them to buy the securities when they are issued. By paying a commitment fee, the issuer is assured the funds will be available later for the investors to buy the shares.

COMMON MESSAGE SWITCH A computer that connects members with the New York and American stock exchanges over which order instructions are transmitted.

COMMON STOCK A security, issued in shares, that represents ownership of a corporation. Common stockholders may vote for the management and receive dividends after all other obligations of the corporation are satisfied.

COMPARATIVE STATEMENTS Financial documents that cover different time periods (but similar in content), used to compare a company's financial situation and to predict where the company is heading.

COMPARISON The process by which two contra brokerage firms in a trade agree to the terms of the transaction. Comparison can be either through a clearing corporation or on a trade-for-trade basis (that is, ex the clearing corporation).

COMPOSITE LIMIT ORDER BOOK A proposed central computer that would show all buy and sell orders of securities, and ultimately could eliminate the need for exchanges because brokers could execute orders directly through the computer.

COMPOUND INTEREST Interest that is computed on the original amount plus all accumulated interest.

COMPUTER ASSISTED EXECUTION SYSTEM A communication network, sponsored by the National Association of Securities Dealers, that connects broker-dealers to the over-the-counter market makers and through which the broker-dealers can order the execution of certain transactions.

CONFIRMATION SLIP Verification that a broker sends to a client acknowledging a transaction. The confirmation slip sets forth the terms of a contract between a broker or dealer and its customer for the purchase or sale of securities. Details shown on a confirmation slip are trade date, settlement date, number of shares or par value of bonds, security description, contract price, commission, account number and type of account, customer's name and address, and any other information required.

CONSOLIDATED BALANCE SHEET A financial statement that shows a parent company's total assets and liabilities without breaking the numbers down to show the assets and liabilities of the company's subsidiaries.

CONSOLIDATED STATEMENT OF FINANCIAL POSITION A document in which a company's current financial status is reported.

CONSOLIDATED TAPE A network that continuously reports on all securities transactions on every exchange.

CONTINGENT ORDER An order to buy one security and sell another only if the deal can be made at a stipulated price difference.

CONTINUOUS NET SETTLEMENT The National Securities Clearing Corporation becomes the intermediary between two brokers involved in a securities transaction, thus creating a securities balance account. Depending on whether the firm was buying or selling, the account is adjusted up or down each day. Most securities are settled in this manner.

CONTRA BROKER The broker handling the other side of a trade. When buying, the seller is the contra broker.

CONTRACT BROKER One stock exchange member who trades for other exchange members.

CONTRACT SHEET The Securities Industry Automation Corporation prepares this sheet daily from information provided to it by brokers. The sheet covers transaction information, including whether there are problems or disagreements over the pending settlement.

CONVENIENCE SHELF A registration statement for a security that will be offered publicly for sale. While this particular registration does not require information concerning the price or the underwriter, it does stipulate the maximum number of shares that can be sold.

CONVENTIONAL PASS THROUGH A security issued by a financial institution that represents a part of a mortgage pool. The government does not guarantee interest or principal.

CONVERSION The exchange of one type of security for another.

CONVERTIBLE ISSUE (BOND) A security's feature that permits the issue holder to convert into another issue, usually common stock. This privilege can only be used once. The preferred stock- or bondholder can convert from that issue to another, but not back.

COOLING OFF PERIOD A period of time, usually 20 days, that must elapse between the filing of a registration statement with the SEC and the offering of securities to the public.

CORNERING THE MARKET Holding enough shares of a security to be able to manipulate the price.

CORPORATE BOND A debt instrument issued by a corporation. It is usually fixed income, that is, it carries a fixed rate of interest.

COST OF CAPITAL The amount of money a company could make if it invested in another venture with an equal risk.

COST OF CARRY Out-of-pocket expense paid by an investor during the period that a security position is maintained. Also called carry.

COUPON A certificate that accompanies a bond and carries the amount and the date interest is due. The certificate is torn off and presented when the investor wants an interest payment.

COUPON BOND A bond instrument with a detachable coupon. Anyone who has physical possession of the coupon can present it to an agent for payment of any interest due.

COUPON RATE A bond's annual rate of interest, expressed as a percentage of the bond's face value.

COUPON ROLLOVER DATE The day a new interest rate on a floating-rate security will be established.

COUPON YIELD Divide a bond's yearly interest rate by its face value, which equals the coupon rate.

COVER (1) Corporations: the ability to pay fixed charges on debt securities by earned income. Important in ratings of bonds. (2) Clients who have sold short: the act of buying an equivalent number of shares or bonds and instructing the broker to deliver against a short position. Also used in short against box when the client instructs the broker to deliver box securities against the short position.

CRASH A dramatic drop in the securities market and in the economy in general.

CREDIT AGREEMENT A contract between a broker-dealer and client when the client uses credit to purchase securities. The contract stipulates terms of the credit and the amount of margin to be maintained, as well as how interest will be charged.

CREDIT BALANCE	The funds available to a client in a cash or margin account. In a short sale, this balance represents the customer's liability.
CREDIT SPREAD	When the value of the long option on a security is less than that of the short option on the same security, the investor gets credit in his or her brokerage account.
CROSSED MARKET	When one broker's bid is higher than another's lowest offer. While crossed markets sometimes occur, the National Association of Securities Dealers Automated Quotations prohibits brokers from intentionally crossing the market.
CROSS ORDER	One client asks a broker to buy a security, and another client asks the same broker to sell the same security. Such orders cannot be directly paired, and must be executed through the stock exchange.
CROSS PURCHASE	When a broker improperly executes a cross order directly without going through the stock exchange.
CUMULATIVE PREFERRED	A preferred stock feature that entitles the holder to the later payment of dividends that were not paid when due. The dividends are, in this sense, "cumulative." The dividends accumulate and must be paid before common stockholders may receive any dividends.
CURRENCY	Any form of money that is in public circulation.
CURRENCY IN CIRCULATION	A popular misnomer for money in circulation. Currency is only coins and paper money. Money is a broader term and includes demand deposits, which are balances in checking accounts.
CURRENT	In budget and accounting practices this designates the operations of the present fiscal period.
CURRENT ASSETS	All of a company's assets that probably will be converted into cash within the company's fiscal year. For example, accounts receivable are considered current assets.
CURRENT LIABILITIES	All of a company's debts that are payable within the company's fiscal year. For example, a mortgage payment is considered a current liability.
CURRENT MARKET VALUE	The value of a security based on its closing price of the previous day.
CURRENT MATURITY	The amount of time left on a bond before it matures.
CURRENT VALUE ACCOUNTING	An accounting system in which a person's assets are measured according to current prices instead of the prices the person paid when buying the assets.
CURRENT YIELD	A security's dividend divided by its current market value.

CUSIP NUMBER	A number assigned by the Committee of Uniform Security Identification Procedure that appears on the face of all securities documents. Each security is given its own number so it can be easily identified.
CUSTODIAN	An agent such as a broker or a bank that stores a customer's investments.
CUSTOMER'S NET DEBIT BALANCE	The New York Stock Exchange provides credit to its member firms so the firms can, in turn, finance their own customers' securities purchases.
D	Lowercase, it appears in stock transaction tables and indicates the stock has reached its lowest price in the last year.
DATED DATE	The first day that interest starts to accrue on newly issued bonds.
DATE OF MATURITY	The designated day an obligation must be paid.
DATE OF RECORD	The last day a new purchaser will be entitled to a dividend. If an investor buys stock before the date of record, he or she will be entitled to receive a dividend from the stock.
DATE OF TRADE	The day a buy or sell order is executed.
DAYLIGHT TRADING	Buying a security and then selling it the same day (see Day Trade).
DAY ORDER	A buy or sell order that expires when the exchange closes for the day. Usually, all buy and sell orders are day orders unless otherwise specified.
DAY TRADE	The purchase and sell of a stock in one day (see Daylight Trading).
DBO	See delivery balance order.
DEAD MARKET	A market with little trading and little interest or activity.
DEALER	A person who buys and sells securities for his or her own account and at his or her own risk. A company can also be a dealer.
DEALER ACTIVITIES	Usually refers to a bank that takes on the responsibilities of a dealer by trading and underwriting securities.
DEALER BANK	A commercial bank that makes a continuous market in government and agency securities.
DEALER MARKET	A market in which all securities are traded between principals for their own accounts, not for the accounts of clients.
DEALER PAPER	Commercial paper an issuer sells to a broker-dealer, who then marks it up and sells it to institutional investors.
DEALER'S TURN	A broker-dealer's profit when he or she buys a security at bid and sells at the offer price.

DEBENTURE A long-term debt instrument issued without collateral.

DEBENTURE BOND A long-term debt instrument that has no collateral other than the issuing company's general credit.

DEBENTURE STOCK A security that has fixed payments at designated intervals. As with preferred stock, a debenture stock's liquidity is in its equity, not in its debt like a normal debenture.

DEBIT A bank account entry subtracting a specific amount of money. The opposite of credit.

DEBIT BALANCE The amount of loan in a margin account.

DEBT INSTRUMENT General name for any certificate that evidences a loan between a borrower and a lender. Commonly used equivalent terms, although there are differences in the payment of interest on the debt, are bill, note, bond, certificate of indebtedness, certificate of deposit, banker's acceptance, commercial paper, and receiver's certificate.

DEBT SECURITY Any security that represents a loan.

DECLARATION DATE The day a company announces it will pay dividends, when it will pay them, and how much they will be.

DEEP BID A significant, away-from-the-market bid.

DEEP DISCOUNT BOND A debt instrument issued at par and currently selling for less than 80% of its par value.

DEFALCATION When a fiduciary or representative misappropriates funds.

DEFAULT Used of debts if the debtor fails to meet an interest payment or to repay the principal. The debt agreement, however, may define default in other ways.

DEFERRED ASSET An asset that cannot be converted easily into cash.

DEFERRED CHARGES Expenditures on an asset carried forward over a period of time. These are usually monies a company spends to improve the long-term outlook of its business.

DEFERRED STOCK A security with a dividend that will not be paid until after a specific date or until after a designated event has occurred.

DEFICIENCY LETTER Written statement from the SEC to an issuer during the registration process. The letter suggests revision or addition of other information to the preliminary registration statement. Although a deficiency letter does not necessarily delay the registration, an effective date will not be assigned until the deficiency is corrected.

DEFICIT A company's liabilities and debts exceed its income and assets or a company's spending exceeds its budget.

DEFICIT NET WORTH Liabilities exceed assets and capital stock.

DELAYED DELIVERY A securities contract is settled after a regular-way delivery of the security, which usually is after five business days.

DELETE OF COMPARED A form, as well as a process, used to delete trades that were compared by mistake through the NSCC.

DELIVERABLE BILLS Treasury bills that meet the requirements on the exchange on which it is traded.

DELIVERY BALANCE ORDER An order issued by the clearing corporation to any firm that, after the day's trades are netted, has a delivery or sale position remaining. The order defines what is to be delivered to whom.

DELIVERY NOTICE The seller confirms that he or she will deliver a stock or commodity on a specific day at a specific place.

DELIVERY VERSUS PAYMENT Payment for a security must be made when the security is delivered. Usually, the payment is made to a bank, which in turn pays for the stock certificates.

DEMAND AS-OF A form used in the NSCC OTC comparison system. Its purpose is to give a firm that is DKing a trade a last chance to accept the trade. After the Dking firm has turned down the demand as-of, the submitting firm is no longer obligated to accept the trade and can take other action.

DEMAND PRICE The amount of money a buyer will pay for a specific security or commodity.

DEMONSTRATION A sudden and unexpected change in a security's activities.

DENOMINATION The number of shares appearing on the face of a security, or the principal amount appearing on the face of a bond.

DEPOSITORY (1) A central location for keeping securities on deposit. (2) A bank that accepts deposits of securities and government funds.

DEPOSITORY TRUST COMPANY (DTC) A corporation, owned by banks and brokerage firms, that holds securities, arranges for their receipt and delivery, and arranges for the payments in settlement.

DEPRECIATION An amount of money that represents a tangible asset's drop in value over time. The amount is subtracted from the asset's purchase price to give its residual value. For example, an automobile depreciates each year the more it is used. In other words, the more miles racked up, the greater the depreciation.

DEPRECIATION FUND Money or securities set aside and designated to replace depreciating fixed assets.

DEPRESSED PRICE A security's price is lower than it should be when considering the issuing company's financial condition.

DEPTH The amount of general interest investors show in the market, representing the number of issued traded compared to the number of issues listed. Logically, the more issues traded, the greater the market depth. Depth also describes the market's ability to absorb a large buy or sell order without a dramatic change in the security's price.

DESCENDING TOPS A bearish chart pattern in which each new price for a security is lower than the security's last high price.

DESIGNATED ORDER TURNAROUND (DOT) An order routing and execution reporting system of the NYSE. Orders up to 599 shares may be entered by member firms through this system.

DIARY A listing of financial instruments' maturity dates.

DIFFERENTIAL A dealer is paid, usually 1/8 of a point, for completing an odd lot transaction, or the dealer increases his or her quoted fee to a customer because the customer is buying or selling a small amount of securities.

DIGESTED SECURITIES Securities owned by an investor who plans to hold onto them for a long time.

DIME Equal to 10 basis points, or 0.1 percent, on a debt security's yield.

DIP A slight drop in securities prices in an upward trend, usually marking a good time to buy.

DIRECTOR A corporate board member elected by the stockholders.

DIRECT PLACEMENT Used of an issuer's sale of a new security to one or more institutional clients without the assistance of a broker-dealer.

DISCONTINUOUS MARKET Securities that are not listed form a separate market.

DISCOUNT The difference between a security's redemption value and its current market price.

DISCOUNT BOND A bond that initially sold near par, but now sells for less.

DISCOUNT BROKER A broker who charges a lower fee because he or she executes transactions, but provides clients no other services, such as investment advice.

DISCOUNT ON SECURITIES The difference in amounts when a security is traded for less than its par value.

DISCOUNTING THE NEWS When the price of a stock or the level of one of the markets moves up or down in anticipation of good or bad news.

DISCOUNT RATE Interest rate charged by the Federal Reserve when member banks borrow from the Fed against eligible securities as collateral.

DISCOUNT WINDOW	Term for the loan facility provided by the Federal Reserve Bank whereby member banks can borrow against the collateral value of eligible securities.
DISCOUNT YIELD	Achieved by dividing a security's discount by its face value, and multiplying that number by the approximate number of days in the year (360) divided by the number of days left to maturity. The figure provides the interest on a security's face value instead of on the amount of money invested.
DISCRETIONARY ACCOUNT	A brokerage account that allows an employee of an exchange-member firm to make investment decisions on the client's behalf, such as buying and selling, choosing securities, when to buy or sell and at what price to buy or sell.
DISCRETIONARY ORDER	An order to buy or sell that an employee of a member firm entered because she has limited power of attorney over a client's account. Industry rules require that such orders be marked discretionary, be entered in accord with the customer's investment objectives, and be approved promptly by a designated person in the member firm.
DISTRESS SELLING	Selling a security out of necessity.
DISTRIBUTION	General term used to designate the sale of a large block of stock. The distribution may be primary, as in an underwriting, or secondary, as in an exchange distribution.
DISTRIBUTION AREA	A security has not changed in price much in a long time. The area is that narrow price range.
DISTRICT BUSINESS CONDUCT COMMITTEE (DBCC)	A committee appointed by the members within 1 of the 13 districts of the National Association of Securities Dealers (NASD). The DBCC is empowered to hear trade practice complaints against a member or a person associated with a member under the Code of Procedure.
DIVERGENCE	When market trends go in a different direction than market indicators predicated, usually signaling the onset of a trend change.
DIVERSIFICATION	An investor reduces his or her financial risk by spreading his or her investment over a large number of securities, instead of risking it all in one area.

DIVERSIFIED Term used of management investment companies - both closed and open-ended - if at least 75% of its assets are represented by four forms: cash, government securities, securities of other investment companies, and other securities. Purpose: so no more than 5% of the management company's total assets are invested in the securities of any one issuer and they hold no more than 10% of the voting securities of any issuing corporation.

DIVIDEND A portion of a corporation's assets paid to stockholders on a per-share basis. Preferred stock is supposed to pay a regular and prescribed dividend amount. Common stock pays varying amounts when declared.

DIVIDEND DEPARTMENT A division of the operations department that is charged with the collection of dividends and the crediting of these dividends to the accounts of customers.

DIVIDEND REINVESTMENT PLAN Instead of receiving cash dividends, investors can put the money into buying more shares of the security.

DIVIDENDS PAYABLE The exact dollar amount of a dividend.

DIVIDENDS PER SHARE The amount of money an investor receives in dividends for each share of stock he or she owns.

DK Abbreviation for don't know. An expression used by a broker or dealer to indicate that a certain transaction which another broker or dealer is attempting to confirm or compare is unknown to it. When mutual understanding is reached, the transaction is properly compared or canceled.

DNI See do not increase.

DNR See do not reduce.

DO NOT INCREASE (DNI) An instruction that informs order handling personnel not to increase the quantity of shares specified on the order in the event of a stock dividend. DNI is placed on buy limit, sell stop, and stop limit GTC orders.

DO NOT REDUCE (DNR) An instruction that informs the order handling personnel not to reduce the price of the order by the amount of dividends, if and when paid by the corporation. DNR is placed on buy limit, sell stop and sell stop limit GTC orders.

"DON'T FIGHT THE TAPE" Some analysts say it is not wise to trade securities against the general market trend.

DOT see designated order turnaround.

DORMANT ACCOUNT A brokerage account that has not had any activity for a long time.

DOUBLE AUCTION MARKET	Buyers and seller constantly vary their prices in an attempt to make the market. When the investor making the highest offer and the seller with the lowest asking price agree on a price, a transaction is made.
DOUBLE BOTTOM	When a stock drops to the same low price twice. Analysts use the double bottom to determine if a stock will continue a decline. Usually, they will predict further decline if the stock drops to that level a third time.
DOUBLE ENTRY	When one financial account entry shows an increase, another entry must show either an increase or decrease so that all the debits equal all of the credits.
DOUBLE TOP	When a stock hits the same peak high price twice. Analysts use the double top to determine if a stock will continue to go up. Usually they will predict further increases if the stock reaches that peak a third time.
DOW JONES AVERAGE	A composite of the price movement of 65 stocks, including 30 industrials, 20 transportation, and 15 utilities.
DOWNDRAFT	A stock market decline.
DOWN GAP	When the lowest price in a given market day is higher than the highest price of the next day, an open space appears on the stock chart.
DOWN MARKET	A trend of declining market prices.
DOWN REVERSAL	A sudden drop in prices after the prices had been moving up.
DOWNSIDE PROTECTION	The range of a security's price must drop before the investor starts to lose money.
DOWNSIDE TREND	A security's price continues a long-term drop.
DOWN TICK	An exchange-listed security is sold for less than the last regular-way transaction involving the same security.
DOWN TREND	A security's price is dropping, and it looks like it will continue to go down.
DOWNTURN	A financial cycle that begins to go down. For example, when a bullish market becomes bearish, the market is experiencing a downturn.
DOW THEORY	No market trend will last longer than a year unless such a trend is indicated by the movements of the industrial, transportation, and utility averages.
DR	Commonly used designation, DR, of a debit in a client's account with a brokerage firm. For example, a client's statement reads $2,500 Dr, which signifies that the client owes the brokerage firm $2,500.
DRAWN SECURITIES	A security ready to be redeemed.
DRIED UP	A buying or selling order is removed from the market.

DRIVE Sellers try to manipulate the market by forcing prices down, which is illegal.

DROP LOCK SECURITY A feature on a floating rate security that allows the holder to exchange the security for a fixed-rate security if the popular interbank loan rate drops to a predetermined level.

DTC Abbreviation for Depository Trust Company. A depository for eligible securities which facilitates clearance between member organizations and banks without the necessity of receiving or delivering actual certificates. See Depository Trust Company.

DUALLY LISTED A security that is listed on more than one stock exchange.

DUE DILIGENCE MEETING The last meeting between corporate officials and underwriters prior to the issuance of the security. At the meeting, the content of the prospectus is discussed, and relevant parts of the underwriting are put into place.

DULL When securities' prices do not change much and trading is relatively inactive.

DUMP To sell a security at a reduced price just to get rid of it.

DUMPING Selling a large number of stocks with little concern about their market price.

DUN & BRADSTREET A firm that deals in collection services and credit reporting, used primarily by brokers and dealers.

DUN'S NUMBER The Dun's Market Identifier, or the Data Universal Numbering System, is included in a list of companies. The list contains identification numbers, firms' names, addresses, numbers of employees, corporate affiliations, etc.

DURATION The difference between a bond's price change and the change in its yield to maturity, which gives the investor an indication of how interest rate changes will affect the bond's price.

DYNAMITER A broker who uses the telephone to try to sell unregistered or outright fraudulent stocks and bonds.

EACH WAY Commissions earned by a broker on the buy and sell of a trade.

EAGLE A restricted and tightly controlled computer system at the New York Stock Exchange containing corporate information.

EARNING POWER The amount of money an asset or security is expected to earn and the current value of those earnings.

EARNINGS A company's profits after paying all expenses, but before paying dividends.

EARNINGS BEFORE TAXES (EBT) The amount of money a company has after it pays dividends but before it pays taxes.

EARNINGS PER SHARE (EPS) A company's net profit minus its preferred stock obligations, with the difference divided by the number of outstanding shares of common stock.

EARNINGS STATEMENT A written review of a company's earnings, such as an income statement.

EARNINGS YIELD A security's earnings divided by its market price.

EASIER Bid prices are dropping.

EFFECTIVE ANNUAL YIELD The amount of money an investment makes as expressed in its equivalent simple interest rate.

EFFECTIVE PAR A preferred stock's par value that corresponds to a specific dividend rate.

EFFECTIVE DATE The first date after the cooling-off period of a new issue that the security can be offered.

EFFECTIVE RATE The yield on a debt security based on the coupon rate, price, time between interest payments, and the amount of time to maturity. This rate determines the overall yield.

EFFECTIVE SALE Common expression for the price of the round-lot transaction on an exchange that determines the execution of an odd-lot order.

EITHER/OR ORDER An investor advises his or her broker to have one of two orders executed. When one is executed, the other alternative is automatically canceled.

EITHER WAY MARKET When a bid on a security is identical to an offer price.

ELECTRONIC ACCESS MEMBER For a fee, the New York Stock Exchange gives some people the right to use electronic communications to buy and sell securities on the trading floor, even though they are not exchange members.

ELIGIBLE LIST (ELIGIBLE SECURITY) A list of securities that banks and other financial institutions can buy. Securities on this list may include the following: (1) Securities traded by the Federal Open Market Committee, (2) Securities that the Federal Reserve will accept for loans at the discount window, (3) Securities that have loan value under Regulation T, whether in the general, special bond, or special subscription accounts, (4) Securities that a carrying broker may deposit at the Options Clearing Corporation as collateral for short options positions, (5) Securities that exchange members may trade in the OTC market although they are listed on the exchange.

ELIGIBLE STOCK A security in which charities and financial institutions can invest.

ENVELOPE A graduated listing of securities' price extremes.

EQUITY (1) A company's value after all of its liabilities have been discharged (2) The portion in an account that reflects the customer's ownership interest.

EQUITY CAPITAL Money a company earns by selling shares of its stock. Equity capital reflects ownership, while a bond represents a debt.

EQUITY EARNINGS A portion of a subsidiary's surplus earnings that exceed dividend payments and that the parent company does not report.

EQUITY NET WORTH The amount of interest a company's stockholders own based on capital, retained earnings, and surplus.

EQUITY SECURITIES Term applied to common stocks or to debentures or preferred stocks which are convertible into common stocks.

ESCROW RECEIPT A guarantee of delivery issued by a qualified bank to a clearing corporation, such as OCC, on behalf of the bank's customer. The member brokerage firm acts as a conduit for this document.

ESTIMATED BALANCE SHEET An estimate of what the company's assets and liabilities will be at the end of the company's next fiscal year.

EUROBOND A company issues a bond through the international market, with interest and principal payments due in the currency in which the bond was issued.

EURODOLLAR Common term for dollars held by banks in European countries.

EURODOLLAR CD Short-term time deposits issued by European banks.

EXACT INTEREST Financial institutions pay interest based on 365 days per year, instead of the usual 360 days when calculating the daily interest accrued on large deposits.

EX-ALL A security is sold without any rights, dividends, warrants, or other privileges.

EXCESS MARGIN Dollar value of a client's equity above initial Regulation-T margin or maintenance requirement.

EXCHANGE The physical location where brokers transact business for their clients.

EXCHANGE ACQUISITION An order to buy a large block of stocks is combined with several orders to sell the same security, with the deal being put together on the exchange floor.

EXCHANGE DISTRIBUTION An order to sell a large block of securities is combined with several orders to buy the same stock, with the deal being put together on the exchange floor.

EXCHANGE FLOOR The physical area of a stock exchange where securities deals are put together.

EXCHANGE RATE How much of one currency is worth another. For example, if 1,000 Italian lira is worth one US dollar, that would be the exchange rate.

EXCHANGES Any financial instrument given to a clearing house for collection.

EXCHANGE SEAT Stock exchange membership, with a limited number of seats available.

EX-CLEARING HOUSE When two contra brokers complete a transaction without using a clearing house.

EX-COUPON A stock sold without a coupon.

EX-DIVIDEND Security contract that does not entitle the buyer to the next dividend on the security. The trade is ex-dividend because the settlement date is after the record date that determines the holders who will receive the dividend.

EX-DIVIDEND DATE The first day on which the purchaser of the security is not entitled to the dividend. It is also the day that the price of the security drops to the next highest fraction of the dividend amount.

EXECUTION Filling a buy or sell order, or completing a securities transaction.

EXEMPT SECURITIES Securities such as government and municipal bonds that do not have to be registered or that do not have to comply with some securities laws, such as those governing margin, dealer registration, and reporting requirements.

EXERCISE PRICE The price for which a call holder can buy, or a put holder can sell, the underlying security. See strike price.

EXPIRATION The last day an option can be exercised.

EX-RIGHTS Status of the underlying security on the day after the rights and their accompanying prospectus are distributed to present security holders. On or after that date, the security and the rights trade separately and the buyer of the security from a previous holder will not get the rights.

EXTENDED A rise or fall in a security's price that continues a trend.

F Describes large, rapid, price fluctuations in the commodities market.

FACE AMOUNT The principal amount of money involved in a financial agreement or designated on a financial instrument.

FACE VALUE The amount of money for which a coin, note or other financial instrument can be redeemed in cash, or the amount of money for which a financial instrument can be redeemed for cash at maturity.

FACILITATION ORDER An order for a broker-dealer's proprietary account that is crossed with a customer's order.

FACTOR TABLE A table used to compute the outstanding principal on pass-throughs - Ginnie Maes, Freddie Macs, and Fannie Maes.

FADED Prices that were quoted earlier have been either adjusted down or withdrawn altogether.

FAIL FLOAT The cash balance left after a securities transaction falls through because the security was not delivered by the settlement date.

FAIL POSITION A broker-dealer cannot deliver securities to the buyer because the broker-dealer's client has not delivered the securities to him or her.

FAILS A broker is unable to complete a transaction by the agreed upon settlement date.

FAIL TO DELIVER An overdue agreement in which the seller has not delivered the security to the buyer on settlement date.

FAIL TO RECEIVE An overdue agreement in which the buyer has not paid for a security because the seller has not paid for the security on settlement date.

FAIR MARKET VALUE The price at which a buyer and a seller are willing to exchange an asset. The term is synonymous with the current market value.

FAIR PRICE A regulation that requires a bidder to make the same offer for all shares of the same security he or she purchases during a specific time.

FALL The seller does not deliver the securities to the buyer by the specified delivery date.

FEDERAL AGENCY SECURITY A federally issued debt instrument that has a higher safety rating because it is government sponsored.

FEDERAL FUNDS The amount of money that exceeds the Federal Reserve System's requirement for daily trading by member banks. These funds can be lent out overnight to other member banks.

FEDERAL FUNDS RATE The interest rate charged when one Federal Reserve bank borrows money from another Federal Reserve bank.

FEDERAL HOME LOAN BANK (FHLB) A corporation, sponsored by the US government, that issues bonds, with the proceeds providing mortgages to the home building industry. The bank was established to promote home financing during the Great Depression.

FEDERAL HOME LOAN MORTGAGE CORPORATION (FHLMC) Commonly referred to as Freddie Mac, this government-sponsored company buys conventional residential mortgages from company members, then assures the mortgage and resells it publicly.

FEDERAL NATIONAL MORTGAGE ASSOCIATION (FNMA) Commonly referred to as Fannie Mae, the FNMA is a government-sponsored corporation that buys and sells Farmers Home Administration, Veterans Administration mortgages, and some non-governmentally backed mortgages.

FED WIRE A computer system that connects the Federal Reserve System with its banks and with some dealers in government securities. Banks can use the computer to transfer the ownership of some securities.

FEEDING THE DUCKS An investor sells his or her stock as the stock's price is going up.

FEVERISH MARKET When market prices fluctuate so erratically that no common direction can be detected easily.

FICTITIOUS ORDER A person orders a broker to buy or sell a security, but never intends to honor the contract. The buy or sell is filed only to manipulate prices by making it look like there is a lot of activity in the market.

FIDELITY BOND Insures employees, officers, and partners of broker-dealer firms against misplaced money or misplaced securities, forged checks, forged securities, and fraudulent trading.

FIGURATION The computation of trades in the purchase and sale (P&S) department.

FILL An order to execute a buy or sell for securities.

FILL OR KILL ORDER A broker is ordered to trade an order entirely as soon as it reaches the trading post. If it is not executed immediately, it is canceled automatically.

FINANCIAL FUTURE Futures contract for interest-sensitive securities: T-bills, T-notes, T-bonds, CDs, and GNMA pass-throughs.

FIREWORKS A security's price shoots up quickly.

FIRM The acceptance of an obligation.

FIRM BID A bid that pledges a specific amount of money for a definite number of securities, with the bid binding on acceptance.

FIRM COMMITMENT In a securities offering, the underwriter will assume the risk of selling the entire offering.

FIRMING OF THE MARKET When, after a downturn, the prices of securities stabilize.

FIRM MARKET A nonnegotiable asking or selling price.

FIRM ORDER An investor tells his or her broker to buy or sell a specific quantity of securities at a specific limit price.

FIRM PRICE A broker tells a client that a specific cost for a security is nonnegotiable and will be good only for a limited time.

FIRST IN, FIRST OUT (FIFO) For accounting and tax purposes, inventory and assets are presumed to be sold in the same order in which they were purchased. Therefore, inventory costs begin with the oldest asset, and move forward toward the most recent purchase.

FISCAL YEAR The twelve-month period during which a business maintains its financial records. Since this cycle does not have to coincide with the calendar year, it is known as the fiscal year.

FIVE PERCENT RULE Set by the National Association of Securities Dealers, this is an ethical standard for markup, markdowns, and dealers' commissions on securities transactions.

FIXED ASSET Any asset a company expects to use in its current operations for at least a year.

FIXED CAPITAL The capital that securities investors invest in fixed assets, as opposed to current assets, such as land, buildings, machinery, etc.

FIXED EXCHANGE RATE A narrow range in which the exchange of two countries' currencies must fall when trading on the open market.

FIXED INCOME MARKET A debt-bearing instrument such as money market, a corporate bond or financial future.

FIXED INTEREST RATE An interest rate on a debt instrument that remains the same until the debt is retired.

FIXED LIABILITIES A debt obligation that will mature in a year or more.

FLAT A bond trading without accrued interest is said to be trading flat.

FLAT MARKET A market that is typified by a horizontal price movement because of little or no market activity in the security.

FLEXIBLE REPURCHASE AGREEMENT A long-term contract, with securities as collateral, between a lender and borrower in which the borrower is required to buy the collateral back in the future. During the life of the loan, the principal and interest is adjusted according to current market conditions.

FLOAT The number of shares in the hands of the public; thus, it gives insight into the number of shares available for trading.

FLOATING DEBT Term primarily used in municipal security analysis for debts that will mature within five years.

FLOATING SECURITIES An investor buys a security in his or her broker's name and sells it immediately to make a quick profit.

FLOATING SUPPLY The number of shares of a security that normally is available to be traded.

FLOOR The physical area of an exchange where securities are traded.

FLOOR BROKER A person who executes security or commodity orders, as agent, on the floor of an exchange.

FLOOR BROKERAGE The commission charged by one broker or dealer to another for executions of transactions on exchanges.

FLOOR REPORT After an order has been executed on the exchange floor, the price, number of shares, and the name of the security are confirmed.

FLOOR TICKET Entered by an investor's broker, this contains all the information necessary to complete a buy or sell order.

FLOOR TRADER An exchange member who trades only for his or her own account or for accounts in which he or she holds some financial interest.

FLOWER BOND A Treasury bond that can be redeemed at par value when the owner dies so the proceeds can be used to pay any inheritance taxes.

FLUCTUATION Changes in a security's market price between transactions, with the movements caused by such factors as supply and demand.

FOCUS REPORT Broker-dealers must submit Financial and Operational Combined Uniform Single (FOCUS) reports to self-regulatory organizations monthly and quarterly. The statements must include the firm's earnings, capital, and other trade information as required by rule 17A-5 of the Securities Exchange Commission.

FOREIGN SECURITIES A security issued by a company incorporated outside of the United States which does most of its business outside of the United States.

FORM 3 A document filed with the Securities and Exchange Commission by officers, directors, and holders of 10% or more of equity securities of a company registered with the SEC. The document states beneficial ownership of stock or other security that may be converted into equity securities: rights, warrants, options, or convertibles. The form is available from the SEC.

FORM 4 A document filed with the Securities and Exchange Commission by officers, directors, and holders of 10% or more of equity securities of a company registered with SEC to reflect net changes in security ownership. The document must be filed within 10 days after the end of the month in which the changes occur. The form can be obtained from the SEC.

FORM 8-K A public report that must be filed with the Securities and Exchange Commission by a reporting corporation. The report must be filed in the month following any material event that affects the company's financial situation.

FORM 10-K An annual report, released publicly, that all companies with registered securities must issue. The report must include such information as sales, revenue, and operating income.

FORM 10-Q A quarterly report a company must file with the Securities and Exchange Commission; copies must also be sent to stockholders.

FORWARD EXCHANGE TRANSACTION Buying or selling foreign currencies with the price fixed at a current price, but with delivery to be made later.

FOURTH MARKET When two large institutions execute a securities deal without using a broker.

FRACTIONAL DISCRETION ORDER A broker has the right to buy or sell for a client using the broker's own discretion, up to a certain order or price limit.

FREE BOX Industry slang for a bank vault or other secure location used to store fully paid customer securities. Many broker-dealers use the Depository Trust Company (DTC) as a free box for their customer-owned securities.

FREE RIDE After a person makes a buy order, the stock price goes up and he or she sells the stock before actually paying for the buy order. This illegal practice allows a person to profit without actually risking any money.

FREE RIGHT OF EXCHANGE An investor can change his or her security from bearer to registered, or from registered to bearer, without having to pay a fee.

FREE STOCK Loanable securities, that is, securities that can be used for loan or hypothecation. These securities are firm-owned shares or stock in a margin account that represents the debit balance.

FRONT-ENDING ORDER A broker-dealer agrees to buy part of a block order as long as he or she is allowed to act as the agent for executing the rest of the block.

FROZEN ACCOUNT Any account in which no transactions can be made, usually because the bank or carrier of the account has accused the holder of some rules violation, or because of account discrepancies.

FULL A bond that is trading with accrued interest.

FULL COUPON BOND A debt instrument with a coupon rate higher than the market's current interest rate.

FULL DISCLOSURE All pertinent facts about a security and the issuing company must be revealed when the security is offered for sale as required by the Securities and Exchange Acts of 1933, 1934, and the major stock exchanges.

FULL STOCK Any equity stock that has a par value of $100.

FULLY DILUTED EARNINGS PER SHARE A company's earnings figured as if all of the company's convertible securities had been changed into shares of common stock.

FULLY MODIFIED PASS-THROUGH SECURITIES A debt instrument with fractional claims on a multi-mortgage portfolio, with the issuer distributing guaranteed principal and interest to the holder. If the payments were not guaranteed, the securities would not be fully modified.

FULLY PAID SECURITIES Securities an investor has paid for, or legal issues for which a company has received cash, goods, or services equal to its par value.

FULLY VALUED The point at which a stock has reached a price that accurately reflects its underlying company's actual earning power. If the price goes above this price, it is overvalued, and if it drops below this price, it is undervalued.

FUTURES CONTRACT An agreement to sell or buy a specific amount of a commodity or security at a specific time, with the contract executed on one of the exchanges.

_G_ In newspaper stock listings, this designates earnings in Canadian dollars.

GAIN An investment's realized or unrealized profits.

GAIN ON DISPOSAL Selling an asset, which wasn't expected to be sold or converted to cash, for more than its book value.

GAP A period when a stock's high and low prices do not overlap its high and low prices from the previous day during which no trade was made. This will occur when some extraordinarily positive or negative news is received on a stock or a commodity.

GENERAL ACCOUNT A customer's margin account in which a broker makes equity transactions for that customer.

GENERAL LEDGER A balance sheet that contains all of a company's financial statements, including the offsetting credit and debit accounts.

GENERAL OBLIGATION BOND A municipal bond whose issuer's ability to pay back principal and interest is based only on its full taxing power.

GILT-EDGED Term applied to the security of a corporation that has proved, over time, its ability to pay continuous dividends or interest. It refers more often to high-quality bonds than to stocks.

GINNIE MAE Nickname for the Government National Mortgage Association.

GINNIE MAE MORTGAGE-BACKED SECURITIES Mortgage bank-issued securities backed by Ginnie Mae bonds and protected by the full faith and credit of the government.

GIVE UP When one broker executes an order for another broker's client, they split the commission, but the client does not have to pay anything extra.

GLASS STEAGALL ACT A Federal law that prohibits commercial banks from owning broker-dealer affiliates. Bank holding companies, however, may own such affiliates. The law forbids commercial banks from owning, underwriting, or trading corporate securities for proprietary accounts. The law also forbids banks from underwriting most municipal revenue bonds.

GLUT To oversupply.

GNMA See Government National Mortgage Association.

GOOD DELIVERY A stock certificate that is in good condition, is properly endorsed, and is accompanied by any required legal documents when presented to transfer the stock's ownership from one investor to another.

GOOD FAITH DEPOSIT A deposit required by member firms when a customer, unknown to the firm, enters an order to buy or sell. Usually a good faith deposit is 25%.

GOOD MONEY A common expression for federal funds. Federal funds are called good money because they can be used immediately without going through bank clearance.

GOOD NAME BROKER When a mismatch exists between the buying and selling broker, the Securities Industry Automated Clearing will suggest the name of this contra broker so an easier and quicker settlement can be reached.

GOOD-THIS-MONTH ORDER (GTM) An investor tells his or her broker to buy or sell a specific amount of securities within a specific price limit, with the order expiring at the end of the month.

GOOD THROUGH An investor tells his or her broker to buy or sell a specific amount of securities, usually with a specific price limit, within a predetermined time frame.

GOOD-TILL-CANCELED ORDER (GTC) An investor makes an order to buy or sell a specific number of a particular security, with the order remaining effective until the order is filled or until the investor cancels the order.

GOOD TO THE LAST DROP If a clearing house member fails to transfer the debits and credits from a day's trading, the other clearing house members must make good on the transactions.

GOODWILL An intangible asset between the book value of a company and the price at which the company is purchased. A company can build goodwill when they treat their customers well.

GO SHORT An investor who expects a particular stock's price to drop sells shares of that stock, even though he or she does not actually own the stock.

GOVERNMENT AGENCY SECURITIES Debt securities, such as Ginnie Maes, issued by branches of the US government, but not guaranteed by the government.

GOVERNMENT BILLS US government issued debt securities that mature in a year or less.

GOVERNMENT BOND A 10 year or longer US government-issued debt security that carries the highest rate available.

GOVERNMENT NATIONAL MORTGAGE ASSOCIATION (GNMA) A government corporation that buys Veterans Administration and Federal Housing Administration mortgages, then issues bonds on pools of the mortgages. An investor in such a bond, commonly referred to as a Ginnie Mae, receives monthly dividends through the mortgagee's payments on principal and interest.

GOVERNMENT NOTES Conservative, US government-issued debt securities that trade easily and mature in one to 10 years.

GOVERNMENTS Nickname for US Treasury securities.

GRAVEYARD MARKET A bear market in which investors who sell their shares lose money, and other potential investors stay away from the market altogether. The market is so named because the people who are inside can't get out, and the ones who are outside don't want to get in.

GROSS The total amount of cash or assets before taxes are paid.

GROSS SPREAD The dollar difference between the public offering price of a new issue of securities and the proceeds to the issuer. The gross spread is further subdivided into the manager's fee, the dealer's (or underwriter's) discount, and the selling concession.

GROSS YIELD A discounted bond's yield to maturity before any taxes are paid.

GUN JUMPING (1) The illegal act of soliciting buy orders before an SEC registration is effective. (2) Buying a security based on information that is not yet public.

HAIRCUT A way of computing a broker-dealer's net capital by valuating securities; the manner varies depending on the type of security and its market risk.

HALF STOCK Any stock that has a $50 value.

HARD DOLLAR Payments made by a customer for services such as research and investigations.

HARD SPOT Securities that remain strong in a weak market.

HEAVY A lot of offers to sell a particular security, which will cause its price to drop.

HEAVY MARKET When sell orders exceed buy orders, securities and commodities prices drop.

HEDGE A measure used to offset losses or potential losses. For example, gold and oil often are used as investments to hedge, or offset, inflation.

HICCUP A temporary market drop.

HIDDEN ASSETS A company's assets that are not readily apparent by studying the company's balance sheet.

HIT The dollar amount lost on any particular investment.

HOLDER OF RECORD The person who holds a stock on the close of business on the record date. That person will be entitled to receive the dividends.

HOLDING PERIOD The length of time a person holds on to an investment or a company holds on to an asset.

HOT STOCK (1) Securities that are stolen. (2) Securities that rise rapidly in price on the initial sale date.

HOUSE A broker-dealer company or a firm involved in investment banking.

HOUSE ACCOUNT The account a brokerage firm uses for its own transactions.

HOUSE CALL A broker notifies a customer that the equity in the customer's account has dropped below maintenance level. If the customer fails to bring the account to a higher level, the broker can liquidate the account.

HOUSE RULES A broker-dealer firm's rules regarding how customer accounts should be handled.

HYPOTHECATION Term refers to the pledging of securities or other assets as collateral for a loan while still keeping ownership.

HYPOTHECATION AGREEMENT A client signs this document to open a margin account, pledging securities so that money can be borrowed against those securities.

I Appears in stock listings to indicate that a dividend already has been paid or has been omitted or deferred.

ILLIQUID Used of a security that does not enjoy an active secondary market; thus the holder may find it difficult to sell the security and thereby go back to cash.

IMBALANCE OF ORDERS Market situation in which there is such an excess of either buy or sell orders that no orderly market is possible. If this happens before the opening, the opening of the market will be delayed; if it occurs during the market day, the specialist will suspend trading until sufficient contra orders are obtained to resolve the imbalance.

IMMEDIATE FAMILY Under the National Association of Securities Dealers' (NASD) rules on free riding and withholding, certain sales are prohibited to brokerage employees and each immediate family. Immediate family includes parents, mother- or father-in-law, brothers or sisters, brothers- or sisters-in law, children, and any relative to whose support the prohibited employee contributes.

IMMEDIATE-OR-CANCEL An instruction on an order that requires as many lots as can be filled immediately and the rest canceled.

INACTIVE ACCOUNT A brokerage account in which there has been no activity over a long period of time.

INACTIVE ASSET A brokerage account in which there has been no activity over a long period of time.

INACTIVE MARKET When the market's trading volume drops below its normal level.

IN-AND-OUT TRADER A day trader, who generally keeps no overnight position in a security or commodity and who endeavors to profit from intra-day price fluctuations.

INCOME ACCOUNT Part of a portfolio that is devoted to holding onto money that is available for spending.

INCOME BASIS The amount of interest or dividend dollars compared to the amount the investor paid for a security.

INCOME BONDS Bonds issued when the ability of the issuing company to pay interest is questioned. They are speculative instruments that pay high rates of interest.

INCOME PORTFOLIO Securities designed to provide investors with short-term high income instead of long-term growth.

INCOME STATEMENT A part of a company's annual report that tells how much money the company made or lost in the previous year after all expenses are deducted.

INCONVERTIBILITY When a security or other investment cannot be exchanged for another security or for cash.

INCURRED LOSSES The number of transactions in which a company or an individual has lost money, with the transaction occurring within a specific time period.

INDICATION The price range in which a security can be traded.

INDIRECT EXPENSE Any business expense that is not associated with a particular department or function, such as rent, utilities, insurance, and taxes. Such costs usually are distributed evenly over a company's departments because all of the departments benefit equally from them.

INDUSTRIAL REVENUE BONDS A form of municipal bond whose issuer's ability to pay interest and principal is based on revenue earned from an industrial complex.

INSIDE INFORMATION Information known by a company's directors and officers, but not available to the public. Generally, all facts concern conditions that could affect the price of a company's securities. Trading securities using the advantage of having inside information is illegal.

INSTITUTIONAL INVESTOR Industry term for an investor who, because of the size or frequency of transactions, is eligible for preferential commissions and other special transaction services. The term is often used of banks, mutual funds, insurance companies, and large corporate investment accounts.

INSTRUMENT Any security.

INTERBANK RATE Interest rate at which banks are willing to buy and sell excess reserves among themselves. Similar to the federal funds rate.

INTEREST The amount of money a lender loans a borrower to pay for using the borrower's principal.

INTEREST ACCRUED The amount of interest that has been earned, but not yet paid.

INTEREST BEARING A debt instrument that pays interest instead of dividends.

INTEREST CHARGES The cost of carrying a customer's margin account, including brokerage fees.

INTEREST ON INTEREST Compound interest, which is computed with each forthcoming interest payment based on the principal plus the previous earned interest amount. With simple interest, payments are based only on the principal amount.

INTEREST YIELD The interest rate on a security, computed using the price at which the security was purchased to amortize premiums paid or to accrue discounts received.

INTERNAL AUDIT A department of a company that conducts audits of that same company's financial records.

INTERNAL CONTROL A company's system of maintaining an efficient and well-managed business with protected assets and well-regulated policies.

INVENTORY A balance sheet entry that represents all materials involved in a company's manufacturing processes, including all goods produced as well as all raw materials.

INVESTMENT ASSETS Cash, bonds, stocks, other assets, or other investments that will produce income for the investor or that will appreciate in value.

INVESTMENT BANKER General term for a broker-dealer who assists corporations with the distribution of securities or with other money management or public relations services.

INVESTMENT COMPANY ACT OF 1940 Public legislation that regulates the issuance of investment company securities. The law is administered by the SEC. The act sets standards for the organization, operation, and pricing of investment company securities, their public sale and reporting requirements, and, in many cases, for the allocation of portfolio investments.

INVESTMENT INCOME Any money earned from an investment.

INVESTMENT OBJECTIVE The amount of money an investor expects to realize on an investment. Also, the goals of a portfolio.

INVESTMENT SECURITIES All investments purchased for a portfolio instead of for a quick sale.

_IO_ An interest only bond. See stripped Bond

ISSUE (1) The process by which a new security is brought to market. (2) Any security.

ISSUED AND OUTSTANDING Term used for the number of a corporation's authorized shares that are held by investors, including corporate officers. The term does not include unissued shares and those treasury shares repurchased by the company.

ISSUER A corporation, trust, association, municipality, or government that is legally empowered to distribute its own securities.

JAJO Represents January, April, July, and October, which are the expiration months of successively offered option contracts. It also represents interest and dividend payments that are due quarterly.

JUNIOR SECURITIES A stock or bond that falls subordinate to other claims on the issuer's cash or assets. For example, preferred stock is junior to a debenture, and common stock is junior to preferred stock.

JUNK BOND A speculative bond with a rating of BB or lower from Moody's or Standard & Poor's.

_K_ Follows a number to indicate that the number should be multiplied by 1,000.

KICKER A special feature or added benefit of a security.

KILL To cancel an order.

KIND ARBITRAGE Profitably buying and selling identical securities in the same market at about the same time, with the profit coming from the price differences in separate trading values.

KNOCKED DOWN A price that has been reduced.

KNOW YOUR CUSTOMER An Industry obligation, imposed by the New York Stock Exchange's Rule 405 but equally implied by other industry rules, that requires a brokerage firm and its registered representatives to know the important facts about the customers with whom they do business. The rule requires due diligence because what may be unimportant for one customer may be very important for another.

LAST IN, FIRST OUT (LIFO) A company that lists the production costs of the items most recently added to its inventory first on its inventory balance sheet, as opposed to the first in, first out (fifo) method.

LAST SALE A security's most recent transaction, often used to describe the closing sale on the last trading day.

LATE TAPE Term used if the exchange tape is significantly behind schedule in the reporting of completed transactions.

LEDGER The final bookkeeping entry record which accounts for every type of transaction and has an entry for every transaction within every account.

LEGAL ASSET Any asset a person or company can use to pay a debt. For example, securities would be considered a legal asset.

LEGAL LIST Various states restrict the investments of fiduciaries to specific securities on a list prepared by the state. As a general rule, the securities are specified high-quality debt and equity securities.

LEGAL TRANSFER A type of transfer that requires legal documentation, in addition to the normal forms. Usually, in the name of a deceased person, a trust, or other third party.

LENDING AGREEMENT An investor signs an agreement with his or her broker that allows the broker's firm to lend out securities held in the investor's margin account.

LENDING FLAT When a borrower doesn't pay a fee and a lender doesn't pay interest; typically done when a person borrows securities using cash as collateral.

LENDING SECURITIES The securities a client borrows from his or her broker to make a short sale, with a cash amount equal to the value of the securities.

LEVEL The price at which a security can be bought or sold.

LEVEL 1 SERVICE OF NASDAQ A computer subscription service, available to brokerage firms, that provides the highest and lowest price offers of securities traded through the National Association of Securities Dealers Automated Quotation.

LEVEL 2 SERVICE OF NASDAQ A computer subscription service, available to institutional investors and traders, that provides the names of market makers and their bids on securities traded through the National Association of Securities Dealers Automated Quotation.

LEVEL 3 SERVICE OF NASDAQ A computer subscription service, available to registered market makers, that provides the names of market makers and their bids on securities traded through the National Association of Securities Automated Quotation.

LIABILITY Any debt, both current and potential.

LIBOR See London Interbank Offering Rate.

LIFT A market-average measure of a security's price increase.

LIFO See last in, first out.

LIMIT ORDER An investor tells his or her broker to buy securities or commodities at or below a specific maximum price, or to sell securities or commodities above or at a specific minimum price.

LIMIT-OR-MARKET-ON-CLOSE-ORDER An investor tells his or her broker to buy a specified number of shares of a certain security at a certain price. If the broker cannot execute the order as specified, he or she is to execute it as a market order as close to the specifications as possible and as close to the end of the trading day as possible.

LIMIT PRICE The maximum amount at which a broker can buy a security for a client, or the minimum amount at which a broker can sell a security for a client, with the client determining that amount.

LIMIT SYSTEM A computer network through which subscribers can find out about securities traded on all participating exchanges, and including information such as the specialist, the number involved in the deal, and the bid and offer prices.

LIMIT UP, LIMIT DOWN The most a commodity's price is allowed to move during one trading day.

LIQUID MARKET A market in which securities or commodities are easily bought and sold because of the willingness of interested buyers and sellers to trade large quantities at reasonable prices.

LIQUID SECURITIES Stocks and bonds that are easily converted to cash.

LIQUIDATION (1) Closing out a position. (2) An action taken by the margin department when a client hasn't paid for a purchase.

LIQUIDITY The characteristic of a market that enables investors to buy and sell securities easily.

LISTED OPTION A put or call option that a particular securities exchange has approved for trading.

LISTED SECURITIES Any security that a particular registered exchange has accepted for trading.

LISTING Achieved through meeting all of an exchange's trading requirements and through receiving that exchange's approval for trading.

LISTING AGREEMENT A company and a stock exchange sign such a contract when the company wants its shares listed for trading on that exchange.

LISTING REQUIREMENTS Rules and regulations a security must meet before it can be traded on a particular exchange.

LITTLE BOARD Nickname for the American Stock Exchange, which has the second-largest trading volume of all exchanges. The Big Board is the New York Stock Exchange, which has the largest trading volume.

LOAD The sales charge on the purchase of the shares of some open-end mutual funds.

LOAN VALUE The maximum amount a brokerage firm can lend to a client for buying securities on margin.

LOCKED MARKET When bid and offer prices are the same in a highly competitive market.

LONDON INTERBANK OFFERING RATE (LIBOR) In England's Eurodollar market, this is the interest rate banks charge each other on short-term money.

LONG BOND A bond that doesn't mature for at least 10 years.

LONG MARKET VALUE The daily market value in an investor's margin account, as determined by the value of its long-position securities.

LONG POSITION (1) Denotes ownership of securities. An investor achieves a long position through buying a sec (ownership) before selling because of a increase. (2) In a customer's accou either fully paid for (a cash account) (a margin account). (3) Any position records that has a debit balance.

LONG SALE Any item an investor sells securities he

LONG SIDE A long interest.

LONG-TERM CAPITAL GAINS The amount of money an investor earns by holding on to an investment for more than a year.

LONG-TERM CAPITAL LOSSES The amount of money an investor loses by holding on to an investment for more than a year.

LONG-TERM INVESTMENT An investor buys a security and holds on to it for more than a year because its growth potential is much greater than its short-term profits through a sale would be.

LONG-TERM LIABILITY A debt that falls due in more than a year, but usually indicating an obligation that will last 10 or more years.

LOW The lowest price a security, or the market in general, reached during a specific time period.

M The abbreviation for one thousand; when following a number, it indicates the number is to be multiplied by 1,000. For example, 3M would equal 3,000.

M1 A money supply category consisting of currency in public circulation, credit union share account balances, NOW account balances, automatic transfer balances, demand deposits, and travelers checks.

M2 A money supply category consisting of all money in the M1 category plus Euro dollar deposits, savings and other small deposits, and private holdings in money market mutual funds.

M3 A money supply category consisting of all money in the M1 and M2 categories, plus large deposits and institutional shares in money market mutual funds.

M4 A money supply category consisting of all money in the M1, M2, and M3 categories, plus banker's acceptance, commercial paper, and US savings bonds.

MAINTENANCE The amount of cash and securities an investor has deposited in his or her account to fulfill his or her margin requirements.

MAKE A MARKET The maintaining of firm bid and offer prices on a specific security by always being ready to buy and sell round lots of the security at the prices quoted publicly. The dealer on the over-the-counter market is called the market maker and is called a specialist on the exchanges.

MARKETABILITY Although marketability is synonymous with liquidity on the sell side, on the buy side the term implies that buyers can purchase reasonable amounts of a security without severely raising its market price. Thus, a security has good marketability if it can be easily resold or readily purchased in an active secondary market.

MAKING UP A PRICE A delivered security's price.

MARGIN The amount of money a client deposits with his or her broker and against which the client can borrow when he or she wants to buy securities.

MARGIN DEPARTMENT The operations department responsible for ensuring that customers' accounts are maintained in accordance with margin rules and regulations.

MARGINABLE SECURITIES Securities that can be used for buying on margin.

MARGIN ACCOUNT The brokerage account established for a client who wants to buy securities. The client borrows against the account.

MARGINED SECURITIES Securities an investor buys on credit and holds as collateral in his or her margin account.

MARGIN SECURITY A security a customer can buy or sell in his or her brokerage margin account.

MARKET BREADTH The number of shares of a particular security that are traded during a particular time period. Generally, this term refers to the overall strength and trading volume of the market by such measures as advance/decline figures and volume momentum.

MARKET CYCLE When an increase in price follows a period of lower prices of its outstanding shares of stock.

MARKET MAKER Another term for dealer or specialist. In the interest of maintaining orderly trading, a market maker stands ready to trade against the public and therefore to make a market in an issue.

MARKET ORDER An investor's order to buy or sell a security or commodity at the best price.

MARKET POTENTIAL The amount of a commodity or security that is expected to sell during a specific time period.

MARKET PRICE The last price at which a security or commodity is publicly sold.

MARKET REPORT A verbal or written statement from the exchange floor that a transaction has been executed at a specific price.

MARKET SECURITIES Stocks or bonds that are publicly traded.

MARKET TIMING When economic factors indicate the economy is strong and interest rates are favorable for buying or selling securities.

MARKET VALUE The last price for which a security or commodity was bought or sold.

MARKET VOLUME The number of shares traded in one day on a particular exchange.

MARK TO THE MARKET (1) A securities portfolio is weighted to make sure the investor's margin account complies with his or her margin requirements. A customer may request the excess equity, or the firm may call for the deposit of additional funds. (2) Process by which security position values are brought up to their current market values.

MARK DOWN The amount that a security's selling price is reduced to cover commissions to a market maker in the over-the-counter market. A reduction in the price of an underwriter's municipal bond offering to entice buyers when there is a lack of interest at the original price.

MARK UP The amount a dealer adds to a security's actual price to arrive at the purchase price to cover commissions to the market maker in the over-the-counter market.

MATCHED BOOK A securities dealer's account when his or her borrowing costs equal the interest he or she earned for loaning money to customers and other brokers.

MATCHED ORDERS Purchases and sales of the same security by the same beneficial owner at the same time and price. The purpose is to give the impression of extensive trading in the security. Matched orders, which are usually made through different brokers, are violations of the Securities Exchange Act of 1934.

MATURITY The date on which a loan becomes due and payable - when bonds and other debt instruments must be repaid.

MBS See Mortgage Backed Security.

MCC See Midwest Clearing Corporation.

MEMBER BANK A bank that is a member of the Federal Reserve System.

MEMBER CORPORATION A broker or dealer that is organized as a corporation and that has at least one director-holder of voting stock who is a member of an organized stock exchange.

MEMBER FIRM A brokerage firm or a company that is a member of an organized stock exchange.

MERGER The combination of two or more companies into one through the exchange of stock.

MIDWEST CLEARING CORPORATION (MCC) The clearing corporation of the Midwest Stock Exchange.

MINIMUM 'INTENANCE Established by the exchanges' margin rules, the level to which the equity in an account may fall before the client must deposit additional equity. It is expressed as a percentage relationship between debit balance and equity or between market value and equity.

MINIMUM VARIATION One-eighth of a point in securities transactions, [illegible]/32 of a point in transactions of bonds and government notes.

MINUS TICK Industry jargon for any transaction price that is lower than the previous transaction price. For example, if the previous sale was 20 and the next sale is 19 7/8, the sale is said to be on a minus tick.

MISCELLANEOUS LIABILITIES A bookkeeping entry that represent liabilities for which payments, for tax or legal reasons, have not been determined yet.

MISSING THE MARKET Term describing the fact that an agent failed to execute a transaction at a price that was available, and that the subsequent transaction was disadvantageous to the customer. In this case, the agent must make up the amount lost by the client.

MIXED ACCOUNT A margin account that holds both long and short positions in the securities market.

MM The abbreviation for one million; when following a number, it indicates the number is to be multiplied by 1,000,000. For example, 3MM would equal 3,000,000.

MO Follows some newspaper stock listings to indicate the stock is listed and traded on the Montreal stock Exchange.

MONEY MARKET An international market for dealers who trade short-term government and corporate financial instruments such as banker's acceptance, commercial paper, negotiable certificates of deposit, or Treasury bills.

MONEY MARKET SECURITIES High quality securities with market prices that are tied more closely to the prevailing interest rates than to the underlying company's general economic health.

MORTGAGE BACKED SECURITY (MBS) A debt instrument with a pool of real estate loans as the underlying collateral.

MORTGAGE BOND A debt instrument issued by a corporation and secured by real estate owned by the corporation such as factories or office buildings.

MORTGAGE PARTICIPATION CERTIFICATE A mortgage purchased by the Federal Home Loan Mortgage Association and resold as a pass-through security. The security represents an undivided interest in a mortgage pool.

MORTGAGE PASS-THROUGH SECURITIES A pool of residential mortgage loans, with the interest and principal distributed to the investor each month.

MUNICIPAL BOND A long-term debt instrument issued by a state or local government. It usually carries a fixed rate of interest, which is paid semi-annually. The interest on these instruments is exempt from Federal taxation. However, if issued in the bondholder's state of residence, the instruments will also be exempt from state and local taxes.

MUTUAL FUND An investment company that puts investors' money in a variety of areas, usually securities, and that must redeem the shares at net asset value upon demand.

N Used in stock listings to designate that a security's primary market is the New York Stock Exchange.

NAKED POSITION A long or short position the holder has not hedged as prices fluctuate. The write of a call option, for example, is naked if the investor doesn't own the underlying security, and is partially hedged if he or she does own the underlying security because the potential risk is much greater if the price rises.

NARROW MARKET Occurs when securities are traded with little difference between the bid and asked prices.

NARROWING THE SPREAD Action by a broker-dealer or a specialist whereby he bids higher or offers lower than the previous bid or offer, thus narrowing the spread between bids and offers. Also called closing a market.

NASD See National Association of Securities Dealers.

NASDAQ See National Association of Securities Dealers Automated Quotations.

NATIONAL ASSOCIATION OF SECURITIES DEALERS (NASD) An organization of brokers and dealers who trade securities in the United States. Supervised by the Securities and Exchange Commission, the NASD regulates all over-the-counter brokers and dealers.

NATIONAL ASSOCIATION OF SECURITIES DEALERS FIVE PERCENT POLICY A non-binding NASD recommendation that brokerage commissions, markups, and markdowns should be near five percent on most transactions. NASD members do not need to adhere to this policy when executing small transactions, transactions that are difficult to complete, or mutual fund transactions.

NATIONAL ASSOCIATION OF SECURITIES DEALERS RULES OF FAIR PRACTICE NASD regulations that cover the ethics of brokers and dealers to make sure that they all deal fairly with their customers.

NATIONAL QUOTATION SERVICE (NQS) A National Quotation Bureau system that lists corporate bonds, over-the-counter securities, their market makers, and bid and ask prices. The NQS reports on those OTC stocks that are not quoted by the National Association of Securities Dealers Automated Quotation system.

NATIONAL SECURITIES CLEARING CORPORATION An independent clearing organization that member firms use to execute transactions with other member firms.

NATIONAL SECURITIES EXCHANGE Any securities exchange that has been registered with the Securities and Exchange Commission.

NATIONAL SECURITIES TRADE ASSOCIATION An organization of over-the-counter brokers and dealers. Among other activities, the association provides lobbying services on behalf of brokers and dealers.

NATURAL SELLER An investor who is selling a security he or she actually has in his or her portfolio.

NC Abbreviation for non-callable. Often used on bond offering sheets to designate bonds that are non-callable. See non-callable.

NEAR MONEY A debt instrument such as a bond that is near its redemption or maturity date.

NEGOTIABLE (1) Any instrument that is readily transferable, (2) a security in registered format that has an assignment and power of substitution signed by the registered owner, either on the certificate or on an accompanying stock or bond power, and (3) a price that is not firm and thus is subject to further clarification and discussion.

NET ASSETS The difference between a company's assets and its liabilities.

NET ASSET VALUE Determined by subtracting the liabilities from the portfolio value of a fund's securities, and dividing that figure by the number of outstanding shares.

NET BALANCE The amount that falls due after any refunds have been subtracted.

NET-BY-NET Originated at the Pacific Clearing Corporation (PCC), a method of merging fail positions into settling trades. This process greatly reduced the number of fails open on firms' books.

NET CAPITAL (1) A company's net worth minus assets that cannot be sold at their full value. (2) Net worth of a broker or dealer less certain items such as exchange memberships, carrying value of securities which are not readily marketable, "haircuts" on marketable securities in proprietary accounts, and furniture and equipment as defined in the net capital rules.

NET CAPITAL REQUIREMENT A securities and Exchange Commission regulation that outlines the net capital ratio, which is the aggregate, customer related indebtedness along with cash and other assets that an be converted easily into cash.

NET CHANGE The difference between a security's current price and the price at which it closed after the last trading session.

NET CURRENT ASSETS The amount by which a company's current assets exceed its current liabilities.

NET DOWN Occurs when a taxpayer offsets short-term gains with short-term losses, and long-term gains with long-term losses to reach a final figure in both columns. If the investor ends up with a net loss in one column and a net gain in the other, he or she must offset the gains and losses again.

NET INCOME The profit after all expenses have been deducted.

NET OPERATING INCOME A company's net operating income after minority interest and taxes are subtracted and before investment profits and losses and preferred dividend payments are added and subtracted.

NET PROCEEDS The amount of money an investor receives from selling a security, with the cost of completing the sale subtracted.

NET PROFIT Earnings after all debts, expenses, and taxes have been deducted.

NET TRANSACTION When the buyer and the seller of a security are charged no additional fee in the transaction.

NET WORTH The dollar value by which assets exceed liabilities. Also called stockholders' equity when used on corporate balance sheets.

NEW ACCOUNT REPORT A document required to be prepared, maintained, and updated by all broker-dealers who conduct business with customers. The new account form must contain essential information about the customer: the background, financial circumstances, and investment objectives of the customer.

NEW HIGH A security has reached its highest price during a given time period.

NEW HIGHS A group of securities has reached its highest price in a year.

NEW ISSUE A security publicly offered for sale for the first time.

NEW LOW A security has reached its lowest price during a given time period.

NEW LOWS A group of securities has reached its lowest price in a year.

NEWS TICKER A brokerage house machine that provides business news that could have an effect on securities prices.

NEW YORK FUTURES EXCHANGE (NYFE) A commodities market located at 30 Broad Street, New York, New York, specializing in index futures.

NEW YORK STOCK EXCHANGE (NYSE) The largest stock exchange in the United States, with over 1,500 security listings.

NEW YORK STOCK EXCHANGE AVERAGES A composite market indicator that profiles the general market condition through the prices of 25 industrial and railroad stocks.

NEW YORK STOCK EXCHANGE COMPOSITE INDEX A gauge which averages the trading prices of all of the common shares of companies listed on the New York Stock Exchange. The four subgroup indexes are the financials, industrials, transportations, and utilities.

NEW YORK STOCK EXCHANGE VOLUME All shares traded on the New York Stock Exchange in one day.

1933 ACT See Truth in Security Act and Securities Act of 1933.

1934 ACT See Securities Act of 1934.

NO-LIMIT ORDER An investor's request to have his or her broker buy security with no price restrictions.

NO-LOAD MUTUAL FUND A mutual fund that carries no sales charge.

NOMINAL A security's face value.

NONCALLABLE A security that cannot be redeemed before it matures.

NONCLEARING HOUSE STOCK Any securities that have not been cleared through the New York Stock Exchange Clearing Corporation. Over-the-counter securities are considered nonclearing house securities.

NONCLEARING MEMBER A member of the National Association of Securities Dealers or a member of a securities exchange who does not maintain his or her own operations. Such a person pays another member a fee to use his or her operations to execute settlements.

NONCURRENT ASSET Any asset that will not be sold, converted to cash or transferred within a company's normal cycle, which usually lasts one year. Fixed assets, intangible assets, and leasehold improvements all are considered noncurrent assets.

NONCURRENT LIABILITIES	A claim that will not fall due for one year or more.
NONINTEREST-BEARING BOND	A discounted bond or note that earns no interest, but is redeemable at its face value at maturity.
NONMARKETABLE SECURITIES	Securities that are difficult to sell for some specific reason, e.g., their lack of secondary trading market.
NONPUBLIC INFORMATION	Any information about a company that could cause the company's stock to go up or down in price if it were released publicly. Corporate officers who are privy to nonpublic information cannot legally trade shares using the information because doing so would give them an unfair advantage over other investors.
NO PAR VALUE	A security that has no face value.
NORMAL BETA	The desired portfolio risk.
NORMAL TRADING UNIT	The minimum number of security shares that can be bought or sold. When fewer are involved in a transaction they are considered odd lots.
NOT A DELIVERY	When a document or instrument is invalid because it does not meet the necessary requirements to complete the transaction.
NOT HELD	An indication on an order that the execution does not depend on time; the broker or trader should take whatever time is necessary to ensure a good execution.
NOT RATED	Indicates that a recognized rating service has not rated a particular security.
NOT SUBJECT TO CALL	A bond or note that cannot be redeemed before maturity.
NYSE	See New York Stock Exchange.
O	In newspaper stock listings, this indicates that the security is traded over the counter (OTC).
OBLIGATION	Any legal debt.
OCC	See Options Clearing Corporation.
ODD LOT	A quantity of stock that amounts to less than 100 shares. A deal involving 100 shares or more is considered a round-lot transaction.
OFF BALANCE SHEET FINANCING	A system of financing that is not clearly defined, described, or displayed on a company's balance sheet.
OFFER	(1) To present for sale. (2) The price at which someone is willing to sell a security. Also called asked price.
OFFERED DOWN	Securities sold at prices that are lower than the last price quote or the last transaction involving the same securities.
OFFERING	A security that is being presented for sale.
OFFERING DATE	The first day a security is publicly offered for sale.

OFFERING SALE The prices or yields to maturity at which an underwriter offers the different maturities of a serial bond issue.

OFFER WANTED A term used by a dealer who wants another dealer to make an offer on a particular security.

OFF-FLOOR ORDER An order made off of the New York Stock Exchange floor, usually taking precedence over orders made on the floor.

OFFICE OF SUPERVISORY JURISDICTION A department or office that oversees National Association of Securities Dealers members to make sure that the members follows NASD procedures. Every NASD member must have at least one office of supervisory jurisdiction at its firm.

OFFSHORE Describes a financial institution, organization, or fund outside of the United States that is not restricted by US securities laws unless its securities are sold in the United States.

OFF THE CURVE Describes a corporate debt security when the Treasury yield curve is used as a benchmark in the corporate debt security's pricing.

OFF-THE-RUN ISSUE An equity security that is inactively traded and that attracts little interest.

ON BALANCE The difference between the quantity of securities involved in offsetting sales and purchases. For example, if a person sold 3,000 shares of a security, then bought 4,000 shares of the same security, he or she bought 1,000 shares on balance.

ON BALANCE VOLUME The net of volumes of transactions executed at price increases and transactions executed at price decreases. When the former is higher, the net is considered positive.

ONE CANCELS THE OTHER An alternative order in which the client wants one of two orders executed. When one order is executed, the other automatically is canceled.

ONE-MAN PICTURE A price quote from only one market maker.

ONE PERCENT BROKER A broker who charges a fee to arrange the borrowing and lending of securities between dealers and institutional investors. The fee is 1 percent of the interest rate the lender pays to use the cash collateral.

ON MARGIN Securities an investor buys when he or she has borrowed at least part of the purchase price from his or her broker.

ON THE MONEY When the strike price in a put or call option equals the price of the underlying security.

OPD A stock symbol used to indicate a security's opening transaction when that transaction is at a price that went up or down substantially from the previous closing price. OPD also can indicate the first transaction of the day following a delayed opening.

OPENING BLOCK A security's first transaction during a particular trading session.

OPENING PRICE The price of a security at its first transaction during a particular trading session.

OPENING PURCHASE The transaction that creates or increases an investor's long position in an option trade.

OPENING RANGE The difference between the highest and the lowest opening prices of a particular commodity; often, a commodity will have several opening and closing prices during one trading session. Orders can be filled within this range at any time during that trading session.

OPENING ROTATION The trading rotation in which the price and volume of buy and sell orders are in balance.

OPENING SALE The transaction that creates an investor's short position in an option trade.

OPEN MARKET OPERATION The market through which the Federal Reserve System publicly buys and sells government securities to expand or contract the credit supply.

OPEN ORDER Any unexecuted order to buy or sell securities that has not been canceled; a good-till-canceled order.

OPEN TRADE A deal that has not been closed or canceled.

OPERATING ASSET Any asset involved in a company's operations that directly and regularly creates income for a company. Stocks and real estate, while creating some income, are not considered operating assets because they do not produce income regularly, and they are not directly related to the company's production or operations.

OPERATING CAPITAL Money a company uses to pay for its daily operations.

OPERATING INCOME The total amount of money a company makes through its earning assets and services.

OPERATING LOSSES Any loss a company incurs during its normal operations.

OPERATING PROFIT Any profit a company makes through its normal operations.

OPERATING RESERVES A company's balance sheet accounts that represent the net accumulated balances for amortization, damages, injuries, pensions, and insurance.

OPERATING STATEMENT A financial statement that includes the company's net costs, expenses, profits, and sales during a specific time period.

OPERATIONS A broker-dealer's functions in clearing, executing, settling, and recording his or her customer's transactions.

OPTION A contract that provides the right, but not the obligation, to buy or sell a specific amount of a specific security within a predetermined time period. One call option contract gives the buyer the right to purchase, or a put buyer to sell, 100 shares of the underlying stock in exchange for a premium based on the time value. The one selling the contracts is called the writer.

OPTIONS CLEARING CORPORATION (OCC) A clearing corporation owned jointly by the exchanges dealing in listed options. OCC is the central or main clearing corporation for listed options. Options traded on any SEC-regulated exchange can be settled through OCC.

OR BETTER An investor's limit order to buy or sell at the price indicated or at a better price, if possible.

ORDER A customer's instructions to his or her broker for buying or selling a security. Such an order may specify price, time limits, or quantity.

ORDER CONFIRMATION TRANSACTION Permits members of the National Association of Securities Dealers to negotiate over-the-counter option transactions for more than three contracts while using the National Association of Securities Dealers Automated Quotations Options Automated Execution System, which normally limits the number of permitted contacts to three.

ORDER DEPARTMENT The broker-dealer's office that routes buy and sell instructions to the trading floors of different exchanges and executes over-the-counter transactions.

ORDER GOOD UNTIL A SPECIFIED TIME A market order or a limit order that a broker will hold in the trading crowd or will execute until a specific time, after which any unexecuted portion will be canceled.

ORDER TICKET A document that provides a customer's directions to the registered representative concerning each specific securities transaction.

ORDINARY ASSET An asset a company regularly buys and sells as part of its business. For example, real estate would represent an ordinary asset to a real estate broker.

ORDINARY DISCOUNT The difference between an item's current value, with an assumed interest rate that will accumulate to the value at maturity, and the item's value at maturity.

ORDINARY GAIN The amount of money a company will make selling an asset that is not a capital asset.

ORDINARY INCOME Any and all income except that earned from capital gains.

ORDINARY INTEREST Simple interest based on a 360-day year. The difference when figuring ordinary interest and exact interest, which is based on a 365-day year, can be substantial when a large sum of money is involved.

ORDINARY STOCK Common stock or equity stock.

ORGANIZED EXCHANGE The place where securities or commodities are bought and sold according to a prescribed set of rules and regulations.

ORGANIZED MARKET An organization of traders that operates under a specific set of rules and regulations and, using those guidelines, trades in commodities or securities.

ORIGINAL COST All costs that were incurred when buying an asset.

ORIGINAL MARGIN The amount of money a brokerage customer is supposed to have when beginning a transaction.

OTC See over-the-counter.

OTHER INCOME Appears on a profit and loss statement to indicate income received from sources that would not normally be income sources. Other income can indicate a one-time profit, or income received infrequently.

OTHER LOANS FOR PURCHASING OR CARRYING SECURITIES The loan one broker will make to another broker for buying or carrying securities.

OTHER LONG TERM DEBT A long term debt that is neither a mortgage bond nor a debenture Serial note, for example, would be classified as "other long-term debts."

OUTBID To offer a securities seller a higher price than any other bidder.

OUTSIDE BROKER A trader who deals in unlisted stocks and who is not a stock exchange member.

OUTSIDE SECURITY A security that is not listed on one of the major exchanges in the issuing company's region.

OUTSTANDING Any instrument that has not been redeemed, paid, or canceled, or any stock issued to shareholders.

OUTSTANDING STOCK All of a company's ownership shares of stock that have been publicly purchased or that are owned by the company's officers. Shares that the company has repurchased are not considered outstanding stock.

OVERALLOTING Offering a security for sale publicly when more shares are confirmed than are available because the issuer mistakenly believed that some investors would not confirm their orders.

OVERBOUGHT Occurs when speculative buying pushes a security's bid price unreasonably high.

OVERHANG A large block of securities or commodities contracts that would push prices down if released into the market.

OVERNIGHT POSITION A broker-dealer's description of his or her securities inventory at the end of a trading day. The securities in inventory represent the broker-dealer's overnight long position in those securities.

OVERSOLD Occurs when, during heavy selling, a security's price is higher than the established downside trend. Because the price is extended, an upward movement probably will occur.

OVERSOLD MARKET This occurs when speculative long interest drops sharply, and the speculative short interest subsequently increases. Usually, the market increases again quickly following an oversold market.

OVERSPECULATION Occurs when speculators cause the market activity to be unusually heavy.

OVERSTAY THE MARKET Describes a person who has held on to a long position for too long and subsequently will suffer a financial loss.

OVERSUBSCRIBED Occurs when investors want to buy more shares of a new security than will be available. When this happens, the price of the security immediately goes up.

OVER THE COUNTER The market for securities that are not listed on one of the major exchanges. The National Association for Securities Dealers Automated Quotations provides prices for over-the-counter securities.

OVERTRADING A dealer, who also is an underwriter, offers to pay more for a security than it is worth if the customer agrees to buy a portion of a new issue.

OVERVALUED Describes a security with a current market price that is too high (considering the company's earnings, history, and price-earnings ratio). A security that is overvalued probably will drop in price.

P As lower case appears in newspaper stock listings to designate a put option, as upper case, used in the newspaper listings of corporate earnings to designate that the principal market for the security is the Philadelphia Stock Exchange.

PAID-IN-CAPITAL The amount above par value that a company received for selling its stock.

PAID-IN-SURPLUS A company's balance sheet entry of the difference between the dollar value actually received from issued shares and the shares' par value.

PAID-UP CAPITAL The total of the par value of a company's stock and the given value of its no-par securities for which the company receives full consideration.

PAID-UP-STOCK Capital stock that the buyer has paid for in cash, goods, or services in an amount that equals or is greater than the stock's par value.

PAINTING THE TAPE A form of manipulation in which a broker illegally enters matched orders to create the false impression of an active market and heavy trading in a particular security.

P & L An abbreviation for a profit and loss statement, which is a financial statement issued by a corporation to reflect its gross income and expenses and thus its profits or losses.

P & S General industry term for the purchase and sale function of a broker-dealer. Although the function may include other aspects of the operations area, P & S normally is responsible for comparing and reconciling the terms of completed transactions to facilitate securities and money settlements.

PAPER Short-term notes such as corporate commercial paper.

PAPER INVESTMENT A paper claim, or a promise backed investment.

PAPERLESS Proof that a person owns a security electronically, even though the owner does not physically hold a certificate.

PAPER LOSS The loss an investor would incur if he or she sold a security or closed his or her position, but that is unrealized because he or she holds on to the security.

PAPER PROFIT The profit an investor would make if he or she sold a security or closed his or her position, but that is unrealized because he or she holds on to the security.

PAPER TITLE Although not a proper title, a paper title is written verification that proves ownership of a security.

PAR Any security whose market value is equivalent to its face value at the time of redemption. A bond with a face value of $1,000 is at par when it is selling for $1,000.

PAR BOND A bond with a current market value that is equal to its redemption value.

PAR ITEM Any instrument that can be redeemed for its par or face value on demand.

PARITY Price or value equality. For example, if a bond is convertible into 100 shares of common stock, with the stock's market price at $5 per share, the bond, to be selling at parity, would have a value of $500.

PARKING An investor will put money into a safe investment to protect it while looking into other investments.

PARTIAL DELIVERY A delivery against a contract sale with the delivery amount less than the contract's total amount.

PARTIALLY PAID BONDS The initial public offering of a dollar-denominated bond sold to a foreign investor when that investor pays 20 to 30 percent of the purchase price immediately and the balance at a specified future date.

PARTICIPATE BUT DO NOT INITIATE Instruction given on some very large orders to buy or sell. The instruction says, in effect, buy or sell, but do not initiate a new price - let the market forces create the new price.

PARTICIPATING CERTIFICATE A document that verified partial ownership in a stock.

PARTICIPATION CERTIFICATE A security that reflects an undivided interest in a mortgage pool.

PARTLY PAID Stocks held in an investor's margin account.

PAR VALUE The stated amount of a bond. If the bond sold above the stated amount, it would be selling at a premium; if it sold below that amount, it would be selling at a discount. The par value for a stock share would be the stock certificate's face value.

PASS-THROUGH SECURITY A debt instrument strategy that reflects an interest in a mortgage pool, with monthly payments divided between the interest on the unpaid principal balance and the repayment of principal.

PAY A bond's currency denomination.

PAY-DOWN (1) Used of a refunding of one debt by another if the new debt is smaller than the originally outstanding debt. (2) Used of Ginnie Mae modified pass-throughs pools if the experienced reduction in the unpaid principal balance is greater than the anticipated reduction.

PAYMENT DATE Date on which a cash payment, either dividend or interest, will be made by an issuer.

PAY UP An investor pays an above-the-market price for a security that he or she believes is a wise investment.

PEAK The highest point a security or a market indicator reaches during a specific time period. Prices will begin to drop after reaching a peak.

PEGGING A security's offer price is maintained by a bid that is slightly below that price.

PEGGING THE MARKET An illegal form of manipulation in which an underwriting syndicate sets up a fund to stabilize the stock's price by fixing a bid at the offering price during the offering's initial stages.

PENNANT A security's chart pattern that forms a triangle, or pennant. Usually, this indicates that the security's price either will rise or fall as the apex is reached.

PENNY STOCK A low-priced share of stock that is usually traded for less than $1 a share. These stocks are normally issued by speculative companies with a short or erratic revenue and earnings history.

PERCENTAGE ORDER A customer's order to his or her broker to buy or sell a specific number of shares after a particular number of the same shares have been traded in one trading day.

PERMANENT ASSET A fixed asset.

PERPETUAL INVENTORY A company's accounting system in which the on-hand inventory continuously is reflected in the book inventory through a daily record of physical inventory and the dollar amounts, each of which is periodically reconciled.

PER SHARE NET The number of outstanding shares divided into the company's earnings after it has paid taxes.

PERSONAL FINANCIAL STATEMENT An individual's account of obligations and income sources.

PETTY CASH Money set aside, in a cash or a bank deposit, to be used as change for small transactions.

PICTURE The prices at which a dealer will trade.

PINCH A quick rise in prices.

PITI The abbreviation for principal, interest, taxes and insurance.

PIVOTAL STOCK A stock that does or can influence the market activity of other stocks.

PLACEMENT Securities distribution, either public or private.

PLEDGED SECURITIES Securities used as collateral for long- or short-term debt.

PLUNGE A quick, sudden drop in the market or a security's price.

PLUNK DOWN To pay for in cash.

PLUS Follows a security's price quote to indicate a point fraction in 64ths.

PLUS TICK Expression signifying that a transaction in a listed security occurred at a higher price than the previous regular-way transaction in that security. Thus, 74+ means that the prior regular-way transaction in the security was at 73 7/8 or below.

PO A principal only bond. See stripped bond.

POINT Used to quote securities prices. One point for a stock equals $1; for a bond, one point equals $10 assuming a $1,000 par value.

POINT AND FIGURE CHART A measure of price changes and the direction of the changes without any consideration for volume or time.

POOL A group of debt instruments, with another security representing an undivided interest.

PORTFOLIO Either a combination of assets, or all of a person's investments.

PORTFOLIO BETA SCORE A portfolio's volatility, determined by the beta coefficients of its securities, with beta 1 reflecting the same volatility as the general market. A higher beta would reflect securities that are more volatile, and a beta of less than 1 would be less volatile than the general market.

POSITION The nature of investment account holdings. For example, an investor who owns securities has a long position in those securities, and an investor who sells short, which is selling securities he or she doesn't own in anticipation of buying them back at a lower price, holds a short position.

POSITION BID A broker's bid when that broker wants to buy a large block of securities for his or her own account to accommodate an institutional client.

POSITION BUILDING The establishment of net long or net short positions for a portfolio, which cuts down on the number of securities the account executive must follow while increasing the risks.

POSITION LIMITS An options exchange regulation that prohibits investors from holding 2,000 or more put or call contracts against the same underlying security on the same side of the market.

POSITION OFFER A broker's offer when that broker wants to sell a large block of securities for his or her own account to accommodate an institutional client.

POSITION TRADER A commodities broker who tries to achieve long-term profits by taking only calculated risks and by dealing in contracts that have durations of six months or longer.

POSITIVE YIELD CURVE A graph that displays the relationship between the maturities and yields of securities with the same issuer or with similar credit ratings. When the graph has a positive yield curve, the longer-term securities have higher yields than the shorter-term securities.

POST 30 A special New York Stock Exchange trading post for transactions involving inactive stocks and round lots of fewer than 100 shares.

PRECAUTIONARY LIQUIDITY BALANCE The cash, securities, or other assets that an investor holds onto and uses only in case of an emergency.

PRECEDENCE broker's right to buy a security before other brokers, even though the other brokers could complete the transaction. A broker is given precedence based on the time of his bid and the size of that bid.

PRECEDENCE OF ORDER One security's priority over another security when buy or sell orders are received.

PREFERRED STOCK Stock shares that represent a portion of ownership in a company, with the shares normally carrying fixed dividends and voting rights.

PREMIUM The amount for which a security is selling above its par value.

PREMIUM BOND A bond that is selling at a price that is higher than its face value. The amount the price exceeds the bond's face value is the premium.

PREMIUM FOR RISK An investment's yield after subtracting its basic, prevailing yield at the time.

PREMIUM ON BOND The percentage over a bond's face value for which it can be bought, sold or redeemed.

PREMIUM ON CAPITAL STOCK The amount over a stock's cash value for which it can be bought or sold.

PREMIUM ON SECURITIES The amount over a security's value for which it can be bought or sold.

PREMIUM OVER BOND VALUE The difference between a convertible bond's market value and the general market price of a regular bond from the same issuer.

PREMIUM OVER CONVERSION VALUE The difference between the market price of a convertible stock or bond and the price at which it can be converted.

PREMIUM STOCK A stock that generates profits at a greater rate than that displayed by the general market.

PREPAID EXPENSES A balance sheet entry that includes items that normally must be paid in advance.

PREPAYMENT When a brokerage firm pays a selling client for a security before the transaction's predetermined settlement date.

PRESENT VALUE The discounted value of an amount that will be payable at a specific future date.

PRESOLD ISSUE	An issue of government or municipal securities that has been sold even before the coupon rate or price has been announced.
PRETAX EARNINGS	A company's net income before federal taxes have been subtracted.
PRETAX RATE OF RETURN	A security's yield before taxes have been subtracted.
PRICE ALERT	Occurs when a security's price pushes above or below a previous resistance level and exceeds its previous high or low point during a specific time period. A strength or weakness in the market can be measured by totaling all stocks that have upside or downside breakouts.
PRICE AVERAGING	Buying several equal amounts of a security at different prices to achieve a better overall price per share. For example, if an investor bought 100 shares of a stock at $10 a share, then bought 100 shares at $16 a share, and then bought 100 shares at $20 a share, the overall price per share would be $15.33, while the stock's price continued to climb.
PRICE CHANGE	The net rise or drop in a security's market price.
PRICED OUT OF THE MARKET	Occurs when an item is priced so high that no one will buy it, which ultimately leads to a drop in sales.
PRICE GAP	Occurs when a security's price range in one day does not overlap its price range from the day before.
PRICE POTENTIAL	A technical, analytical estimate of a security's future market value.
PRICE RANGE	The prices that fall between a security's highest and lowest prices during a specific time period.
PRICE SPREAD	The difference between a security's bid and ask prices.
PRICE TAKER	An investor whose securities transactions are so small that they have no impact on the market.
PRICE-VOLUME ALERT	A price breakout combined with a volume breakout. A breakout occurs when a security's price pushes above or below a previous resistance level.
PRICEY	An underpriced bid or overpriced offer.
PRIMARY DEALER	A group of dealers and banks that can buy and sell government securities while working directly with the Federal Reserve Bank of New York.
PRIMARY DISTRIBUTION	The first time a new securities issue is offered publicly for sale. The primary distribution usually involves an investment banker selling the issue as an over-the-counter security.
PRIMARY EARNINGS	A company's net income after taxes and preferred dividends, divided by the number of common shares the company has outstanding.

PRIMARY MARKET The market in which investment bankers first sell newly issued securities to investors.

PRIMARY OFFERING The first time a company publicly sells its stock.

PRIMARY TREND A market trend or price movement that lasts for a long period of time, sometimes as long as several years.

PRIME PAPER Commercial paper that Moody's Investors Services has given a rating of P, with the rating broken into three categories: P-3 is high quality, P-2 is higher, and P-1 is the highest quality.

PRIME RATE A preferential rate of interest on short-term loans granted by commercial banks to their most credit-worthy customers. Theoretically, it is the lowest rate of interest for bank loans that are not backed by items of value pledged as collateral.

PRINCIPAL The client for whom a broker makes an investment. Also the basic amount of money invested, or the balance of an obligation.

PRINCIPAL AMOUNT A debt security's par value, or a loan's face amount.

PRINCIPAL SUM The same as "principal", or the total amount of a financial obligation, such as loan, less interest.

PRINT The exchange-tape record of securities transactions.

PRIORITY The first broker to make the highest bid or the lowest offer. Because the broker has priority, he or she always receives at least partial execution of the order.

PRIVATE SECTOR PASS-THROUGH A bank-issued, non-government, mortgage-backed security that sometimes is privately guaranteed.

PROCEEDS The profit a seller receives for selling assets. The amount of the proceeds is calculated by subtracting all fees and commissions from the total sale price.

PROCEEDS SALE Securities sold in the secondary market, with proceeds from the sale used to buy securities in the secondary market.

PROFESSIONAL A person who buys and sells securities for a living.

PROFIT AND LOSS ACCOUNT An account transferred from the accounts receivable to a different account and subtracted from the accounts receivable balance because it is considered uncollectable.

PROFIT AND LOSS RESERVE An amount of money a company sets aside to take care of uncollectable accounts.

PROFIT AND LOSS STATEMENT A company's accounting statement that shows net profits, losses, income sources, and expenses.

PROFIT AND LOSS SUMMARY ACCOUNT A company's account of all income and expenses, transferred to this summary ledger at the end of the company's fiscal year.

PROFIT MARGIN A company divides its net sales into its net income to measure, through a percentage figure, its profitability.

PROFIT-TAKING Describes when a stock is being sold for capital gains.

PRO FORMA A financial statement reflecting the company's financial condition using hypothetical data to determine the effects of an idea that has been proposed, but not yet consummated.

PROPERTY CAPITAL Ownership of debts or securities.

PROPRIETARY ACCOUNT An account that reflects the company's actual financial condition by providing such numbers as the exact inventory count, the dollar amount of earnings, and the dollar amount of the company's reserves.

PRO RATA A method of equally and proportionately allocating money, profits or liabilities by percentage. For example, if a gas company is found to have overcharged consumers and is subsequently forced to pay rebates, each consumer would get an amount proportionate to the amount he or she overpaid in the first place.

PROSPECT Any potential business customer or potential investor.

PROSPECTUS A document the Securities and Exchange Commission requires a company that is newly issuing securities to provide to prospective investors. The prospectus includes such information as the financial background of the company or the company's officers, and the company's investment potential.

PROXY DEPARTMENT The area of a brokerage firm that distributes financial statements, voting information, and other corporate publications to beneficial owners. The department acts as an intermediary between the issuing company and the beneficial owners, and votes on behalf of those owners.

PUBLICLY HELD A company with stock shares owned by a large number of people.

PUBLIC MARKET A securities market with relevant information publicly available.

PUBLIC OFFERING A company offers a large number of its shares to the general public for sale.

PUBLIC OFFERING PRICE A company's asking price for its securities during the first public sale.

PUBLIC SECURITIES ASSOCIATION A trade association representing banks, dealers, and brokers who underwrite and trade municipals, governments, and federal agency securities.

PULL To cancel a securities order, to increase the offering price, or to lower the bid price.

PULL THE PLUG ON THE MARKET To cancel supporting bids that were entered just below a leading security's prevailing market price.

PUNT A stock that probably will not bring the holder any profit.

PUP An inactive, low-priced security.

PURPOSE LOAN Money borrowed to buy, carry, or trade securities which uses other securities as collateral.

PUT See put option.

PUT OPTION An agreement that gives the buyer the right to sell a specific quantity of a particular security by a specific date. The option is not obligatory and is traded during its life. The holder hopes the stock will drop in price.

Q Signifies a company operating under federal bankruptcy law that will ultimately be liquidated or reorganized.

QUALITATIVE ANALYSIS A subjective analysis of a security, with the judgment not based on financial information such as that found on a balance sheet or on an account statement. Instead, the judgment may be based on such issues as labor relations.

QUALITY RATING An evaluation, such as the Standard and Poor's and Moody's rating, given to a security, with the grading based on such factors as the issuing company's financial condition, strength, and proven management ability.

QUALITY STOCK A highly graded stock.

QUANTITATIVE ANALYSIS An analysis of a security, with the judgment based on financial information such as that found on a balance sheet or on an income statement.

QUARTER STOCK Any stock with a $25-a-share par value.

QUESTIONABLE TRADE (QT) A form used when an NYSE-originated trade cannot be compared by the morning of trade date plus three.

QUICK ASSET A current asset that can be readily converted into cash.

QUICK TURN Occurs when a security is sold immediately after it is purchased, with the investor seeking short-term profits.

QUIET PERIOD The 90 days, as required by the Securities and Exchange Commission, between an issuer's first public offering and the first time underwriters distribute research information about the issuing company. The purpose of the quiet period is to make sure that traders do not try to influence investors because the trader has a beneficial interest in the offering's secondary market.

QUOTE The highest bid and lowest offer on a given security at a particular time.

QUOTATION A figure that reflects a security's current transaction, bid, or ask price.

QUOTATION BOARD A security's exchange board that displays a security's daily market prices, ticker symbol, transaction price, and the number of shares traded.

QUOTATION TICKER An exchange's ticker tape that displays transaction prices.

QUOTED PRICE The last transaction price of any stock, bond, or commodity.

QUOTE MACHINE An electronic system that provides securities' transaction prices.

QUOTE WIRE An electronic connection between a brokerage house and the New York Stock Exchange that carries a listed security's highest bid and lowest offer prices.

R Appears in newspaper stock listings to describe an option that has not been traded.

RAG STOCK A security with a low price.

RAID A manipulative move to drive stock down.

RALLY A short, sharp rise in the general level of the market, commodity futures, or a security's price after a period of a downward or sideways movement.

RAN See revenue anticipation notes.

RANDOM WALK The path of stock prices, in that past prices cannot always be used to determine future prices because of the many and varied influences that can affect the prices.

RANGE All of the prices that fall between a highest and lowest price during a specific time period.

RANKING The rating of a security's performance during a specific time period compared to the performance of other securities rated during that same period.

RATE OF RETURN A measure of a company's profitability, the rate of return is determined by dividing stockholder's equity into net income. This produces a security's yearly after-tax profit, expresses as a percentage of the original capital investment.

RATING OF SECURITIES The determination of an issuing company's financial strength and stability, based on the company's management ability, debts, and payment history.

RATIO The comparison of different financial variables and their relationship to one another.

REACQUIRED STOCK Stock shares that a company has issued to stockholders, and then bought back.

REACTION Occurs when a security's price changes directions then stabilizes, usually following a lengthy and strong up or down price movement.

READING THE TAPE An investor can determine a stock's price performance by reading the stock exchange's ticker tape, which regularly displays prices. The investor can then judge whether the stock's price will go up or down.

REAL ACCOUNTS Accounts with balances that are carried over to the next fiscal period instead of being canceled. Liabilities, for example, would be included in a real account.

REAL CAPITAL Equipment or machinery that is used in a company's production.

REAL INVESTMENT An expense that creates a new capital asset.

REAL MONEY Coins, as opposed to paper currency, that contain intrinsic value.

REAL STOCK A long stock position versus a short position.

REAL TERMS A measure of the degree to which inflation has affected purchasing power.

RECEDING MARKET A period when the market's prices are dropping.

RECEIVABLES Accounts receivable.

RECEIVE AND DELIVER DEPARTMENT A division of the operations department responsible for the physical receipts and/or delivery of incoming and outgoing securities. Often it is also responsible for the daily balancing of cash entries made by the various operations departments.

RECEIVE BALANCE ORDER (RBO) An order issued by the clearing corporation to any firm with a long (or buy) position remaining after the day's compared trades have been netted. It states what will be delivered, what must be paid, and who is to deliver.

RECEIVE VERSUS PAYMENT A buyer pays the seller in cash for a security when the security is delivered.

RECIPROCAL BUSINESS One investor wants to buy or sell securities in a deal with a person who later will enter another deal with the investor.

RECLAIM A security certificate is recovered after a flaw was found and corrected.

RECORD DATE The date an investor must be registered with the issuing company as a security's owner of record to receive dividends or other ownership privileges.

RECORDS OF ORIGINAL ENTRY A record of all cash receipts and expenses, with entries recorded before they are made in the general ledger.

RECOVERY A period in which securities prices are climbing steadily after a period in which they dropped or were inactive.

REDEEM The issuing company repurchases a bond at maturity by paying the holders its face value.

REDEEMABLE BOND A bond that the issuing company can buy back before maturity, usually by paying the holder a premium.

REDEEMABLE STOCK Any preferred stock that the issuing company can call in for redemption.

REDEMPTION When a security's issuer repurchases the security.

REDEMPTION NOTICE A document that tells stockholders whose securities are being called in with the time and terms through which their securities will be redeemed.

REDEMPTION PRICE The price at which a bond can be redeemed before maturity or the price at which the shares from a mutual fund can be redeemed.

REDEMPTION VALUE The amount for which a security can be redeemed.

REDUCIBLE RATE BOND A bond on which the issuer can reduce the interest.

REFERENCE CURRENCY Any cash that is used to pay bondholders.

REFINANCING An issuer sells new bonds at lower interest rates to raise money to pay off an older debt that had a higher interest rate.

REFLEX RALLY A price correction from an oversold condition. The security price moves up, but does not change the price's established trend.

REFLEX REACTION A price correction from an overbought condition. The security's price drops, but does not change the price's established trend.

REGISTER To formally record.

REGISTERED AS TO INTEREST ONLY Bonds with interest that is sent directly to the registered holder and with the face value payable only to the bearer.

REGISTERED AS TO PRINCIPAL ONLY A coupon bond with its face value payable only to the registered holder at maturity.

REGISTERED BOND A bond registered in the owner's name and payable only to that owner, as opposed to a bearer bond.

REGISTERED COUPON BOND A bond registered in the owner's name, but with interest coupons paid only by delivering the coupon to a disbursing agent.

REGISTERED EXCHANGE A securities exchange governed by the Securities and Exchange Commission, or a commodities exchange governed by the Commodities Exchange Commission.

REGISTERED FORM The recording of a security's ownership on the issuer's central ledger. Anyone delivering the security must prove that he or she is, in fact, the person to whom the securities is registered.

REGISTERED REPRESENTATIVE An employee of a broker-dealer who is a member of the National Association of Securities Dealers (NASD).

REGISTERED SECONDARY Term for a sale of securities by an owner under an effective registration with the SEC. Generally such registered secondaries are made by a control person or other holder of restricted securities as a: (1) part of a combined primary-secondary offering under a prospectus issued by the corporation, (2) a shelf registration, that is, an offering by the owner using currently filed disclosure documents of the issuer as his disclosure document in the sale of the securities to the public.

REGISTERED SECURITY A security that has been recorded with its issuer.

REGISTERED TRADER A member of an exchange who is responsible for adding "liquidity" to the marketplace by purchasing or selling assigned securities from his or her inventory. Also known as competitive market makers or option principal members.

REGISTRAR A commercial bank or trust company that controls the issuance of securities.

REGISTRATION A procedure through which the Securities and Exchange Commission must review and approve publicly traded securities before they can be publicly sold.

REGISTRATION STATEMENT Document filed with the Securities and Exchange Commission (SEC) explaining an impending issue and pertinent data about the issuer. Based on the information provided, the SEC either permits or prevents the issue from being offered.

REGULAR WAY CONTRACT The fist contract sheet received from NSCC that contains compared, uncompared, and advisory data.

REGULAR-WAY DELIVERY (SETTLEMENT) A securities transaction in which the selling broker delivers the security to the buying broker, who in turn pays the selling broker within five business days after the transaction transpired. Other securities such as governments, options, and money market funds settle on the next business day.

REGULAR-WAY SALE Any sale that is not a short sale.

REGULATED INVESTMENT COMPANY An investment company that meets IRS eligibility requirements as a regulated company. They: (1) do not pay taxes on income received; (2) the income, if passed through to the fund holders, is taxable to the fund holder. The net income passed through to the fund holders retains the quality it had when the fund received it; thus, long-term gains remain long-term gains and dividend income remains dividend income.

REGULATION A Securities offerings between $50,000 and $300,000 must file a prospectus, though a less-detailed one than is required from an offering of more than $300,000.

REGULATION G Regulates the amount of credit that can be extended for buying securities in some situations that otherwise are unregulated.

REGULATION Q A Federal Reserve System ceiling on the interest rates that banks pay.

REGULATION T Regulates the amount of credit that brokers or dealers can extend to customers who want to buy securities.

REGULATION T CALL A brokerage firm's margin call.

REGULATION T EXCESS The amount of credit a broker-dealer can extend to a margin account customer above the amount of credit the customer already is using.

REGULATION U Regulates the amount of credit a bank can extend to customers who want to buy securities.

REGULATION X Regulates the type and amount of credit extended to people for buying, carrying, or trading securities.

REGULATION Z Regulates, oversees, and enforces the Truth in Lending Act, which covers disclosure requirements.

REINVESTMENT When dividends and capital gains are put back into buying more shares.

REJECTION A buyer's refusal to accept delivery of a security.

RELATIVE STRENGTH A security's market performance compared to other securities in its industry.

RELATIVE VALUE The value comparison of one security or commodity to another.

REMARGINING When an investor puts up additional securities or money because the equity in his or her margin account has fallen below accepted levels.

REOPEN AN ISSUE Used of government securities if the Treasury sells more of an issue that is already outstanding, with the same terms and conditions, at prevailing price levels. For example, rather than auction a new issue of notes with a new coupon rate, the Treasury reopens an older issue and sells notes with the same coupon priced to compete with current prices.

REORGANIZATION DEPARTMENT A division of the operations department that processes securities involving corporate reorganizations, mergers, consolidations, subscriptions, and the exchange of convertible securities into common stocks.

REPEAT PRICES OMITTED Designated on the consolidation tapes. It means that the tape is late, and to save time, only the first transaction in a series of trades for the same security is printed.

REPURCHASE A security's issuer buys back shares.

REPURCHASE AGREEMENT An agreement in which an investor sells an investment to another investor with the provision that the first investor can buy it back for a specific price by a specific date.

REQUEST FOR A REPORT An investor's inquiry to a brokerage house on the status of a securities order.

RESERVE REQUIREMENT The money that a member bank of the Federal Reserve System must keep on deposit with the nearest Federal Reserve District Bank. Cash in the vault of the member bank is included in the computation of the reserve. The required reserve differs for demand deposits and for time deposits.

RESTING ORDER Any securities order that remains in effect until the order cannot be filled because of high market prices if it is a buy order or because of low market prices if it is a sell order.

RESTRICTED ACCOUNT As defined by Regulation T, a margin account in which the debit balance exceeds the loan value.

RESTRICTED LIST A list of securities issuers and specific issues that cannot be traded, but can be sold only for a customer who does not solicit the sale. A broker-dealer usually gives the restricted list to the firm's selling employees.

RETAINED EARNINGS The portion of a company's earnings that it does not pay out to stockholders.

RETAINED EARNINGS STATEMENT A detailed financial record of annual and past dividend payments, which accompanies the company's annual report.

RETIRE To cancel or redeem a securities issue.

RETIRED SECURITIES A company's outstanding shares that the company calls back in or cancels and thus can no longer be sold.

RETREAT Describes a drop in prices.

RETURN An investment's profits, whether through interest or dividends.

REVENUE ANTICIPATION NOTE (RAN) A short-term debt instrument that is issued by municipalities and that is to be paid off by future (anticipated) revenue.

REVENUE BOND A municipal bond whose issuer's ability to pay interest and principal is based on revenue earned from a specific project.

REVERSAL Occurs when a security's price movement changes, with the new direction continuing at least for several days.

REVERSE REPURCHASE AGREEMENT A customer sells a group of securities to a broker-dealer under the provision that the customer will buy them back by a predetermined date for a specific price. The difference between the amount the customer received for the securities and the amount he or she will pay the broker-dealer when buying them back represents the interest.

REVERSE SPLIT Term used if a corporation reduces the number of outstanding shares by increasing the par value of the shares. Also called a split down.

RICH A price that is too high.

RIGGING Any illegal stock price manipulation.

RISK The probability that an investment will earn the amount of profit that it is supposed to earn. The chance an investment will drop in value.

RULE 144 A Securities and Exchange Commission regulation that covers the selling of restricted securities.

RULE 405 A New York Stock Exchange regulation that members must know specific information about their customers, their customers' accounts, and their customers' transactions. This know your customer rule deals with the suitability of certain investments for individuals with different conditions.

RULE OF 72 To determine how long it will take for an investor to double his or her money, divide the fixed rate of compound interest into 72.

RULES OF FAIR PRACTICE National Association of Securities Dealers' regulations that govern ethical practices, such as fair pricing and proper disclosure.

S (1)Indicates a stock split or stock dividend when it appears in newspaper stock listings. (2) On the consolidated tapes, a transaction that is multiplied of 100 shares. For example, 3s = 300 shares.

S&P INDEXES See Standard and Poor's Indexes.

SADDLED A situation in which an investor pays more than the market price for a security, then is forced to hold onto it because its value has failed to increase up to that price paid.

SAFEKEEPING A brokerage action to store and protect an investor's securities by segregating and identifying the securities.

SAFETY A minimal risk that creates the investor belief that an investment will not lose money.

SAFETY ON INCOME The probability that a company will continue making timely interest and dividend payments.

SAFETY ON PRINCIPAL The probability that money invested with a particular company will remain stable.

SAFETY STOCK A group of securities held to prevent stockouts.

SAG Occurs when a security's price drops slightly after demand for the security has been depleted.

SALE Occurs when a buyer and a seller agree on a price in a securities transaction.

SALES CHARGE A fee that an open-end investment company charges for buying fund shares.

SALES LITERATURE Any communication by a broker-dealer for distribution to customers or to the public that describes the services provided by the issuer of the sales literature. Such sales literature must be truthful and must accurately describe the services provided by the broker-dealer. Industry rules require that sales literature be approved by a person within the firm who is appointed to do so.

SALES LOAD See sales charge.

SALT-DOWN STOCK Occurs when an investor buys securities and keeps them for a long time, even if the securities show large paper profits.

SAME DAY SUBSTITUTION Occurs when an investor sells one security and buys another of equal value in the same day.

SATURATION Occurs when supply exceeds demand to such a degree that the prices must drop to absorb any further supply.

SAVINGS BOND A US Treasury bond that cannot be traded on the public market.

SCALPER A market maker who excessively marks up or marks down securities that carry little risk to the market maker.

SCALPING An unethical and sometimes illegal practice when a trader buys securities for his or her firm's account, then improperly tries to influence investors to buy the securities in an effort to drive the price up.

SCHEDULE C A National Association of Securities Dealers regulation requiring principals, financial principals, and representatives to be registered.

SCHEDULE 13-D	A form of the Securities and Exchange Commission requires the buyer of 5% of a registered security to file within 10 days of the purchase.
SCHEDULE 13-G	A short form the Securities and Exchange Commission requires the owner of 5% of a registered security to file at the end of the year.
SCIENTER	To knowingly transact a fraudulent securities deal.
SCREEN	To search for securities that meet certain investment goals and criteria, such as a certain price/earnings ratio.
SCRIP	A fractional share of stock distributed by a company on the occasion of a stock dividend, a split-up, or the spin-off of an asset. The recipient can hold the scrip, sell it, or, in most cases, purchase the remaining fraction of the share to have a full share.
SEASONED SECURITY	A publicly held security, so any future transaction would involve a deal between two investors and not between the issuer and an inventor
SEAT	A securities or commodities exchange membership.
SEC	See Securities and Exchange Commission.
SECONDARY DISTRIBUTION	Generally, any sale of securities, whether by an effective registration or not, made by a selling holder of the bonds or stocks. More specifically, a method of selling a large block of securities to investors by a previous holder.
SECONDARY MARKET	A securities transaction that takes place after the initial distribution.
SECONDARY MOVEMENT	A sharp price rally in a bear market, or a sharp drop in a bull market.
SECONDARY REACTION	A price change that moves against the general market trend.
SECOND MARKET	The over-the-counter securities market with the exchanges being first.
SECURITIES	Usually describes stocks and bonds, but can be expanded to describe any financial instrument.
SECURITIES ACT OF 1933	A law that regulates securities markets by requiring, among other things, registration before any sale and by requiring disclosure of all pertinent information about the issuing company.
SECURITIES ACT OF 1934	A law that created the Securities and Exchange Commission to govern securities markets, which outlawed price manipulation, the misrepresentation of facts, and other possible abuses.
SECURITIES ACTS AMENDMENTS OF 1975	A law that calls for a national market system and a national process through which securities transactions can be cleared and executed.

SECURITIES ANALYST A brokerage employee who reviews and judges securities investments and the financial condition of publicly held companies.

SECURITIES AND COMMODITIES EXCHANGES National exchanges which trade securities, options, and futures contracts by members for their customers and personal accounts.

SECURITIES AND EXCHANGE COMMISSION (SEC) The government agency that regulates and supervises the securities industry. The commission administers federal laws and formulates and enforces rules to protect against malpractice and provide investors the fullest possible disclosure.

SECURITIES AND EXCHANGE COMMISSION FEE The SEC imposes a one-cent charge on every $300 involved in a securities transaction. The seller normally pays the fee, which applies only to exchange-registered equity securities.

SECURITIES AND EXCHANGE COMMISSION ORGANIZATION MEMBER A broker-dealer who is registered with the SEC and is not a member of the National Association of Securities Dealers or of a national exchange.

SEC RULE 10A-1 The so-called plus-tick rule. This rule prohibits the short sale of securities registered on an exchange unless the sale, wherever made, is effected at a price that is above the last different regular-way transaction on the principal exchange where the security is traded.

SEC RULE 10B-2 This rule prohibits anyone from soliciting purchase orders for a security on an exchange while involved in a distribution (i.e. a sale) of that same issue.

SEC RULE 10B-4 The rule prohibits the short sale of securities in response to a tender offer. Thus, a person could not sell borrowed securities to a person making a tender offer to buy.

SEC RULE 10B-6 This rule prohibits issuers, underwriters, broker-dealers, or anyone with an interest in a distribution of securities from purchasing or inducing anyone else to purchase, the issue prior to the start of the public offering. Underwriters, however, may accept indications of interest in such issues from prospective buyers, but no sales may be made.

SEC RULE 10B-7 The rule sets the terms and conditions under which an underwriter may use a stabilizing bid to facilitate a distribution of securities.

SEC RULE 10B-8 Prohibits the manipulation of the open-market price for a security by persons involved in the distribution of that security through a rights offering.

SEC RULE 10B-10 It regulates the preparation and distribution of purchase or of sale confirmations by a broker-dealer to customers. The rule sets forth the minimum information required, the necessary disclosures required, and the frequency of such confirmations to customers.

SEC RULE 10B-13 The rule prohibits persons involved in an exchange or tender offer from making other purchases of the same security, either publicly or privately, until the tender offer has expired.

SEC RULE 10B-16 This rule, which is the security industry's response to the truth-in-lending law, requires broker-dealers who extend credit to customers (e.g., a margin-account customer) to provide complete information about the financing terms, conditions, and arrangements.

SEC RULE 11A A series of rules that govern the trading by exchange members for their own accounts.

SEC RULE 13D This rule, which has sub numbers 1 through 7, requires the filing of certain disclosures by anyone who acquires a beneficial ownership of 5% or more in any equity security registered with the SEC.

SEC RULE 13E This rule, which has sub numbers 1 through 4, regulates the purchases by an issuer, or an affiliate of the issuer, of its own securities in the public marketplace.

SEC REGULATION 14A It governs the preparation and distribution of proxy material to stockholders. It also sets forth the kind of information that must be included with the proxy statement, the supporting documents, the format, and the need for prior submission to the SEC of such material.

SEC RULE 15C2-1 This rule regulates the safekeeping of customers' securities left with a broker following their purchase in a margin account. In substance, this rule prohibits commingling customers' securities with the broker's securities and prohibits the broker from hypothecating more of the securities than is justified by the customers' indebtedness to the broker.

SEC RULE 15C3-1 The "net capital" rule governing the liquid capital that a broker-dealer must maintain in terms of his aggregate indebtedness to customers. The rule dictates the minimum net capital and the ratio of debt-to-equity capital of a broker-dealer; but from the viewpoint of a member firm customer, the most important aspect is the coverage that a broker-dealer's net capital provides for customer indebtedness. Although other measurements criteria may be used, the rule of thumb is that customer-related indebtedness may not exceed capital by more than 15 to 1.

SEC RULE 15C3-2 It governs the use of credit balances left with a broker-dealer by a customer, if the credit balance may be freely withdrawn. The rule requires a broker-dealer to notify customers that such credit balances may be withdrawn at any time. If the customer does not request the withdrawal of these balances, the broker-dealer may use the credit balance in the conduct of its ordinary course of business. The customer, of course, retains his or her right to the money left on deposit with the broker-dealer.

SEC RULE 15C3-3 This rule regulates the handling of fully paid securities and money on deposit with a broker-dealer. In substance, the rule requires the proper segregation of customer securities that are fully paid and requires that, at least weekly, money on deposit be deposited in a special account for the benefit of all customers of that broker-dealer.

SEC RULE 17F-1 It requires that broker-dealers, banks, and transfer agents report promptly any knowledge of lost, stolen, counterfeit, or misplaced securities to a centralized computer service maintained for this purpose. This service, called the National Crime Information Center (NCIC), acts as a central clearing service for anyone who wishes to inquire about the report of a missing or stolen security.

SEC RULE 19C-3 This rule permits securities listed on an exchange after April 26, 1979, to be traded by exchange members on or off the exchange, as they see fit. Purpose: to establish an experiment for the widest possible market for listed securities.

SEC RULE 144 In substance, this rule permits a holder of unregistered securities to make a public sale of such securities, without the need for a formal registration, if certain conditions are met. The rule is complex and legal advice is needed, but as a rule of thumb, sales that represent less than 1% of outstanding shares during a 90-day period will not require a formal registration with the SEC.

SEC RULE 145 It sets forth the conditions under which persons who receive securities as a result of a reclassification, merger, consolidation, or transfer of corporate assets may sell these securities without the need for an effective registration statement.

SEC RULE 156 It prohibits the issuance or use of false or misleading sales literature in conjunction with the sale of investment company securities.

SEC RULE 174 This rule lists the circumstances under which a dealer must continue to deliver a prospectus in connection with secondary market transactions in securities that were recently registered.

SEC RULE 254 It sets forth the dollar limitations on sales made under the provisions of Regulation A. At present, issuers may sell securities worth $1.5 million or less--using a short-form registration and providing buyers with an offering circular--without the need for a full and formal registration with the SEC.

SEC RULE 433 This rule outlines the conditions under which a dealer may use a preliminary (i.e., a red herring) prospectus.

SECURITIES DEPOSITORY The place where a security's certificate is physically filed before a bookkeeping transfer.

SECURITIES INDUSTRY ASSOCIATION (SIA) An organization of broker-dealers that is aimed at training members' employees and lobbying for members' interests.

SECURITIES INDUSTRY AUTOMATION CORPORATION A company that handles a trading communication system for the American and New York stock exchanges.

SECURITIES INVESTOR PROTECTION CORPORATION (SIPC) A private, government-sponsored company that insures brokerage accounts for up to $500,000 in securities with $100,000 for cash in case the brokerage firm goes bankrupt.

SECURITIES LOAN When one broker-dealer loans securities to another broker-dealer to complete a short sale.

SECURITIZATION Pooling loans into packages of securities.

SECURITY ELEMENT Any type of collateral.

SECURITY RATINGS Evaluations of the credit and investment risk of securities which are rated by independent agencies.

SEEK A MARKET To try to find orders for the appropriate security to complete a transaction.

SEGREGATE To separate clients' securities from the broker's securities.

SEGREGATED SECURITIES Client's securities kept separate from a broker-dealer's securities and that a broker-dealer cannot use to transact the firm's business.

SELECTED DEALER AGREEMENT An underwriting syndicate's contract for distributing new securities, with the agreement stipulating the syndicate members' rights and responsibilities, such as the obligation to sell the securities at the agreed upon price.

SELF-LIQUIDATING An asset that easily can be converted to cash, or with a value that ultimately can be recovered in full.

SELF-REGULATORY ORGANIZATION A stock exchange, securities, or commodities organization that is registered with the Securities and Exchange Commission and that is responsible for making sure members obey rules and regulations.

SELL AT BEST This is said when an over-the-counter broker-dealer asks another broker-dealer to help sell part of a market order at the best available price.

SELL-DOWN The security shares an underwriting syndicate offers to those who are not syndicate members.

SELLER'S MARKET Occurs when demand exceeds supply, which benefits anyone trying to sell a security or other asset.

SELLER'S SEVEN SALE Occurs when the seller agrees not to deliver the security certificate to the buyer for at least seven days.

SELLING AGAINST THE BOX A short sale in which the client is also long the security. This tactic is used to "box" a profit or loss for application at another time.

SELLING AWAY Occurs when a broker sells a security that his or her firm has not authorized the broker to sell.

SELLING BELOW THE MARKET Occurs when one security is selling for less than other similar securities.

SELLING CLIMAX Describes a downward price trend that suddenly creates a volume increase, which plunges the price dramatically.

SELLING CONCESSION Brokers who receive a commission to help distribute a securities offering.

SELLING FLAT Occurs when an investor buying a bond does not have to pay any additional amount, such as accrued interest, other than the bond's actual purchase price.

SELLING, GENERAL, AND ADMINISTRATIVE EXPENSES (SG&A) An expense section of a company's profit and loss statement that includes items such as advertising, salaries, commissions, travel, entertainment, and promotion.

SELLING GROUP A group of dealers that helps an underwriting syndicate distribute a new or secondary issue by distributing the securities to the public. The group, in turn, receives a commission from the sales.

SELLING ON BALANCE Occurs when supply exceeds demand and thus prices are falling and securities are being sold in high volume.

SELLING ON GOOD NEWS Occurs when an investor sells his or her holdings in a security after the release of positive information about that security. They believe the stock has reached its top price and that profit taking will occur.

SELLING SHORT See short sale.

SELL OFF Occurs when prices are dropping because of heavy selling pressure.

SELL ORDER An investor's directions to his or her broker to liquidate a specific number of shares.

SELL OUT Occurs when a buyer refuses to accept delivery or pay the agreed upon price. A sell out also occurs when a broker liquidates a margin account because the investor has failed to bring the account up to the minimum level following a margin call.

SELL-OUT NOTICE A notice from a broker to a client telling the client he or she must pay an amount due immediately or the broker will begin selling the client's securities to satisfy the debt.

SELL-OUT PROCEDURE When a buying broker fails to honor a contract by refusing to pay for securities he or she agreed to buy, the selling broker can turn around and sell the securities to someone else without notifying the defaulting buyer, or the seller can hold the buyer liable for any losses incurred because of default.

SELL PLUS A market order to sell a security at a price higher than that security's last transaction price.

SELL SIGNAL A market gauge that indicates a security could soon drop in price.

SELL THE BOOK A seller's request to sell as many shares as possible at the best bid price.

SENIOR BOND A bond that has priority over other bonds in claiming assets and dividends.

SENSITIVE MARKET Also describes an insecure market in which the release of either positive or negative information will cause major price shifts.

SENTIMENT INDICATOR A market gauge that indicates changes in investors' moods, psychology, and strategies.

SEPARATE CUSTOMER Describes the highest level of customer protection that the Securities Investor Protection Corporation (SIPC) provides. The SIPC keeps one investor's cash, margin, and special bond accounts separate from another customer's by listing each individual ownership under the investor's name.

SEPARATE TRADING OF REGISTERED INTEREST AND PRINCIPAL OF SECURITIES (STRIPS) This is a US Treasury method of selling interest and principal payments separately on certain qualified government-issued securities (See also stripped bond).

SEQUENTIAL TRANSACTIONS When a security is heavily traded on an exchange, the exchange's ticker tape lists the transactions in consecutive order by volume and by price, but without constantly repeating the identifying stock symbol.

SERIAL BONDS A group of bonds from the same issue that have different maturity dates.

SERIES BOND One bond that is offered publicly on a number of different dates instead of on one particular issue date.

SERIES 7 EXAM A test of the basic understanding of the securities industry required and administered by the NASD of all registered representative candidates. The multiple choice test is developed by the New York Stock Exchange.

SESSION One trading day.

SETTLE To finalize a securities transaction, usually with the physical delivery of the security and the payment of the purchase price.

SETTLEMENT DATE The day that securities must be delivered and paid to complete a transaction.

SETTLEMENT DATE INVENTORY The total of all positions in a security on settlement date, including vault, transfer, fails, and elsewhere.

SETTLEMENT PRICE A commodity's closing price.

SG&A See selling, general, and administrative expenses.

SHADOW PRICE The price at which a security would sell under equilibrium conditions.

SHARE A single stock unit that represents a portion of company ownership.

SHAREHOLDER Any person who owns units of a company's stock.

SHARE REGISTER	A company's record of who owns the publicly held shares.
SHARES AUTHORIZED	The maximum number of stock shares a company can sell as prescribed in its articles of incorporation. The company can sell more shares only if the board passes a charter amendment increasing the maximum number of shares authorized.
SHAVE	An extra charge added to a security purchase when the buyer wants to extend the delivery time.
SHEARED	An unsuccessful broker or dealer.
SHELF REGISTRATION	A Securities and Exchange Commission registration that carries the right for a security to be sold at some unspecified future date.
SHOP	A broker-dealer's office, or the production area of a company.
SHORT	A stock record position (street side) which presents location (such as box, transfer, and so forth) or due from (such as fail-to-receive, or owed to the brokerage concern by a customer on account of a short sale).
SHORT AGAINST THE BOX	Occurs when an investor sells the same number of securities short that he or she owns.
SHORT BOND	Either a bond that once had a long maturity but that is now nearing that maturity date, or any bond that has been sold short.
SHORT COUPON	A newly issued bond with a first coupon due in less than six months.
SHORT COVERING	Occurs when an investor buys securities or commodities to close a short position or to return a security that previously was borrowed.
SHORT EXEMPT	A phrase used to describe a short sale that is exempt from the short sale rules. For example, buying a convertible preferred, submitting conversion instructions, and selling the common stock before the stock is received.
SHORT MARKET VALUE	The current market value of securities sold short.
SHORT OF THE MARKET	Occurs when an investor holds a short position in a security because he or she believes the security's price will drop.

SHORT POSITION (1) Industry term for a client account in which the completion of a sale was made by the delivery of a borrowed certificate. The client is said to have a short position because the client owes the security borrowed to the broker. (2) Industry term for a client account in which a client has written an option, either a put or a call, and has not yet made a closing purchase, has not been exercised, or the option has not expired. (3) Industry term for a client commodity account in which the client has contracted to sell the commodity at a future date for a fixed price. (4) A investor's situation after shorting a security, option, or futures contract.

SHORT PURCHASE Occurs when an investor buys stock to cover a previous short sale in the same security.

SHORT SALE The sale of a security that the seller does not own, based on the belief that the seller will be able to buy it back at a lower price, thus profiting from the difference. Short sales can be executed only through a brokerage margin account, with the brokerage firm loaning the seller the security so he or she can deliver it to the buyer.

SHORT SALE RULE A Securities and Exchange Commission regulation that all short sales must be on a zero-plus tick or on an uptick.

SHORT SQUEEZE A situation in which the price of a security or futures contract moves up sharply, forcing traders with short positions to buy back the position in order to cover and prevent losses.

SHORT SWING Occurs when a company's directors, officers, stockholders, or others with access to inside information transact a profitable deal by buying and then selling back the company's securities within six months, or selling the securities and then buying them back within six months. Such transactions normally are prohibited, and the company often can recover any profits, because a US securities laws assume the directors, officers, or stockholders acted on inside information, which is illegal.

SHORT TENDER An illegal practice in which a person accepts a tender offer by delivering borrowed securities. According to the Securities and Exchange Commission, only long securities can be included in a tender offer.

SHORT TERM For purposes of capital gains tax, an investment of one year or less.

SHORT-TERM CAPITAL GAIN The profit from an investment held for one year or less.

SHORT-TERM CAPITAL LOSS The loss from an investment held for one year or less.

SHORT-TERM DEBT A bond or other debt instrument that will mature within the next five years.

SHORT-TERM SECURITY A security that is payable on demand and that matures in a year or less.

SHORT-TERM TRADING Holding an investment for a brief period of time with the hopes of making a quick profit.

SHORT-TERM TRADING INDEX (TRIN) To determine a stock exchange's intraday market movements, divide the advance-decline volume ratio into the advance-decline ratio. The New York and American stock exchanges calculate the short-term trading once every minute. The TRIN measuring less than 1.0 is bullish while a higher number is bearish.

SICK MARKET A weak market.

SIDE-BY-SIDE TRADING Occurs when an investor simultaneously trades a security and an option on that security on the same exchange.

SIDEWAYS MARKET Occurs when market prices remain relatively stable, not moving up or down to any great degree.

SIGNAL A gauge that indicates when a price is expected to rise or fall, thus giving an investor a way of knowing when to buy or sell a particular security.

SIMPLE ARBITRAGE Arbitrage that an investor can achieve by using three markets.

SIMPLE INTEREST Interest that is based on the original principal amount instead of compounding.

SINGLE CAPITAL STRUCTURE COMPANY A company that has issued only one class of securities.

SIPC See Securities Investor Protection Corporation.

SIZE The number of stock shares available at the bid and ask prices.

SKIMMING PRICES A high initial price followed by several price drops. Skimming allows the seller to attract as many buys as possible at the highest before dropping the price some more, which attracts more buyers at that next level.

SKIP-DAY SETTLEMENT Occurs when a security is to be paid for and delivered on the second day after the transaction date.

SLD LAST SALE Appears on an exchange's consolidated tape to indicate "sold last sale" when a great change has occurred between transactions in a securities issue, with the change usually consisting of one or two points depending on the issue's price.

SLEEPER An underpriced stock that unexpectedly rose sharply in price.

SLOW MARKET A market with little trading activity.

SLUGS Nonmarketable US Treasury securities sold to states and municipalities, which deposits the securities into escrow accounts until they need them to pay off their own bonds upon maturity.

SLUMP A temporary, but steady, decline in market prices.

SMASH A dramatic drop in market prices.

SOCIETY FOR WORLDWIDE INTERBANK FINANCIAL TELECOMMUNICATIONS (SWIFT) A computer network for transferring financial data and foreign currencies.

SOFT ARBITRAGE An arbitrage achieved between the public sector and private paper.

SOFT DOLLARS Research and brokerage services, instead of hard dollars, are used to pay for underwriting credits and portfolio transaction commissions.

SOFT MARKET A relatively inactive market with little demand and in which a small amount of selling pressure will drive prices down.

SOFT SPOT Securities that are weak when the rest of the market is strong and on the upswing.

SOLD TO YOU One trader's reconfirmation to another that the offer was accepted.

SOURCE AND APPLICATIONS OF FUNDS STATEMENT The comparison of a company's financial situations in two or more different accounting periods.

SPACE ARBITRAGE Simultaneously selling and buying the same security on two different exchanges to take advantage of price differences.

SPECIAL ARBITRAGE ACCOUNT A margin account in which a customer receives advantageous credit terms when he or she simultaneously buys a security and sells it in a different market, or simultaneously buys one security and sells an equal one in the same market to profit from any price differences.

SPECIAL BID A fixed bid for a block of stock in which the buyer pays for all transaction costs.

SPECIAL BOND ACCOUNT A brokerage account used to show the firm's purchasing power from bonds that were bought on margin.

SPECIAL CASH ACCOUNT A margin account in which a customer can buy or sell any security long, with all securities delivered within seven days.

SPECIAL DEAL Occurs when the underwriter of investment company securities pays another dealer's employee in connection with the sale. The National Association of Securities Dealers prohibits this practice.

SPECIAL DEPOSITORY Any bank that the US Treasury allows to receive deposits from the sale of government bonds.

SPECIAL MISCELLANEOUS ACCOUNT (SMA) A special brokerage account that shows how much unpledged money a customer has available in his or her margin account.

SPECIAL OFFERING An issuing company's secondary distribution that has been registered in detail with the Securities and Exchange Commission.

SPECIAL OMNIBUS ACCOUNT A broker-dealer account in which a second broker-dealer who is registered with the Securities and Exchange Commission can transact for the customers without giving those customers' names.

SPECIAL SUBSCRIPTION ACCOUNT185 A margin account through which a client can receive credits to buy a margin security by exercising a right or warrant.

SPIKE A quick, dramatic price increase.

SPIN OFF A dividend made up of assets, such as another company's stock, that is distributed to stockholders. Also, a company divestiture resulting in the transfer of assets of an entire subsidiary.

SPLIT Occurs when stock shares are divided into a larger or smaller number of stock shares. For example, the issuing company will issue two stocks for every one turned in, which could cut the stock's par value in half.

SPLIT COMMISSION A transaction commission that is divided between the executing broker and the person who brought the deal to the broker's attention.

SPLIT OPENING Occurs when a security opens at two different prices, usually because traders simultaneously but separately entered their first quotes on the same security.

SPLIT ORDER A large securities transaction that is broken down into several smaller transactions to avoid causing market fluctuations in the security's price.

SPLIT RATING Occurs when two bond rating services give the same issue two different ratings.

SPLIT UP See split.

SPOT Available for immediate delivery.

SPOT EXCHANGE RATE The amount of one country's currency needed to buy a unit of another country's currency, with the purchase requiring immediate delivery.

SPOT NEWS A sudden news report that could temporarily affect market prices.

SPOT PRICE The price quoted for a cash commodity.

SPOT SALE The purchase of an item to be delivered immediately.

SPOTTED MARKET A market with small up and down price movements, but showing no major trends.

SPREAD (1)The difference between the bid price and the ask price. (2) A long and short option position in either puts or calls on the same underlying stock but in a different series. (3) In underwriting, the difference between what the issuer receives from the underwriter and what underwriter sells the security for to the public on the offering.

SPREAD SHEET The ledger sheet of a company's financial statement, with all income and expenses laid out in columns and rows.

SQUEEZE Occurs when securities or commodities futures begin increasing in price and investors who sold them short must cover their short positions to avoid major losses, thus driving up the prices even more.

STABILIZATION A lateral price movement usually preceding a change in price direction.

STABILIZATION BID The bid price that an underwriter will offer immediately after a new security is issued to maintain the security's market level.

STAMPED SECURITY A security certificate that has been stamped to indicate it has been altered since it was originally issued.

STANDARD AND POOR'S An investment service that rates securities.

STANDARD AND POOR'S INDEX As a market performance gauge, this index checks the movement of 500 of the most commonly held stocks and generalizes the findings to predict the potential movements of other securities and market volatility.

STANDARD AND POOR'S INDEXES An average of securities traded on the New York Stock Exchange as determined by multiplying the price of each issue by the number of outstanding shares.

STANDARD AND POOR'S RATING A rating of stocks and bonds of risk with AAA, AA, A and BBB considered investment grade, indicating minimal risk.

STANDARD COST Normal production costs that include no unforeseen conditions. A company can determine its cost efficiency by calculating the difference between standard costs and actual costs.

STANDBY COMMITMENT A contract between a company and a banking group in which the banking group agrees to buy a portion of a securities issue offered in a rights offering after the current shareholders fail to buy all that was offered during the prescribed period.

STATED CAPITAL The amount of money that stockholders contribute to the company.

STATED PERCENTAGE ORDER An order to buy a block of stock large enough to represent a specific percentage of the security's market volume.

STATED VALUE As opposed to a market value or par value, this is a per-share value a security carries only for accounting purposes.

STATEMENT A summary of charges, expenses, and purchases, as well as a description of financial condition.

STATEMENT ANALYSIS An analyst studies a company's accounting statements and analyzes such ratios as turnover and current, then determines the company's future potential.

STATEMENT OF CHANGES IN FINANCIAL POSITION The part in a company's annual report that shows changes in the company's working capital.

STATEMENT OF CONDITION A summary of the status of a company's assets, liabilities, and equity.

STATUTE OF LIMITATIONS US securities laws prohibit civil actions on most securities matters after three years.

STATUTORY UNDERWRITER A person who inadvertently performs underwriting functions and therefore subjects himself or herself to Securities and Exchange Commission regulations regarding the sale of unregistered securities.

STAYING POWER An investor's financial ability to hold on to an investment that has dropped in value.

STEADY A market that is not moving up or down much.

STEENTH Designates a bid that is quoted in 16ths.

STEPPED COUPON SECURITIES A bond series with all issues paying the same interest rate each year, but with that rate increasing periodically.

STICKY DEAL An underwriting issue that probably will be hard to market.

STICKY PRICES Prices that are not subject to major price fluctuations either up or down.

STOCK A unit of company ownership.

STOCK AHEAD Occurs when one investor orders were put in before another investor's orders on the exchange floor, so the price could change before the later investor's order comes up for execution.

STOCK ALLOTMENT The number of shares an underwriting manager sets aside for each syndicate member to distribute.

STOCK/BOND POWER A form used as a substitute for endorsement of a certificate. When completed and attached to the certificate, the security can be processed for delivery or transfer.

STOCKBROKER A person registered to trade securities for customers.

STOCK BUSINESS Describes a dealer who buys a portion of a new municipal bond issue for his or her own account in hopes of making a quick profit by reselling the bonds.

STOCK CERTIFICATE A document that verifies stock ownership and details such information as the security's par value, the number of shares involved, the issuing company's name and the owner's name.

STOCK COMPANY A company with stockholders providing all of the operating capital, paying all losses, and sharing all profits.

STOCK DISCOUNT The amount a stock's par value exceeds its paid-in-capital.

STOCK DIVIDEND A portion of a company's retained earnings that are distributed to stockholders, with the amount dependent on the number of shares the stockholder owns.

STOCK EXCHANGE An institution wherein members can trade stocks, bonds, and other financial instruments.

STOCKHOLDER A person who has ownership units in a publicly held company.

STOCKHOLDER OF RECORD The stockholder whose name is registered with the issuing company or with the transfer agent and who is entitled to dividend payments.

STOCKHOLDER'S EQUITY A company's net worth, which is its liabilities subtracted from the value of its assets.

STOCK JOBBING Price manipulation.

STOCK LIST A registered exchange's investigation into a company that wants to list its securities on that exchange or wants its securities approved for unlisted trading.

STOCK LOAN BUSINESS A brokerage firm branch designated for earning profits from lending securities.

STOCK MARKET The organized trading of securities on one of the many exchanges.

STOCK OPTION The privilege an issuing company gives to people to buy a specific number of shares within a particular time period and for a price below the market value.

STOCK RECORD The record of individual securities on which both the "long" and "short" positions are shown, the total of the "long" positions and the total of the "short" positions being in balance.

STOCK RECORD DEPARTMENT A brokerage firm department responsible for handling and following all of the firm's securities, identifying their owners, and keeping track of the securities' locations daily.

STOCK SPLIT The exchange of existing shares of stock for more newly issued shares from the same corporation. Since the number of shares outstanding increase, the price per share goes down. Splits do not increase or decrease the capitalization of the company, just redistribute it over more shares. The effect is the adjustment to the trading price.

STOCK TABLES A newspaper listing of market information, such as stock opening and closing prices, trading volumes and price/earnings ratios.

STOCK TICKER An old device that printed trading information on a narrow ticker tape.

STOCK WATCHER A New York Stock Exchange computer network used to follow the movements and transactions of NYSE-listed securities.

STOCK YIELD A security's rate of return, as determined by its market value and dividend payments.

STOP The lowest rate the central bank will charge dealers who trade their government securities in for cash.

STOP-LIMIT ORDER A request to buy or sell a security, directing the broker to make the order a limit order as soon as the security's price hits a predetermined stop level.

STOP-LOSS ORDER An investor's order to his or her broker to sell a security if its price drops to a specified level.

STOP ORDER A request to buy or sell a security as soon as the security's price hits a specific level.

STOP-OUT PRICE The lowest price that will be accepted at a Treasury auction.

STOP-OUT RATE The lowest rate the Federal Reserve will allow a nonbank dealer to pay on a repurchase agreement.

STORY A scenario for buying a specific stock as described by an analyst. For example, the analyst may tell the potential investor about positive factors that are influencing the issuing company's management.

STRADDLE Simultaneous long or short positions of puts and calls having the same underlying security and same series designation.

STRAIGHT BOND An investment made because of its current value and income and not because of any expected increase.

STRAIGHT-LINE DEPRECIATION A method in which the company's cost of a qualified asset can be apportioned in equal amounts over the length of the asset's life. To obtain the amount that can be depreciated, subtract the asset's salvage value at the end of its useful life from the asset's original cost.

STRAIGHT-LINE INTEREST Annually computed interest payments based on a percentage of the unpaid balance.

STREET Nickname for Wall Street and any other area's major financial center.

STREET BROKER Any over-the-counter broker who is not an exchange member.

STREET CERTIFICATE A securities certificate with a blank endorsement by an owner with a guaranteed signature, which allows the security to be transferred without the transfer having to be recorded on the company's books.

STREET NAME Describes securities that are being held in the name of a broker for a customer.

STREET PRICE The price of a security that is involved in a transaction not connected to one of the exchanges.

STREET SIDE The brokerage side of a broker-customer relationship.

STRIKE FROM THE LIST An exchange order to stop all transactions in a specific security.

STRIKE PRICE The exercise price, or the price at which an option holder can buy an asset.

STRIPPED BOND A bond which can be bought in either a principal only (PO) or interest only (IO) package.

STRIPPED TREASURY OBLIGATIONS Zero-coupon Treasury bonds that mature in three months to 29 years and are backed by the full faith and credit of the US government.

STRONG MARKET Occurs when demand exceeds supply.

SUBJECT MARKET A traders quote that has yet to be confirmed and authorized by the trader's customer.

SUBJECT PRICE A negotiated, estimated price that is subject to confirmation.

SUBJECT TO PRIOR SALE When the market is strong, the supply of a security limited, and buy orders exceed the security's supply, bid orders often will be filed early so the investor will be able to obtain whatever amount of the limited security is available. Those investors filing their bids later will not be able to buy the security because none will be left.

SUBORDINATED A security with a lower priority than other securities when dividends and assets are distributed in liquidations or bankruptcies.

SUBSCRIBER An investor who promises to buy a specific number of shares of a newly issued security.

SUBSCRIPTION An agreement to buy a certain number of shares of a newly issued security.

SUBSCRIPTION CAPITAL The money an issuer receives from the public in a new securities offering.

SUBSCRIPTION CASH RECORD A cash record of all capital stock subscriber's payments, including the down payment.

SUBSCRIPTION LIST A document a subscriber signs verifying the number of shares he or she has agreed to buy.

SUBSCRIPTION PRICE The set, established price at which a new security is offered publicly for sale.

SUBSTITUTION One security is sold and another purchased to replace it in order to take advantage of price differences while maintaining the same volume of ownership.

SUBSTITUTION OF COLLATERAL Occurs when a borrower substitutes one collateral, such as property, for another collateral, such as securities.

SUITABILITY Guidelines that brokers who deal in speculative securities must follow to make sure the investors actually can afford to assume such risks.

SUMMARY COMPLAINT PROCEEDINGS A National Association of Securities Dealers code that says that a person charged with NASD code violations may, in some case, plead guilty to a minor infraction as long as the person pays a fine and promises not to appeal.

SUNDRY ASSET An asset that the company does not use in day-to-day production, but that it plans to hold on to for a long period of time. Undeveloped land, for example, would be considered a sundry asset.

SUPER DOT An automated order processing and trade reporting system through which New York Stock Exchange members can quickly execute price orders.

SUPER STOCK A security that will multiply several times in value.

SUPPLEMENTAL CONTRACT A contract issued by the clearing corporation that includes the total of the regular way contract, adjustments made through advisories, and adds by seller processing.

SUPPLY The number of shares available publicly for sale.

SUPPLY AND DEMAND INDICATORS A gauge that measures how much money is coming in and out of the market.

SUPPLY AREA The place on a price chart that indicates the price's resistance level.

SUPPORT Occurs when an investor buys securities at prices that will keep the securities' values from dropping in an effort to discourage people from exercising their put options.

SUPPORTING ORDERS Buy orders entered to support a security's price.

SUPPORTING SCHEDULES A supplementary report of information added either to a company's balance sheet or to its profit and loss statement.

SUPPORTING THE MARKET Occurs when a bid falls at or slightly below a security's prevailing market price. The bid is usually designed to balance the price and to encourage it to go up.

SUPPORT LEVEL The price at which buyers have tended to purchase a security, thus overcoming the downward pressure from sellers.

SURETY A security that protects the holder in case a party owing money to the issuer defaults, or for example, if a company officer embezzles money from the company.

SURPLUS EQUITY The amount by which a margin account security's market value exceeds the amount needed to satisfy a margin requirement.

SURPLUS RESERVES A company's financial reserve that is not available for paying dividends.

SURVEILLANCE DEPARTMENT OF EXCHANGES An exchange department that watches for unusual securities transactions that could indicate illegal activity is under way.

SUSPENSE ACCOUNT A broker-dealer's account of security balance discrepancies.

SUSPENSION Occurs when a brokerage employee is either permanently or temporarily stopped from working because he or she has violated securities regulations.

SUSPENSION OF TRADING Occurs when an exchange temporarily halts trading in a particular security to stabilize the market.

SWAP Occurs when a government agrees to borrow a foreign currency from the issuing country to pay for an intervention in the foreign exchange market. Also, the sale of one security to purchase another security with similar features.

SWIFT See Society for Worldwide Interbank Financial Telecommunications.

SWIMMING MARKET A strong, active securities market.

SWING A price movement, usually in the opposite direction of the previous movement.

SWITCHING Selling some securities from a portfolio and replacing them with different securities.

SWITCH ORDER An investor's request to simultaneously buy one stock and sell another because of beneficial price differences.

SYMBOL An acronym used to identify securities that are traded on a ticker tape or exchange, or are listed in newspapers.

SYNDICATE A group of investment bankers that underwrites and distributes a new securities issue.

T Appears in newspaper stock listings to indicate the security's main trading place is the Toronto Stock Exchange.

TAG ENDS Indicates that only a small number of debt securities are available from the underwriting syndicate because the rest have been sold.

TAIL The difference between the lowest bid accepted and the average bid in a US Treasury auction.

TAILGATING Occurs when a registered representative buys a security for a customer, then buys more shares of the same security for his or her own accounts.

TAKE Indicates that buyers are accepting another broker's offering price to complete a transaction.

TAKE A POSITION Occurs when an investor creates a long or short position.

TAKE IT A broker's indication that he or she will buy a specific security at a specific price.

TAKE ON A LINE Occurs when an investor buys a large block of stock over a period of time because he or she expects the stock's price to climb.

TAKE-OR-PAY CONTRACT A contract that binds the buyer to pay the seller a minimum amount of money, even if the seller does not provide the buyer with the promised goods or services. Such contracts protect bondholders.

TAKEOUT The amount of money an investor withdraws to sell one security and buy another at a lower price.

TECHNICIAN An analyst, also called a chartist, that uses indicators such as ratios and graphs to predict future market trends instead of studying the issuing companies' management and fundamentals.

TECHNILIST A newsletter a financial institution sends to subscribers with recommendations on what securities to buy or sell and at what prices.

TEMPORARY AGENT TRANSFER PROGRAM Using the National Association of Securities Dealers' Central Registration Depository, the North American Securities Administrators Association designed a program through which salespeople can obtain temporary registration before they file their permanent registration forms.

TEMPORARY RECEIPT A document acknowledging security ownership until the engraved certificate is ready.

TENDENCY The probability or likelihood of a security's price to shift up, down, or sideways.

TENDER To formally bid on a security.

TENDER OFFER One company's public announcement that it plans to buy as many shares of another company securities as possible, usually in an effort to take that company over.

TEN-K REPORT The annual report that any company issuing listed securities must file with the Securities and Exchange Commission.

TENOR A bond's maturity.

TEN PERCENT GUIDELINE A city's bonded debt never should exceed 10 percent of the city-owned real estate's market value.

TERM The time between the issuing date and the date of maturity.

TERM BOND An issue with all bonds in the series maturing on the same date.

TERM REPURCHASE AGREEMENT A repurchase agreement that lasts a longer-than-normal period of time.

TERTIARY MOVEMENT Small, unimportant, daily price shifts.

TEST Occurs when a price is challenging a resistance level. If the price does not break through the level, the resistance level is said to have passed the test.

TESTING A market price that challenges the resistance level, but will not break through that level.

THINLY HELD STOCK Shares owned by a small number of people, which results in wide price fluctuations even when trading volume is low.

THIN MARKET	A market with little interest in buying or selling a particular security, which prompts large price fluctuations in the few shares that are traded.
THIRD MARKET	Occurs when a trader who is not a member of an exchange trades exchange-listed securities either over the counter or off the board.
THIRD-PARTY ACCOUNT	An illegal brokerage account that one person carries in his or her name, even though another person actually owns the account.
THIRD-PARTY BROKER	A broker who routinely executes institutional trades, then returns a portion of his or her fee to a fund such as a pension program.
THIRD-PARTY PURCHASE AGREEMENT	A broker's deal with a bank customer in which the bank guarantees the loan and the broker uses government securities as collateral.
THIRTY-DAY VISIBLE SUPPLY	A list of securities that will be offered publicly within 30 days.
THIRTY-DAY WASH RULE	With this regulation, the Internal Revenue Service prohibits an investor who suffered a loss on a stock sale from using that loss for tax benefits if the investor bought the stock back 30 days after the sale date, or owned the stock for only 30 days before the sale.
THREE-HANDED DEAL	A securities issue that puts together serial maturity bonds with two-term maturity bonds.
THRIFT INSTITUTION	A savings and loan, credit union, or savings bank.
THROUGH THE MARKET	Occurs when a new bond offering has a lower yield-to-maturity than comparable outstanding bonds.
TICK	A security's successive transaction prices.
TICKER TAPE	An exchange's system for physically recording and reporting securities transactions and volume information. The ticker tape is referred to as a ticker or a tape.
TICK INDEX	Subtract an exchange's downtick volume from its uptick volume to determine the net tick volume.
TICKLER	A financial institution's list of bonds and their maturity dates, with such an index reminding the institution of which bonds will fall due and when.
TICK VOLUME	The downtick volume compared to the uptick volume of a certain security in one trading day.
TIER	Differentiates one class of securities from another.
TIFFANY LIST	The nickname for a group of companies that issue high-grade commercial paper.
TIGHT MARKET	An active, competitive market with little difference between bid and offer prices.

TIME BARGAIN	An agreement between a buyer and a seller to trade a specific security at a particular price at a specific future date.
TIME BILL	A bill of exchange with a fixed payment date.
TIME ORDER	A market order that becomes a limit order on a specific date or at a specific time.
TIME WARRANT	A negotiable, government obligation with a term that is shorter than bonds. Time warrants often are used to pay people and companies for goods provided or for services rendered.
TIME WEIGHTED RATE OF RETURN	The investment performance of assets held for a specific time period.
TIMING	The proper time to buy or sell securities according to impending trends.
TIP	An inducement to buy or sell securities, with the tip carrying the assumption that it is based on inside information.
TIPPEE	A person who accepts inside information.
TIPSTER	A person who claims he or she has inside information on an investment.
TIPSTER SHEET	A list of recommended securities.
TO COME	The number of shares that will be sold, but that have not yet been transferred.
TOEHOLD PURCHASE	Buying less than 5 percent of a company's outstanding stock before the company notifies the Securities and Exchange Commission about the purchase.
TO GO	The number of shares that will be purchased, but that have not yet been transferred.
TOMBSTONE	A public announcement that a new security will be offered for sale. A tombstone is not, however, an advertisement to buy the security, but merely an announcement that it will be available.
TOM-NEXT	Tomorrow's business day to the next business day. A next business day settlement.
TON	A nickname for $100 million.
TOP	A security's highest price during a particular time period.
TOP-DOWN APPROACH TO INVESTING	An investment strategy in which an investor studies economic trends, then picks an industry and a company within that industry that will probably benefit the most from the trends.
TOPHEAVY	Occurs when a security, commodity, or the general market is priced so that it is expected to fall.
TOPPING A BID	Occurs when an investor bids a higher amount than the prevailing market price.

TOPPING OUT Occurs when a security's steadily increasing price stabilizes and then begins to decline.

TOPPY Occurs when the general market or an individual security hits its resistance level and subsequently drops.

TOTAL COST The amount of money it costs to buy a security, including the purchase price, fees, and commissions.

TOTAL RETURN An investment's current cash flow combined with its ultimate gains or losses.

TO THE BUCK An offer when the bid and the offer amounts are close, and the offer is a round point.

TRADE A term that indicates the consummation of a security transaction, either a purchase or sale.

TRADE DATE The day a securities transaction is negotiated and executed.

TRADE DATE INVENTORY A term used by trading departments to mean the total of all positions of a security at the start of the trading day.

TRADE FOR TRADE SETTLEMENT A form of settlement in which the buying clearing firm settles a trade directly with the selling firm. It excludes the use of netting, CNS, or clearing system.

TRADE HOUSE A brokerage firm that buys and sells futures and actuals for its own account and for the accounts of customers.

TRADE PROCESSING AND OPERATIONS DEPARTMENT A broker-dealer's area responsible for processing all securities transactions.

TRADER A person who buys and sells securities for short-term profits.

TRADER'S MARKET Occurs when market conditions are positive for profiting from short-term investments.

TRADE THROUGH A normally unethical practice in which an exchange member transacts a deal on the exchange floor even though a better price is available through the Intermarket Trading System.

TRADING AUTHORIZATION An agreement in which an account owner allows another person to buy and sell securities for the owner's account.

TRADING DAY Any day a securities exchange is open, normally Monday through Friday except for holidays.

TRADING DIFFERENCE The point-fraction difference between the price in an odd-lot transaction and the price of those securities if they had been purchased in a round lot.

TRADING DOWN Occurs when an investor buys and sells high-risk or low-rated securities in an attempt to increase his or her capital gains.

TRADING FLOOR	The exchange area where securities are bought and sold.
TRADING HOURS	The times a securities exchange is open, normally 9:30 a.m. to 4 p.m.
TRADING INSTRUCTIONS	An investor's orders to his or her broker that limits a transaction through a stop order or other restriction.
TRADING LIMIT	The price range within which a commodity can be bought or sold within a given day, with high and low limits marking the edges of that range. A commodity cannot be sold below the limit or above the high limit.
TRADING MARKET	A low-volume market with few price fluctuations, in which professional traders, not the general public, make up most of the trading business for the day.
TRADING PATTERN	The long-term direction of a security's price movements.
TRADING POST	The area of an exchange where one particular security is traded.
TRADING RANGE	The price difference between a security's highest and lowest transaction price in a specific time period.
TRADING UNIT	A round lot.
TRADING UP	Occurs when an investor trades securities from his or her portfolio for securities with higher ratings, which thereby reduces the investor's portfolio risks.
TRADING VARIATION	The fractions to which a security's price is rounded. For example, stocks are rounded up and down and traded in eighths.
TRADING VOLUME	The number of shares a security has traded on a particular exchange during a specific time period.
TRANCHE	Once class of a bond or securities issue. This is done to meet the needs of the issuer and to meet different objectives of investors.
TRANSACTION	The execution of a securities deal.
TRANSFER	Usually refers to the act of changing ownership of registered securities on the books of the issuing corporation.
TRANSFER AGENT	A person who physically records the transfer of a securities-ownership. A transfer agent keeps a record of the name of each registered shareholder, his or her address, and the number of shares owned. The agent sees that certificates presented to his office for transfer are properly canceled and that new certificates are issued in the name of the transferee.
TRANSFER AND SHIP	A security owner's order to his or her broker to have the security registered in his or her name and shipped to the address on the account.

TRANSFER DEPARTMENT A division of the operations department that matches, processes, and controls securities being transferred.

TRANSFER INITIATION REQUEST A contract issued by the National Securities Clearing Corporation that approves the transfer of securities from one member's account to another's.

TRANSFER JOURNAL A company's book that shows all securities issued, transferred, and canceled.

TRANSFER TAX A modest tax on securities transactions, normally paid by the seller.

TRANS-LUX An electrically run screen in a brokerage firm's board room that projects commodity and security price quotes from the various exchanges.

TRANSMITTAL LETTER The letter a seller attaches to the document or securities he or she is sending to the buyer describing the shipment's purpose and contents.

TREASURIES Nickname for any Treasury security.

TREASURY BILL A short-term discounted, government debt instrument of one year or less, issued in $10,000 denominations that pay its face value at maturity. The government issues Treasury bills weekly.

TREASURY BILL AUCTION A weekly Treasury Department auction in which short-term government obligations are sold.

TREASURY BOND A long-term, Treasury-issued debt instrument issued at par and maturing in at least 10 years in minimum denominations of $1,000. Treasury bonds pay interest, which is exempt from state and local taxes, twice a year.

TREASURY CERTIFICATE A short-term government security with a maturity of six months to a year that has been issued to ease Federal Reserve transfers to banks.

TREASURY INVESTMENT GROWTH RECEIPT (TIGR) A Treasury bond that has been stripped of its coupons, with ownership of individual coupons, or of bond principal sold at a discount as a zero coupon. All interest is paid at maturity.

TREASURY NOTE A medium-term, government debt instrument that is issued at par in $5,000 to $10,000 denominations, and matures in one to 10 years. Treasury notes pay interest that is exempt from state and local taxes bi-annually.

TREASURY RECEIPTS Stripped Treasury bonds.

TREASURY STOCK Stock a company issues then buys back, at which time it is placed in the company's treasury, where it earns no dividends and carries no voting privileges.

TREND A prevailing price movement.

TRENDLESS A price movement that fluctuates up and down to the extent that no specific trend can be identified.

TRENDLINE	A chart slope representing price movements, connecting the highest and lowest prices of a security. Technical analysts use this line to indicate an uptrend or downtrend.
TRIANGLE	A charted price pattern that forms a triangle because the security's price has gone down, then up, then back down again.
TRIANGULAR ARBITRAGE	Arbitrage achieved through the exchange rates of three foreign currencies.
TRIPLE BOTTOM	A chart that shows a security's price has hit three bottom prices within a short time, but will not drop below the most recent low price.
TRIPLE TOP	A chart that shows a security's price has hit three top prices within a short time, but will not rise above the most recent high price.
TRUTH IN SECURITIES ACT (1933 ACT)	A law that requires full disclosure of information concerning publicly issued securities.
TURKEY	A security that has lost money for its investors.
TURN	Occurs when a price movement or trend changes directions.
TURNAROUND	A security with a price that has rebounded.
TURNOVER	The number of securities in an investor's portfolio that were bought and sold within a specific time period.
TURTLE BLOOD	A stable security with low volatility and a price that is not expected to increase quickly.
TWENTY-DAY PERIOD	Also called the cooling off period, this is the time between the day a company files its registration statement with the Securities and Exchange Commission and the day the security can be publicly sold.
TWO-DOLLAR BROKER	An exchange member who executes transactions for other brokers who are too busy to handle their own high-volume businesses. Two-dollar brokers are so named because they used to charge $2 for every 100-share deal.
TWO-WAY TRADE	Occurs when an investor simultaneously buys one security and sells another.
TYPE OF OPTIONS	Indicates either a call option or a put option.
U	Appears in newspaper stock listings to indicate a security has reached a new high for the past year.

U-4 An application used to register agents and representatives with an exchange and with the National Association of Securities Dealers. The registration will provide the personal, legal, and business background of the applicant.

U-5 A document used to notify an exchange and the National Association of Securities Dealers that an agent's registration has been terminated.

UNACCRUED Income from payments made before their due date.

UNAMORTIZED BOND DISCOUNT The difference between a bond's face value and the amount of money the issuing company received for selling the security, minus any amortized portion.

UNAMORTIZED DISCOUNTS ON INVESTMENTS The difference between a security's face value and the amount the issuing company received for selling the security, minus any amortized portion.

UNAMORTIZED PREMIUMS ON INVESTMENTS The unexpensed part of the amount that a security's purchase price exceeded its par or market value.

UNASSENTED SECURITIES Securities that the issuing company wants to change, but which have yet to receive stockholder approval.

UNCOVERED A short option for which the seller does not own the underlying security and is therefore not in a hedged position.

UNCOVERED WRITER A person who sells an option contract without owning any shares of the underlying security.

UNCOVER THE STOPS Depressing a security's price to the extent that investors begin creating stop orders.

UNDERCUTTING AN OFFER An attempt to sell securities below the prevailing offer price.

UNDERLYING SECURITY The security on which an options contract is written. Underlying security is also the common stock which can be issued by a corporation to an investor who exercises a stock option, right offering, warrant, or convertible security.

UNDERPRICED Used to describe a stock price that is low compared to its potential future value.

UNDER REVIEW (UR) Indicates a bond that a rating service has yet to rank.

UNDER THE RULE Occurs when exchange officers buy or sell securities to complete a transaction that a delinquent exchange member entered but failed to settle. The delinquent member is charged with any price discrepancies.

UNDERTONE The market's strong or weak base.

UNDERVALUED Occurs when a security's price is lower that its liquidation price or the market value placed on it by analysts. An undervalued stock justifies a higher market price and price/earnings ratio.

UNDERWRITING The business of investment bankers to assume the risk of buying new issues of securities from a corporation or government entity and distributing them to the public. The underwriters will profit from the difference in the purchase and selling price.

UNDERWRITING AGREEMENT The contract between an underwriting syndicate and the security's issuer, with the agreement spelling out the terms, price, and account settlement details.

UNDIGESTED SECURITIES A securities issue in which more shares are issued than the market can absorb.

UNDILUTED STOCK A security with an earnings per share that has not been reduced for any reason.

UNEARNED INCOME Income such as dividends, interest payments, or other income that is not earned through salaries or wages.

UNEVEN MARKET A market with fluctuating prices.

UNIFORM PRACTICE CODE Part of the NASD rules that govern the dealing of firms with each other.

UNIFORM SECURITIES AGENT STATE LAW EXAMINATION A state test, administered by the National Association of Securities Dealers, given to people who want to become registered representatives.

UNISSUED COMMON STOCK Common stock shares that a company has authorized to be issued publicly but that have not yet been issued. Unissued common stock shares do not include those shares the company has reacquired.

UNITED STATES GOVERNMENT SECURITIES Any debt issued by the US government such as Treasuries and Series EE and HH savings bonds.

UNIT At issuance, a "package" of securities, such as a bond and warrant, which become separable at a later date.

UNIT INVESTMENT TRUST A portfolio made up of a variety of different income securities that are pooled together and sold to investors as units. Each unit represents a fractional, undivided interest in the portfolio's principal and income.

UNLISTED STOCK A security such as an over-the-counter stock that is not listed with a registered exchange.

UNLISTED TRADING An exchange transaction involving an unlisted security. Such a transaction is allowed only with the special permission of the Securities and Exchange Commission.

UNLOADING When an investor sells securities or commodities that have dropped in price to prevent any further losses.

UNMARGINABLE A security that cannot be used as margin for buying stock shares.

UNPAID DIVIDEND A dividend a company has declared, but not yet paid to stockholders.

UNREALIZED APPRECIATION Occurs when a security's market value increases above its purchase price, but the owner does not sell it. The appreciation will remain unrealized, or a paper profit, until the investor sells the security.

UNREALIZED LOSS Occurs when a security's market value drops below its purchase price, but the owner does not sell it. The loss will remain unrealized, or a paper loss, until the investor sells the security.

UNRECOVERED COST The part of an investment that has not been amortized.

UNREGISTERED STOCK Limited-issue stock that is not registered with the Securities and Exchange Commission. The issues are either confined to certain buyers or issued by a small company to raise money for a limited, specific purpose.

UNSEASONED SECURITY A newly issued security with no prior exposure to the effects of supply and demand.

UNSECURED DEBT A debt obligation with no collateral, and backed only by the debtor's creditworthiness.

UNSTEADY MARKET A market in which securities prices fluctuate to the point that specialists cannot identify any trends.

UNSUBSCRIBED SHARES Shares in a securities offering that the underwriting syndicate has not yet sold to the public.

UNVALUED STOCK Stock for which the issuing company has recorded on its books as having no par or stated value.

UNWIND A TRADE A transaction that voids a previous transaction. For example, to unwind the purchase of a security, an investor would sell that security.

UP Follows a number to indicate the dollar amount that a security's price has increased.

UPDATE An upward trend in a security's price.

UPGRADE Occurs when an investor sells the low-quality securities from his or her portfolio, and replaces them by buying higher quality securities.

UP REVERSAL A sudden, short-term price increase in a security that has been dropping in value.

UPSET PRICE The lowest price a seller will consider before selling an item, security, or property.

UPSIDE A security's price increase.

UPSIDE BREAK-EVEN The most a security's price will have to rise before the investor starts to make a profit.

UPSIDE-DOWNSIDE VOLUME RATIO The total number of traded shares that dropped in value divided into the total number of traded shares that rose in value during a specific time period.

UPSIDE GAP A gap that appears on a chart when a security's highest price on one day is lower than its lowest price on the next day.

UPSIDE POTENTIAL The price to which an investor expects a security to rise based on all fundamental and technical predictions. The upside potential of a stock may also be a buy-out price.

UPSIDE TREND A period of at least several months during which prices steadily climb, even if it is a market with a few temporary down reversals.

UPSTAIRS MARKET A brokerage firm area where a transaction involving a listed security is completed without sending that transaction to the exchange floor. The deal, for example, would be negotiated between one broker-dealer and another broker-dealer.

UPTICK A security transaction made at a higher price than the previous transaction in the security.

UPTICK-DOWNTICK BLOCK RATIO The number of security blocks traded on downticks divided into the number traded on upticks. A ratio below 0.4 indicates the market is oversold, and a ratio above one indicates the market is overbought.

UP TREND Occurs when a security's price continues to climb steadily over a period of time.

UR See under review.

VALUATION An appraisal

VALUE ASSET To determine the value asset for each share of common stock, divide the number of common shares outstanding into the issuing company's net resources. To determine the value asset for each preferred stock, divide the number of preferred shares outstanding into the issuing company's net resources.

VALUE BROKER A discount broker who bases his or her rates on a percentage of each transaction's dollar value. Small orders, therefore, are less expensive when settled through a value broker.

VALUE CHANGE The net change of all individual securities weighted to represent the number of shares outstanding.

VALUE DATE A foreign currency settlement date.

VARIABLE COST A cost that will change as production costs (such as labor and equipment) change.

VARIABLE INCOME SECURITY A security with its dividend payments dependent on the company's ability to make a profit.

V-FORMATION On a vertical line chart, a V-shaped pattern indicates a bottoming out, thus a bullish movement, followed by a current uptrend. An inverted-V pattern indicates a bearish movement.

VI Used in lower case in the stock or bond tables in the newspaper to designate that the corporation is undergoing reorganization under the bankruptcy laws of the United States.

VOID A document that has been canceled or that has no legal standing or worth.

VOLATILE Description of a stock, or a bond, or a market in general, whose price is subject to wide, rapid fluctuations.

VOLATILITY The extent to which a security's price fluctuates back and forth within a short time.

VOLUME The total number of shares traded for a market or for a particular stock, bond, option, or futures contract.

VOLUME ALERT Occurs when a security's volume surpasses its moving average during a specific time period.

VOLUME DISCOUNT A discount often given to institutional investors when an order exceeds a certain level.

VOLUME DELETED Announcement on the consolidated tape that only symbols and prices will be given, unless the transaction is over 5,000 or more shares. Normally done when the tape is two or more minutes late in its reporting of securities transactions.

WAITING PERIOD The 20 days between a company's filing of its registration statement, and the date the Securities and Exchange Commission has approved for the company's securities to be publicly sold.

WALLFLOWER A stock that no longer is popular with the investing public.

WALLPAPER A worthless securities certificate

WALL STREET A street in Manhattan that represents the primary financial district in the United States.

WALL STREET JOURNAL A highly respected newspaper that concentrates on financial and corporate news.

WANTED FOR CASH Indicates on an exchange's tape that a buyer will pay cash the same day for a block of securities.

WAR BABIES Securities issued from companies involved in the defense industry.

WARRANT A company-issued certificate that represents an option to buy a certain number of stock shares at a specific price before a predetermined date. A warrant, because it has value of its own, can be traded on the open market.

WARRANTS INTO NEGOTIABLE GOVERNMENT SECURITIES (WINGS)	These are options to buy a specific number of Treasury notes at a predetermined price to be delivered at a stated future date.
WARRANTS TO BUY TREASURIES (WARTS)	These represent rights to buy a specific amount of government issues at specific prices within six months to one year.
WARTS	See warrants to buy treasury securities.
WASH SALE	A transaction in which an investor simultaneously buys and sells a security through two different brokers. Such a transaction is considered a manipulation and is illegal if it artificially increases the security's trading volume or changes the price.
WATCH LIST	A list of securities the exchange is monitoring for potential illegal practices. An exchange will, for example, watch a security that a broker-dealer is about to underwrite, or a security that is heavily traded by the issuing company's officers.
WATERED STOCK	A security issue that adds no extra value to the issuing company's position.
WEAK HOLDINGS	Securities a speculator will keep on margin only long enough to sell them.
WEAL MARKET	A short-term drop in general market prices.
WEALTH	Any item or resource that can be used, exchanged, or sold.
WEEKLY SHEET	A list the National Quotation Bureau publishes each week for market makers, which provides prices for over-the-counter securities.
WEEK ORDER	A buy or sell order that expires automatically if it cannot be executed on the exchange floor within a week.
WE OFFER RETAIL (WOR)	This indicates the seller will assume all transaction costs.
W FORMATION	A chart that shows a security's price fluctuations form a pattern.
WHEN DISTRIBUTED	A security traded before the final certificate has been printed. The investor will receive the certificate as soon as it is complete.
WHEN ISSUED	Denotes a security authorized for issuance but not yet actually issued. The security is traded before it receives final trading authorization with the investor receiving the certificate only after the final approval is granted. The transaction would be canceled automatically if the security failed to receive the approval.

WHIPSAWED	Describes an investor who lost money on both sides of a price swing, such as an investor who bought a security just before the price dropped, then sold it right before the price rose again.
WHITE SHEET	A list the National Quotation Bureau publishes daily for market makers, which provides prices for over-the-counter securities traded in Chicago, Los Angeles, and San Francisco.
WHOLE LOAN	An individual mortgage that is not part of any investment pool.
WIDE MARKET	A market with many investors.
WIDE OPENING	A large price difference between the opening bid and ask prices.
WILD CARD	An investment that carries either the highest interest rate allowed by law or an unlimited yield.
WINDOW SETTLEMENT	The physical place where the selling broker delivers securities to the buying broker. Most deals, however, are settled through a depository instead of the window.
WINGS	See warrants into negotiable government securities.
WINNING A BID	The bid that is attractive and profitable enough to a seller to lead to a completed transaction.
WIPED OUT	An investor who lost all of his or her money in the market.
WIRE HOUSE	An exchange-member firm connected to other offices by a communications system.
WIRE ROOM	A brokerage firm area that changes customer orders into floor tickets so the orders can be executed in the market with the best available prices.
WITHHOLDING	Occurs when a broker-dealer keeps part of the securities from an offering and sells the remaining portion to employees.
WITH INTEREST	Used to indicate that a bond buyer must pay the bond seller all interest that accrued on the bond between the bond's last payment date and the transaction's settlement date.
WITH OR WITHOUT	Instructions an investor gives his or her broker to sell an odd-lot limit order either for the stock quote or in the round-lot market, whichever comes first.
WITHOUT AN OFFER	A one-sided quote in which a dealer is willing to bid a certain price for a security, but is unwilling to sell it at that price, either because the dealer does not want to sell the security short or because the dealer does not actually have possession of the security.

WITHOUT INTEREST When a security that is in default is sold without interest, and the buyer does not make any additional accrued interest payments to the seller.

WOR See we offer retail.

WORKED OFF A slight drop in a security's or commodity's price.

WORKING ASSET An asset, invested in securities, with a price that fluctuates along with common stock prices.

WORKING CAPITAL A company's current liabilities subtracted from its current assets, which gives the company the amount of money it probably will need to maintain operations for a year.

WORKING ORDER An investor's order to his or her broker to buy or sell a large block of stock gradually so that the transaction does not affect the stock's market price.

WORKOUT MARKET An estimated price quoted for a security.

WORTH An asset's or investment's total value.

WRINKLE A security feature that could potentially be profitable to the investor.

WRITE To sell a put or call option in an opening transaction.

WRITE-OFF Charging an asset amount to a loss, which subtracts the asset's value from the company's profits and therefore lessens the company's tax liabilities.

WRITE OUT Occurs when a specialist trades an order that is on his or her books by having the broker who entered the order write the order, after which the specialist becomes the contra broker. The broker who wrote the order receives all fees and commissions.

WRITE UP An asset's book value increase that is not due to added costs or asset account adjustments reflected from an updated appraisal.

WRITTEN-DOWN VALUE An asset's net book value after depreciation or amortization.

X (1)Used in the newspaper tables to designate a security that is trading ex-dividend. (2) Used on the Quotron System to differentiate the number of shares bid and offered. For example, 10 X 11 signifies that 1,000 shares are at the prevailing quote and 1,100 shares are offered.

XCH Used to indicate that a securities transaction will be completed outside of the normal clearing procedures.

XD Appears in newspaper stock listings to indicate a security is trading ex-dividend.

X-DIS Used to indicate that a securities buyer is not entitled to a dividend distribution.

XENOCURRENCY A currency that is traded in money markets outside of its own country.

XR Appears in newspaper stock listings to indicate a security is trading ex-rights.

XW Appears in newspaper stock listings to indicate a security is trading ex-warrants.

XX Used to indicate without securities or warrants.

YANKEE BOND A foreign bond denominated in US dollars and registered with the Securities and Exchange Commission for sale in the United States.

YANKEES American securities traded in Great Britain.

YELLOW SHEETS A list the National Quotation Bureau publishes daily for market makers which provides over-the-counter corporate bond prices.

YEN BOND A bond, originally issued outside the United States, that is denominated in Japanese yen. Such bonds are not registered for sale in the United States, although after the bond is seasoned (traded for a reasonable period outside the United States) it may become eligible for trading here.

YIELD The dividends or interest a security will earn, with the yield expressed as a percentage of the amount paid for the security or of the security's par value.

YIELD CURE General term for the graph depicting yields on the y-axis, and time to maturity on the x-axis, for fixed income securities of the same class (e.g., corporates, utilities, governments, municipalities, and so on).

YIELD TO AVERAGE LIFE Term used by money market funds--and often by dealers in unit investment trusts--to designate the simple interest that a new investor will receive, based on present cash flow and the average life of the securities in the portfolio. The yield is an estimate and presumes no portfolio changes.

YIELD TO MATURITY (YTM) A measurement of the compound rate of return that an investor in a bond with a maturity of more than one year will receive if (1) he holds the security to maturity and (2) he reinvests all cash flows at the same market rate of interest. YTM is an approximation and presumes a flat yield curve. However, it is used extensively in comparing fixed-income instruments, in making fixed-income portfolio decisions, and in financial planning if an investor does not want to spend investment income, but, instead, is looking for an increase in net worth.

YIELD SPREAD A comparison between the yields of different quality issues.

YO-YO STOCK A volatile stock with a price that continually rises and falls quickly.

Z Appears in newspaper stock listings preceding a number to indicate that the number represents total volume, so it should not be multiplied by 100.

ZERIAL BOND A stripped Treasury bond or other zero-coupon debt instrument issued in serial form.

ZERO-COUPON BOND A bond sold at deep discount that pays no interest until maturity, at which time the holder receives the bonds face value plus all accrued interest. While holders receive no interest on the bond until maturity, they are responsible for paying taxes each year on the unpaid interest.

ZEROES Nickname for zero-coupon bonds.

ZERO MINUS TICK Also called a zero downtick, this is a security transaction that occurs at the same price as the previous similar transaction in that same security, but less than the last different transaction in that security.

ZERO PLUS TICK Also called a zero uptick, this is a security transaction that occurs at the same price as the previous similar transaction in that same security, but higher than the last different transaction in that security.

INDEX

A

D

N

R

S